Dearest Michael
Thanks for yo[ur]
and support. [...]
exceptional journey. [...]
for your inspiration.
                    Best,
                    Anan[d]

In Black and White

To my mother and father
To my wife, daughter and son
To all the lead actors and bit players
who have played a role in my story

Thank you for the memories.

In Black and White

A Memoir

Anant Singh

PICADOR AFRICA

First published in 2021 by Picador Africa
an imprint of Pan Macmillan South Africa
Private Bag x19, Northlands
Johannesburg
2116

www.panmacmillan.co.za

TPB ISBN 978 1 77010 740 3
HB ISBN 978 1 77010 742 7
E-ISBN 978 1 77010 741 0

*While every effort has been made to ensure the accuracy of the details, facts,
names and places mentioned, as a memoir this book is partly based on memory.
The publisher and author welcome feedback, comments and/or corrections that
could further enrich the book.*

*Unless otherwise specified, all photographs are courtesy of
the SINGH FAMILY COLLECTION and VIDEOVISION ENTERTAINMENT.*

Editing by Alison Lowry
Proofreading by Sally Hines
Design and layout by Triple M Design, Johannesburg
Cover design by publicide
Cover photographs: front: Anant in 2009; back: The filmmaker photocall after
the world premiere of *Sarafina!* at the Cannes Film Festival: Mbongeni Ngema,
Miriam Makeba, Leleti Khumalo, Whoopi Goldberg, Darrell Roodt and Anant,
11 May 1992; back flap: Anant on the set of *The Stick*, 1987.

Printed by **novus print**, a division of Novus Holdings

Contents

Prelude

I first heard about Anant Singh's pioneering anti-apartheid films and admired his courage to make these films in a very difficult environment. Meeting him at the screening of one of his films in the United States almost 40 years ago was the start of a beautiful friendship, a bond that I truly treasure.

When I visited South Africa with my TransAfrica colleagues in 1991 to meet Nelson Mandela, Anant was about to start the production of *Sarafina!* and we were all invited to the launch. I knew the kids who were in the stage musical when they played on Broadway, and it was so good to see them all grown up. That event was even more special because Madiba was there to give Anant his support for the movie. I knew the potential of *Sarafina!* and I took it upon myself to try to help Anant with the movie in the States through my relationships with the studios.

Visiting South Africa has always been very special. On every visit Anant has hosted really great get-togethers and ensured that all my South African friends were there so that we could see each other and have fun.

Over the years, Anant and I have met all over the world. We became part of the World Economic Forum family in Davos as awardees of the forum's Crystal Award, and forged friendships with the global business community there; we had a great time at the Montreux Jazz Festival, and spent memorable moments with Marlon Brando in London.

For me, Anant's greatest work to date is *Mandela: Long Walk to Freedom*. It was a huge responsibility for him to tell the most important South African story ever. He often discussed the project with me and asked for advice whenever he felt the need to. I am so thrilled that he accomplished his dream and immortalised Madiba's life story on film, so that future generations can be inspired by Madiba like I was.

Anant's story is inspiring – how he rose from humble beginnings to the top of the film world and more ... I salute him for all that he has achieved!

Quincy Jones
Los Angeles
September 2021

Foreword

Anant Singh's celebrated lifelong passion for film, for the magical telling of stories on celluloid, is itself a phenomenal tale and in this book he deftly lays it all bare with a maestro's touch. Never boring, never pedantic nor boastful, often witty, the book is an electrifying account of the passion, hard work and dedication – and the audacity – that has made Anant Singh South Africa's most celebrated and successful filmmaker, both locally and internationally.

We are proud of him (and his remarkable team at Videovision Entertainment, his company) not only because of his high achievement but because, back then, in the days of the all mighty and powerful apartheid state, this young Indian guy from a relatively humble background in Durban, in love with film and its possibilities, resolutely and ingeniously forged his own path in the teeth of all the daunting and demeaning obstacles that stood in his way. Not for him the current currency of fawning business favours via political connectedness. Anant was the real thing from the start, always working seriously hard, getting to know the industry from inside out, learning what he could from a few savvy people and, above all, taking risks that sometimes leaves you both breathless and smiling at the audacity of it all. He is a self-made business person, a maker, not a taker.

I got to know Anant about 30 years ago via my lifelong partner, Ahmed

Kathrada (Kathy), who told the story of how taken he was by this young filmmaker whom he met at the ANC offices shortly after the organisation's unbanning. They forged an enduring friendship which was to last all the years until Kathy died. Akin to a father/son relationship, Anant was in touch almost weekly, and it was wonderful to hear them chatting away on the phone. Over the years we have spent countless happy times together, later with Vanashree and the kids, Gyana and Kiyan, and I will always be grateful for the warmhearted way we were absorbed into the family – very special for both of us. For Kathy, who went to Robben Island as a political prisoner at the age of 34 and came out when he was 60, Anant and his family brought a special magic and meaning to his life in his final years of freedom. But what is not well known is how many people Anant and Vanashree have quietly helped in difficult times with thoughtfulness and no fanfare.

In conclusion, this book is an extraordinary account of the history of film in South Africa, throughout all our turbulent years, during apartheid and beyond. At a time when the apartheid government entombed the country with a dome through which no information could enter or leave South Africa, Anant and others managed to prise open a crack in that dome to allow our stories to filter out and through, which outside stories could, in turn, tunnel their way back in and have resonance for us here. Again, in these later years when telling truth to power remains so important, a film like *Yesterday* retains its resonance and significance for all time to come. For all those who battle to tell the stories, to hold power accountable, we are all truly grateful.

Barbara Hogan
Cape Town
September 2021

Prologue

Thursday, 5 December 2013 – London

There's a buzz in the air, an electricity weaving its way through the bustling crowd in Leicester Square, London. Inside the Odeon a demure hush has descended over the VIPs and other invited guests who are milling around the glamorously lit foyer, cocktails in hand, nervous laughter on their lips, but outside on the pavement the excitement has reached fever pitch. Onlookers are laughing, calling, straining their necks to identify the special guests who pull up in limousine after limousine, and step out to rapturous applause and blinding bursts of camera flashes. This is a significant moment, history in the making, and the crowd can read it. Beneath the towering black granite façade of the Odeon cinema there's a red carpet, roped barricades and a convoy of chauffeur-driven luxury vehicles – the stuff of dreams, of Hollywood, of success.

Tonight, the Odeon Leicester Square, London's most prestigious cinema, is filled to its 1 600-plus capacity for the first premiere in the United Kingdom of *Mandela: Long Walk to Freedom*, the story of Nelson Mandela. It's the crowning moment of my career, bringing together many strands of my life, right here in London. It's an other-worldly experience for me and I can scarcely take it all in.

Adding to the occasion is the fact that the film is being screened as a Royal Film Performance, an event staged every year to raise funds for the Cinema and Television Benevolent Fund in the United Kingdom. This means there will be British royalty in attendance, so there's an added tension, a sense of anticipation reserved for such illustrious occasions.

Then the moment arrives. The hordes lining the red carpet leading to the cinema erupt as an elegant silver Bentley slowly pulls up and the Duke and Duchess of Cambridge, Prince William and Kate, finally emerge. A smile for the cameras, the royal wave, greetings and handshakes and nods of acknowledgement. Joining the royals on the red carpet is a throng of VIP dignitaries and movie stars, among them the film's leads: Idris Elba and Naomie Harris – both stylish in classic black.

The most important guests of all, though, aren't movie stars or princesses. They are two women whom most in the crowd don't even recognise. Two sisters, elegant women in their 50s: Madiba's daughters Zenani and Zindzi. Zindzi was just 18 months old when her freedom-fighting father was arrested, tried and banished to prison for 27 years. Her older sister was four.

'We grew up without him and met him very late in our lives,' the smiling Zindzi says of her 95-year-old father as cameras flash around her and fans and admirers, who suspect that this is a Very Important Person, try to attract her attention. 'It makes us proud that the sacrifices he made are recognised and continue to be recognised.'

'What's so special about this new version of Nelson Mandela's life?' a journalist prods. Zindzi smiles.

'I think most importantly it's because my father trusted Anant Singh with the depiction of his life story on film.'

I cringe a little, embarrassed. Adulation has never sat well with me, and I remember Madiba's comment, 'It's easy to become used to adoration, but it's the most dangerous thing for sobriety.' But it is true that there is some sense of pride, of achievement. Mandela's story would never have been an easy one to tell, and it has taken an inordinate amount of time, of energy, of sensitivity to get this right – 25 years, in fact.

Tonight, as the audience watches the life of Mandela play out on the big screen, a real sense of occasion hangs over the art deco-inspired interior of the Odeon. When we are all finally seated, and the opening credits start to roll, I pray that we have achieved just that, that we have got it right.

Then, around halfway through the movie, before the screen fades to black, there is a hand on my shoulder, a whisper in my ear. I am handed a note by an usher appearing out of the darkness. I nod a thank you and he retreats into the shadows as I unfold the piece of paper, trying not to distract the other audience members focused on the screen. Squinting in the dimness of the theatre, I read.

My blood runs cold.

1

Even the circus was in on it

When Charlie Chaplin first swaggered into my life, it was on a big white sheet attached to the curtain rail in the lounge of our small but comfortable house in Springfield, Durban. This was the only place the sheet would fit so that was where it went. Affixed with pins at its four corners, it formed a screen of roughly 1.5 x 1.0 metres.

Much to the delight of his two sons, my father loved movies and he would hire a projector and bring home films for the family to watch. These were special occasions – Mummy happily ensconced on the brocade settee where she had kept a space for Daddy, for when he wasn't checking the film reel, my grandmother, Parvati Singh, whom we called Ajee, in the small old wingback armchair that was reserved for her and her only. My brother Sanjeev would sit hugging his knees at Mummy's feet, while my place was always cross-legged at the far end of the mottled rug so that I could satisfy my curiosity and keep an eye on Daddy as he readied the machine whirring at the back.

It wasn't always Charlie Chaplin in his ill-fitting clothes tying us up in stitches. We fell in love with The Three Stooges and with Laurel and Hardy – the greatest comedy duo to have ever lived. Buster Keaton was another firm favourite – even without a single word of dialogue. The great stone face never ceased to keep us youngsters enthralled with his ability to maintain his decorum while around him everything went to hell. Sometimes my father kept us guessing. Who would it be tonight – The Tramp, Zorro or The Lone Ranger? Or maybe – yes, maybe – the wild antics of Moe, Larry and Curly?

Such enjoyment was infectious and Sanjeev and I thought of a way to share the entertainment with the neighbourhood children.

'Sanjeev!' This was our father, calling from the top of a chair, which was balanced precariously against the back wall of our lounge, lined with furniture shifted to the side so as to leave empty floor space in the middle. 'Anant! Bring the chair, please!'

We brothers stole a glance at each other, stifling giggles. Daddy liked to act all cross and grumpy but we knew that, secretly, he was happy to help us, to lend a hand, encourage our determination and dedication. Our parents had long resigned themselves to their sons' initiatives, and the Singh boys' 'bioscope', as our mother referred to it, had become something of a talking point among the children in Springfield. It was a source of excitement when word spread that the brothers had hauled out their mother's sheet and were setting things in place.

The screen secured, Daddy would climb down off the chair, wipe his hands on the dishcloth my mother handed him and begin to set up the projector. Keeping one eye on the youngsters at the gate, he unpacked the 8mm reels from their cases and began to loop them in place. When he was done, he banged on the door. 'Anant! Sanjeev! Come, bring your friends. We are ready ...'

And with that pandemonium broke out. Little legs scurried through the gate, up the path and into the house as fast as they could, everyone scrambling for a place on the carpet, tiny ones in the front, the bigger ones at the back. Animated chatter, excited giggles, some prodding and teasing as everyone settled in.

It was my job to flip the switch and dim the light. I always relished that moment as I knew what was to follow. The joy we would soon see on those little faces as, wide-eyed, the neighbourhood children followed every move on the makeshift screen was magical. As soon as the projector ground to life and the whirr of the spooling reel was heard, a hush fell over the room. And then – dead silence, not a sound. Until Stan Laurel and Oliver Hardy waddled onto the screen and our lounge erupted with raucous laughter. Sanjeev and I would turn to each other and smile. This was what it was all about.

For the most part, Sanjeev and I were fortunate, in 1960s apartheid South Africa, in that we were relatively shielded from much of the horror, the harsh reality of the racism and violence experienced by so many elsewhere in the country. Safe in the embrace of our parents, our family, we saw little of what was unfolding beyond our home and the security it offered us.

I was born on 29 May 1956, the eldest son of Hareebrun and Bhindoo Singh. This was the year that African National Congress (ANC) leader Albert Luthuli was arrested and charged with treason alongside 155 others, including Nelson Mandela, Ahmed Kathrada, Walter Sisulu and Oliver Tambo, for daring to challenge the injustice that was apartheid.

I was four years old when the massacre at Sharpeville occurred on 21 March 1960. Police officers shot and killed more than 69 unarmed people, including children, protesting in a township on the goldfields up north in the Transvaal.

As small children, we did not yet know about the minefield of apartheid legislation or the Group Areas Act, which dictated where and how everyone would live, including us. It meant that we would grow up in an Indian neighbourhood and attend schools only for Indians. Springfield was one such Indian community and home, for us, was No 223 Quarry Road, a comfortable tin-roofed house with a single outdoor toilet. People very often lived with multiple family members, sometimes as many as 15 or so, in a single dwelling.

I had the good fortune of being born into a large family. My father was one of nine children – six brothers and three sisters – and he grew up in the same Indian community that had sprung up on the banks of the Umgeni River, the big, lazy, slow-moving mass of water that runs into the Indian Ocean at the Blue Lagoon about seven kilometres further downstream. Sometimes, after heavy rain, the river would become a seething mass of angry floodwater, charging the riverbanks and wreaking havoc along its route. Our home was built only a short distance from the river, in an area known as Tika Singh's Bend. Tika – short for Tikaram – was my great-grandfather, who arrived in South Africa as an indentured labourer to work the sugar-cane fields of the colonial British.

From what we have been able to determine from ships' passenger lists and family records, the 22-year-old Tikaram and his wife Sulwantia, aged 25, disembarked in Durban on 3 June 1877. Tikaram was from the town of Mhow in the state of Madhya Pradesh in central India, and his wife was from Shahabad in the state of Uttar Pradesh. The couple would go on to have seven children: five sons and two daughters.

After completing his indenture, Tikaram opted to take up a plot of land rather than the free passage back to India and the family settled in Quarry Road. Here he became a successful market gardener, in time able to acquire additional plots further west on the banks of the Umgeni on a road that later became known as Siripat Road, and across the river in Sea Cow Lake, where some of his children would later settle on the land he gifted to them – including his daughters, a gesture quite unheard of in his day, when family wealth was deemed to be the right of sons only. Tikaram also leased a tract of land adjacent to the Quarry Road property from the Durban City Council. Here small plots were demarcated and rented out for informal housing, the rent revenue supplementing his income. This was the area that became known as Tika Singh's Bend.

In time, Tika's son Bunsee – my grandfather – continued to maintain the vegetable garden in the same field tended by his father, which became a welcome resource when it came to feeding and nurturing the growing brood that was the Singh family. As a youngster Bunsee spent many long hours working that plot of earth, his back bent, his neck burning in the blazing sun, his brow dripping from the toil. Here, on the banks of the Umgeni, he also tended the rose bushes that became one of his great passions, and which continued to bloom in profusion right into the 1990s after my father transplanted a few of them to our new home in the suburb of Reservoir Hills. Sadly, in the mid-1970s the portion of the land in Quarry Road that had the vegetable garden was forcefully expropriated; and at the same time the Siripat Road property was also expropriated to develop sports fields. The family received a paltry compensation of less than R1 for a square metre. The city official who was despatched to negotiate with property owners was told by my very angry Uncle Jonsy that the price was insulting. One could not even buy fabric for that price, he said.

Balkumar, my father's brother and the eldest of Bunsee's children, took his older brother responsibility seriously: he kept a close eye on his siblings, especially when it came to the river. He and his younger brother Maania would scavenge for shrimps and freshwater crabs (the best, tastiest 'seafood' ever) and other creepy-crawlies that made their home on the banks of the river, digging in and around the swampy shallows, while the other children played nearby. That was how we learned to experience the Umgeni – for leisure, irrigation, food, and the ebb and flow of our lives.

Balkumar was well aware of the dangers posed by the river, the risk of young boys and girls being caught in the swells and eddies. He'd heard the stories, many of them, over and over. He did not want anyone in his family ending up like the neighbours' little Leela, whose head had disappeared under the churning water and who hadn't been seen again. At the same time his siblings knew that their big brother – Barka Bhai (meaning big brother in Hindi), as they called him – would never let that happen to them.

Learning to swim was the first safety measure. Sink or swim. That was how all of us boys, growing up on the banks of the river, learned to swim. For the most part we taught ourselves and from an early age, five or six; girls at the time had fewer freedoms than their male siblings and cousins. In a city with sweltering temperatures, swimming was a way to cool off, but it was also a useful skill, a precaution against drowning. And there were many drownings over the years. Mostly it would be the elderly trying to cross the river to reach the market or young children who strayed too far and ended up in the water.

Balkumar – popularly known in later years as BB – had heard too many tragic tales to ignore the dangers. Becoming more and more concerned about the high rate of drownings, he took it upon himself to do something about it. Life was like that then; there was a sense of responsibility to the community. So it was that, in 1933, he garnered all his organising skills, rounded up some of his friends and founded a voluntary lifesaving club that would later become known as the Durban Indian Surf Lifesaving Club. For the Singh boys it was voluntary in name only, however; all the brothers were forced to join by my grandfather.

The lifesaving club, based in a hut structure at Durban's Indian beach, was often called out to help search the river for a lost child or missing relative whom it was feared had succumbed to the raging torrent when trying to cross the river to get home. At other times, particularly during the hot summer months, they would simply keep a close eye on the river when families converged there to swim.

Areas designated 'White' at this time had all the amenities, while the demarcated Black, Coloured and Indian areas had none. Public swimming pools were reserved for the use of white people only and the beaches that were closest to us – the best beaches – were also reserved for whites. These spaces were off-limits to all people of colour, including us. I remember clearly our days at the beach – our 'Non-White' beach was very different from where white people spent their summer days. The Nest, an eatery in a white beach area, had its own special facilities, toilets and even indoor seating. Of course all these luxuries were for whites only but – because 'business is business' – we were permitted to place an order at the restaurant and be served on trays at our cars. These injustices linger in the hearts and minds of children all the way into adulthood.

Unsurprisingly, given the socio-political context of the time, the lifesaving club had no equipment or amenities, but Uncle BB was determined to change that. After serving in the Second World War in North Africa, he embarked on a fierce campaign for facilities for both the lifesaving club and a swimming pool in Durban where people of colour could be afforded the opportunity to learn how to swim. The struggle was long and hard. His battle against the Durban City Council and its politicians dragged on for nearly 20 years, hampered by the fact that we, part of the majority, had no fundamental rights, freedom or the vote.

Finally, on 2 June 1957 the first swimming pool for Indians only was officially opened in Durban – just one day short of the 80th anniversary of the arrival of Tikaram Singh in South Africa and three days after my first birthday. The pool, named the Balkumar Singh Swimming Baths in recognition of Uncle BB's contribution to swimming and lifesaving, was in the neighbouring Indian community of Asherville. Uncle BB's success here would spur him on to seek further and greater victories for his own community and the city at large. It would become a lifelong mission for him. By the time of his death in 1982 he had been instrumental in the opening of six swimming pools for people of colour in Durban.

Growing up in Springfield, our extended family occupied three separate homes, all of them close to one another and each a haven for all who came and went daily. Ours was very much a communal living experience, with any number of visitors in and out at all times of the day. The modest houses were of wood and corrugated iron, with no more than one or two rooms, sometimes accommodating little more than a bed.

My mother's youngest sister, Niru, who is only two years older than me, remembers the time well, especially the mealtime tradition established when my parents were first married. As a young girl she looked forward to the early-morning markets with her sister Bhindoo. She was in awe of all the sights, sounds and smells that fed her senses. The flower sellers' stalls were a riot of colour – reds, aubergines, oranges and many shades of green – and the vegetable stalls beckoned housewives to come and fill their baskets.

Aware of the weight they'd be carrying back home, but nevertheless content with their purchases, Niru allowed her mind to skip ahead in anticipation. She already knew how each vegetable would be prepared. It would be pumpkin with mustard seeds and dried chillies, green beans with fenugreek seeds and garlic, calabash in dhal or slices dipped in chickpea flour batter and fried, or bhindi (okra) braised in spices and yoghurt or fried crisp with onions.

They would sit around the kitchen table while Bhindoo Bhanie (Bhanie meaning 'sister' in Hindi) served her rotis off the flat cast-iron pan known as a thawa and her unrivalled curried shrimps, sometimes with peas or tharoi, a type of ridged gourd. Fresh sprigs of curry leaves from the tree outside, thrown into the pot of sizzling oil, added to the flavours of fenugreek, cumin, coriander and split fresh green chillies. That curry-leaf tree was the pride of the property. It was the biggest such tree, Niru said, she ever saw in Durban and it probably stands there still, with its tenacious roots, bearing its aromatic leaves. No one left their home without a bunch of those leaves.

When my parents bought their house in Reservoir Hills they were blessed again with curry-leaf trees on the property, providing the essential aromatic herb for cooking. Those trees are still there today. In later years, once the children were all born, the tradition would continue. In the evenings we often had meals together, many times enjoying the fish the uncles had caught on the river. Over weekends the men set traps for shrimp among the reeds and later they would trundle home laden with baskets filled with the juicy catch. This was then cooked on an old wood-fired stovetop in the kitchen of the main home, where my grandmother presided over the work.

Of course, Mummy and her sisters learned from the best – her own mother, as well as, in later years, her mother-in-law Ajee. Although times were tough – there was only one tap inside and ablution facilities were outdoors – the kitchen was always busy. Ajee was an extraordinary cook and the aromas of spicy shrimp that filled the home on Sunday evenings will always be with me. She made roti every single day, the first from her thawa always fed to her cat Champu, who'd be waiting patiently at her feet. I enjoyed a very special bond with my Ajee. Because I was her youngest grandson at the time, she doted on me and I spent a great deal of time at her side, whether it was in the kitchen or when she was tending to her vegetable garden, when I would sit outside the house on the stoep. Like most people of her generation, she spoke Hindi as her first language and I got to learn the language from her. When I conversed with her it was exclusively in Hindi, while I spoke English to the rest of the family. I have since forgotten much of the language as I pretty much stopped speaking Hindi after she passed on in 1962. I was six years old at the time.

As children the centre of our lives was the kitchen table. This was where we would work, eat, study and play, watched over by Ajee as she cooked. Her routine was always the same: first she slipped off her modest bangles, then her ring; these she placed carefully on a tea towel next to the sink, where she could keep an eye on them in case any of the children decided to sneak off with them to play dress-up. When she turned on the tap and allowed the water to flow over her hands and arms, there was a strange silence about her. We were not used to Ajee not jangling and jingling, her bracelets on her arm. It was only here in the kitchen that Ajee didn't ring like bells.

Along the edge of the table, which stood dead centre in the kitchen, as it always had, certainly for as long as we children can remember, Ajee would line up her ingredients. Some were in little bowls, others decanted

into jars or bottles: a bowl of de-veined shrimp, a tub of golden tur-
meric, grated ginger, ground red pepper, a jug of glistening cooking oil
that caught the rays of the afternoon sun and spilled a rainbow across
the table. Cloves, cardamom, cinnamon, garlic that Ajee had already
crushed, an onion and tomatoes – that one of the uncles had brought in
from the garden – chillies and salt and curry leaves and, right at the end,
a jug of mustard oil. There would be not a measuring spoon in sight, just
a teaspoon, a tablespoon and Ajee's ever-faithful enamel cup. Even today,
this is the way my mother cooks.

The heady aromas had the children's mouths watering. We knew her
recipes well – and we all had our favourites.

'Pour this into that pan,' Ajee would say, handing me the jar of oil
and pointing to the heavy-bottomed pan on the counter behind her. 'And
now sprinkle those over the shrimp and turn it over and over. No, no, use
your hands, your fingers, little one … Yes!'

And so it began. The pouring, the mixing, the stirring, the sizzle of
the skillet, the simmering of a pot, Ajee's hands waving in the air all the
while, her sari flapping as she wiped her brow with her wrist in the hot
kitchen filled with steam and fragrances, making your head spin.

We children giggled and whispered among ourselves. We didn't miss a
beat, not a teaspoon of this or a tablespoon of that, not a flick of Ajee's
wrist, nor the smile that played on her lips as she stirred and ladled and
spooned. Not for her the accurate measuring instruments others might
use – with Ajee it was a case of instinctive perfection. We knew dinner
would be ready for serving the minute the uncles came in from work.

This was communal living at its best. We were in the trench, fully
immersed, little realising the impact this would have on us in later years.

As youngsters, our world wasn't very broad, centring mostly around our immediate family and friends.

From a very young age, though, cameras and film were always in there somewhere. My dad would make home movies of the family, and I was no more than six years old when I first saw an 8mm camera and film. It was quite unusual for anyone in those days to have their own 8mm camera, let alone an Indian living in South Africa. Still, my father was one of those who had one – he always was the exception, or perhaps he was blessed with good luck.

The 8mm camera was a simple enough machine. It didn't have the ability to record sound, and the film reel, which lasted just three minutes, had to be processed in a lab. For me, it was exciting because the camera was small enough for even a six-year-old to carry around. Of course, my father didn't just let me loose with it – I was, after all, just a kid – but, thanks to my keen eye watching his guiding hands, I soon picked up the tricks and waited for the opportunity to try them myself. The camera was very basic, manually operated, with limited dials and switches. The trickiest bit was loading the film, but the rest wasn't too hard – although, with each reel limited to only three minutes, we had to be very frugal. Later, my father's home movies flickered to life on the same white sheet on which Charlie Chaplin performed.

One year, 1966, we shot footage of an epic road trip to what was then Rhodesia (now Zimbabwe). I was just 10 years old, but it remains etched in my memory, mostly, I think, because this was not only our first such trip – we had never been anywhere else before – and we saw Kariba Dam, but also because in Rhodesia I saw my very first television set. Unsurprisingly, I was mesmerised to watch *Thunderbirds* – and even by the test pattern as it ticked over in wait for the day's broadcast to commence. South Africans, of course, knew nothing of this extraordinary thing called television. Even as the world was spellbound by earth-shattering news – including in 1967 the first heart transplant in the world by Dr Chris Barnard in Cape Town – we only encountered the breaking story the following day in local newspapers.

In those days, there were no funds for a long, extensive holiday, no possibility of overnighting in hotels en route, especially as most hotels were for whites only. We simply made a call, sent a telegram or wrote a letter to family or friends, or even the family of mere acquaintances we'd never met – this was all about community hospitality – explaining that we would be stopping by on such-and-such a date for lunch or an overnight stay. If you had access to a telephone, you booked a long-distance call via an exchange. To send a telegram, you'd have to go into a post office and they would send a brief message to the recipient's local post office. Then we'd all wait anxiously for a reply, confirmation of our overnight accommodation. Our hosts, be they friends or strangers, were always – always – very warm and welcoming, despite rather modest or humble homes. There would be a warm meal and comfortable bed, albeit more often on the floor piled high with blankets. And, of course, if those families visited Durban we would naturally reciprocate. That was just how it was. It was also how lasting friendships were made.

That trip to Rhodesia was far more significant than all the award-winning road-trip movies that were to engross me in the years to follow. *Thelma and Louise*, *Easy Rider* and *Little Miss Sunshine* had nothing on this. My father drove all the way – over 4 000 kilometres – in his red Opel Rekord. It was a tight squeeze for five of us in that little car, with no air conditioning, Niru, Sanjeev and me in the back. And what an adventurous trip it turned out to be, something of an eye-opener for this little Indian boy who was in many ways cloistered from everyday hardships by his family.

Wherever we travelled we were restricted to certain areas. There were plenty of no-go spots en route, which meant detours and lots of backtracking, and we could only overnight and eat in certain, specially designated places. During apartheid one whole province, the ironically named Orange Free State, was completely taboo for Indian people. If you wanted to pass through the province, you needed official permission and a special permit; and you had to report at a police station when you left. My father had to apply at a police station for all the relevant documentation that allowed us to simply drive – for less than an hour – on public roads in our own country.

Niru is wedged in between the two boys on the back seat of the Opel. On her left, Sanjeev, all arms and elbows and wriggling, is trying to wind the string of his yo-yo, poking Niru in the ribs at every turn. I am on the right, arms crossed, cheeks puffed in a sulk. I've been desperate to wind down the window just a smidgen for a breath of fresh air, but the others won't hear of it. Twice now we've spotted a troop of baboons alongside the road, both guarded by fierce alpha males baring teeth and whooping in warning as the car drove by. Sanjeev and Niru are not taken by the thought of being on the receiving end of those fangs – they'd much rather swelter in the baking heat of the back seat than risk it.

'Stop! Stooooooop!' I shout suddenly.

My mother spins around in the passenger seat. Eyes wide and mouth open, I wind down the window, my arms like windmills.

'Stop, Daddy, stop. Please!'

My father looks up into the rear-view mirror, scanning the back seat to check that all three of us children are safe.

'Anant, you want for me to have an accident? What is the matter with you!'

17

'Monkeys! Monkeys!' Sanjeev and Niru chorus, as much as an alarm to the adults as surprise at the third troop, this time much closer and much scarier, that has made me throw caution to the wind.

'Baboons, Sanjeev. Baboons. Not monkeys,' Mummy says, then turns to my father. 'Hari ... Anant's spotted baboons. He wants us to take a picture.'

My father's camera is on my lap. I am desperate to take a picture of the baboons before they move off. I already know how the camera works, how to load the film, but I also know that Daddy will never allow me, just a boy, to use it. The camera is expensive, the film is expensive, so there can be no second takes. No, if there is any photography to be done, Daddy will be the one who does it, while I watch him. There will be no negotiation on this.

'Please, Daddy, can we stop? Just a quick picture. It won't take long. Promise ...'

My father wants to push on. We need to get to our hosts before night-fall and there's a long way to go still. He turns to my mother and shrugs. They know holidays and road trips are for children and he likes that I am so taken by the camera. While I am still too young to be trusted to use it unsupervised, he doesn't want to discourage my interest.

My mother nods, a smile playing on her lips.

'Five minutes, Anant. Five minutes,' laughs my father as he pulls over on the narrow verge. 'You hear me?' He looks at me through the rear-view mirror, then takes the camera. I watch carefully as my father focuses the camera on the troop, the alpha male strutting up ahead as he leads the oth-ers across the road, turning every now and then to keep an eye on the red Opel and its human occupants. Then I notice something extraordinary.

'Mummy ...' I say, my brow wrinkled in a frown. 'What's wrong with them, Mummy? Are they sick?'

'Sick?' My father is trying hard to be patient. 'What makes you think they are sick? They look perfectly healthy to me.'

'Their bottoms, Daddy. Their bottoms.' My father turns the camera off and follows my pointing finger, which is aimed at the baboon closest to his window and its brightly coloured rear. 'Look. They are wearing plasters [which we now know as band-aids]!' Sanjeev and Niru next to me strain their necks to see, then gasp in unison. I am right! The baboons have band-aids on their butts.

If I notice my parents struggling to stifle their laughter – this, they must be thinking, is going to be a long, long day … I don't understand why. But before my mother can launch into an explanation the three of us will understand, I am already nudging my father to restart the camera and train it on the mother and infant at the back of the line. I am well aware that you can only shoot for a few seconds at a time, no indulgences, because a full film captures only three minutes of footage. I'm too young to know it, but this is an early lesson for me in learning the value of the shot.

My father laughs, that deep-throated chuckle that will later reverberate in our memories. He turns the key in the ignition and we are soon on the road again. He can hear the click of the camera from the back seat as I rewind the film manually.

It's strange how memory functions. That first road trip there were many moments that were as clear as that episode with the baboons and that we'd revisit through my dad's home movies, but others fade. One memorable childhood holiday was one I took without my parents. It was with one of my father's brothers, who we affectionately called Baba. He was a railway policeman and this was my first trip on a train, all the way from Durban to Cape Town, when I was about 14. Strangely enough, my fondest memories of that trip was getting up in the morning and being served a toasted bacon and egg sandwich and how delicious it was. I also remember going up Table Mountain, but the rest of the details are very vague.

I discovered my grandparents' garden early on. My Ajee had green fingers and grew lots of fruit and vegetables, which she handed out to others in the community. She also brought vegetables home for us, but first she'd supply the neighbours and friends. I later learned that this was out of her generosity of spirit, which was reciprocated by the neighbours when they had flourishing gardens of their own. Although I appreciated the virtues of generosity and kindness to others – heaven knows, it had been drummed into us often enough – I struggled to understand Ajee's total lack of business acumen. Although this I don't remember, I am told that one day I said to her, 'Ajee, you mustn't do that. You make the parcels and I'll go and sell them for you.'

You might say this was a first step for an emerging entrepreneur, but in this instance it got no further. Ajee said no. For the time being I'd have to be content to be the delivery guy. In any event our little business venture was curtailed somewhat when I started school.

Springfield Hindu Primary School was my first experience of the classroom. It was 1962 and I was six years old. School was an entirely new adventure – and one that I had been looking forward to – but I must confess I was rather disappointed by it. As it turned out, I would never be an A student.

In the mornings, my cousin Yasmin, the daughter of my father's sister who was of a similar age, and I would make our way to school together. We walked down Quarry Road, past general dealers and, at the corner, the huge Habibia Soofie Darbar mosque, one of the oldest places of worship in Durban, built in 1906. The school, which was right around the corner from the mosque, had originally been founded by Wesleyan missionaries in 1903 but was taken over by the local community in 1947. The two buildings – the mosque and the school, separated only by some vacant land – had been cornerstones of the Springfield community for more than a century.

Despite fond memories of my school years, when it came to the work itself I was a poor scholar. My parents always made sure that my brother and I were well dressed and well behaved – polite, respectful, honest – but that could not make up for my grades. Learning just wasn't for me, and teachers seldom held back their criticism on my annual report cards. The only positive comments tended to be about neatness and attendance. When it came to my studies, most of my teachers agreed that I needed to 'work harder'. One, Mr Ebrahim, wrote rather harshly that I was 'a pupil of average intelligence'. I can't say that those comments bothered me much at the time – I had other interests and pursuits beyond academics that kept me busy and, more importantly, happy – but I'll admit that they have stayed with me all these years.

It was in about 1969, when I was 12, that I had my first and only experience as an actor. It was the stage play *Antigone*, the classic Greek tragedy. One of my uncles, Roy Jithoo, was the director of the theatre at the university's Salisbury Island campus – the campus for Indian students. I played the young pageboy, with one cue and a single line of dialogue. Acting is such a complex craft and so public that I never again felt the urge to become a player in front of an audience or the camera. It has to be said, though, the words of Antigone's uncle Creon had resonance: 'Never grow up if you can help it.' Do we ever grow up?

Under apartheid all schools in South Africa were segregated, so much so that even school holidays were at different times of the year. In fact, it was because of those holidays that I had my political awakening, one of my earliest memories and experiences of segregation at its most terrible – and it all came about because of the circus.

Sanjeev and I loved the circus: the entertainment, the clowns and the animals – the whole shebang. The problem was it was usually quite tricky for us to attend because the circus was in town when we were supposed to be in school. Then one day it dawned on us that the white kids we saw at the circus – when we did manage to go – were all on holiday. It transpired that the travelling circus in South Africa was only ever in Durban during school holidays, but those holidays were geared to white schools, which had different holidays to ours. Sanjeev was incensed.

'How come the circus is never here in *our* school holidays?' he demanded.

I shrugged. 'What do you mean?'

'Well, it's not our holiday and the circus is here!' said Sanjeev in a huff, arms folded. He must have been about seven or eight at the time. 'And these other children all seem to be on holiday. Why aren't *we* on holiday? How does that work?'

That day I realised that we were of different worlds. Separate worlds. There were things in the world of white children that children like us could never have or be. And even the circus was in on it.

2

Sundays, bladdy Sundays

On Sundays, when I was growing up in the 60s, everything in South Africa was closed. Everything. Sundays were church days.

The Nationalists, who were in government, were for the most part Calvinist churchgoers who took their religion so seriously that Sunday was a Holy Day, with no room for negotiation or discussion. Ironically, they seemed to miss the foundation of Christianity, which at its core is to love others as you love yourself. It was truly draconian. Small towns, villages and even the central business districts of big cities were like ghost towns from lunchtime on Saturday to Monday morning. No sport was played. There were no cinemas open. Or shops. Or restaurants. Or bars (so people stayed at home, braaied and had their drinks there). The only concession for public drinking places was that drinks were allowed to be served during specific times, known as 'sessions', and only with an accompanying meal. Naturally, some bars spotted the loophole and got around this by providing a complimentary portion of beans, a boiled egg or fried nuts and chickpeas. Even activities as run of the mill as swimming were frowned upon. The Sabbath was the Sabbath. You were meant to do nothing, except go to church. The added irony of Sunday closures was not lost on an Indian community where Christianity was hardly the dominant religion.

I am Hindu, raised by a Hindu family in a largely Hindu community. Our family was devoted to their faith and prayed daily at the shrine that had pride of place in our front garden. But the experience was much the same in other areas of South Africa with large communities of Jewish or Muslim faithful who were not obliged or bound by their faith to Sunday worship, and yet had no say in the closing of Sundays. This go-to-church thing remained as foreign to them as it was to us. Making things even worse was the fact that when I was a child there was still no television in South Africa.

By the 1960s, colour television had already been introduced in the United States, but in South Africa the National Party, which had ruled South Africa with an iron fist since 1948, considered it a threat.

In South Africa, broadcasting, which was entirely state owned, was a mouthpiece for the racist government and would for decades be limited to radio. And, for us, radio meant the English-language Springbok Radio; there was no Indian radio station, with broadcasts aimed at Indian listeners restricted to weekly windows on Radio South Africa on Saturday and Sunday mornings. Radio thus became a significant part of our lives, integral to our storytelling, giving voice to a narrative that found no outlet elsewhere. On radio the fare was sports results, propaganda news, or the weekly serials *Squad Cars, Money or the Box, Consider Your Verdict* and *The Creaking Door* on a Friday night. And the serials were an exciting treat.

When it came to television, the National Party stand was so outlandish, so laughable, that in 1969 South Africans – those who were able to, that is – watched the moon landing on televisions in neighbouring countries such as Rhodesia. People popped across the border at Musina, watched the *Eagle* land and Neil Armstrong take his giant leap, and then made their way back over the border to TV-less South Africa. Television would only arrive in 1976, more than two decades after the small screen had exploded elsewhere around the globe.

While 15 other African countries already boasted television, South Africa did not, so Saturday nights and Sundays became movie days. Our home – first in Springfield, and then later in Reservoir Hills – embraced that custom and I, in particular, revelled in it.

In June 1964, my parents were able to move the four of us to a new, more modern and bigger neighbourhood 10 kilometres away in an Indians-only area known as Reservoir Hills, north-west of the city. Daddy had bought the house, on its own plot of land and ready-built, for the princely sum of R5 000 (the equivalent of about $250), complete with Swiss parquet floors and all the latest amenities. At the time, the area was still very rural, and as yet undeveloped. Our new home at No 11 Stanton Street was in the middle of the block, one of only three or four houses on the street. It was situated on a steep hill – predictably, given the name Reservoir Hills – with Stanton Street running past our front gate and our yard ending in veld at the bottom of an undulating property. There we planted small patches of mielies and other garden produce for ourselves as well as the community, a legacy of our past.

Initially, it was strange being so removed from the familiarity of extended family, but there was a handful of neighbourhood children, four or five of us of similar age, with whom we bonded – some of these friendships continue to this day. We were in and out of each other's homes all the time. We spent most of our free time outdoors, climbing trees, picking mangoes and bananas, and playing tennis and football and cricket in the streets. Our equipment consisted largely of homemade bats, and makeshift nets and wickets. We played with spinning tops and marbles, flew handmade kites and invented our own games of cops and robbers or cowboys and Indians – copying what the white kids called them at a time of political incorrectness and blissful ignorance. Another favourite game was Three Tins. This consisted of stacking three tins one on top of the other and tossing a ball – usually a tennis ball – from several metres away to try to knock them down. We made walkie-talkies of tin cans and string; guitars out of a one-gallon oil tin, using fishing gut for the strings. Necessity was the mother of invention. And it was fun.

The street was an extended playground for us and posed no serious risk, as there were rarely any cars passing through our side streets. People who could afford cars knew that the street was our playground and drove cautiously. For the most part we had the streets to ourselves and felt completely safe, always.

Another craze was go-karts, which we constructed ourselves in our yards and raced against each other down the street. But ours were no ordinary karts. They were more of an elongated H-shaped box-cart secured to a plank and held in place with a single large nail (to allow it to turn) and a rope tied across the two front wheels for steering. You had to steer using your feet. The go-karts ran on four old ball-bearing wheels we had scavenged from a garage; ball-bearing wheels were ideal because they gave you some real noise and speed. We would fly down that hill as fast as lightning and always somehow make the turn at the end of the road into Riddick Avenue. If you didn't turn in time, you'd go careering into the veld; if you turned too quickly and too far you would somersault into the air and hit the tar. No one wanted that. So our karts included a rudimentary braking system. Essentially this was little more than another plank nailed to the side that you would pull and drag along the road if you wanted to slow down – or else you would just use your feet or an old shoe.

But where there are boys playing, being reckless and careless and fool-hardy, there's always trouble. And this was as true for the boys of Reservoir Hills back in the 60s as it was for kids of that era around the globe.

On this particular day Sanjeev and I were racing with the other neigh-bourhood kids and I was flying. My instinct told me what was about to happen before my brain registered. I was coming down the hill too fast. I immediately started to brake with the plank – or at least try. But then the whole thing came off. The entire plank. It flew through the air like a mis-sile, some oddly shaped unidentified flying object obscuring the sun and then splintering as it struck the pavement and bounced across the veld.

What now? I thought to myself, my brain somersaulting faster than the plank as it leapt through the air. *Am I going to crash? Or can I stop?* Those moments happen so fast.

Immediately, my instincts kicked in. I tried to grab hold of the back wheel with my left hand, trying to latch onto the spinning, rapidly revolv-ing ball-bearing wheel while I steered frantically with my feet towards an inevitable catastrophe.

But then my hand got caught, sucked in under the wheel as it jammed into the tar, dragging and scraping my entire hand as it went. I was lit-erally using my hand to brake an out-of-control go-kart. Something I wouldn't recommend. It was a nightmare. Once the world slowed down and my head stopped spinning and the dead silence of that split second erupted into a cacophony of howls and tears, I discovered my hand was in really bad shape. It had been ripped open, exposing the bone, blood everywhere, with a number of broken bones. Amid my wails and Sanjeev's whimpering, my doctor father put some iodine on the hand and patiently patched me up. Mummy hovered in the background in a slight panic. My hand took a really long time to heal and it's a miracle that I didn't suffer serious permanent damage, but the incident did leave me with three scars that I still look at every day. While these are physical scars, they are also sweet memories of my childhood.

Whether that episode scarred me in any other way, or steered me away from adventures on the street with the other boys, I can't say. But it certainly didn't deter Sanjeev and me from any further antics. My brother and I, and our friend Raj Naidoo, did practically everything together, including our fledgling business enterprises.

One of these was hosting movie viewings for neighbourhood kids. My dad would take out his projector and we would screen films for our friends in our single garage, first for free, and then for a small fee – a blanket 2 cents. We'd regularly get six to eight kids and news spread rapidly by word of mouth. Customers piled in and plonked themselves down on blankets and old carpets spread out on the cold concrete floor of the garage. We were noisy – but they loved coming to our movies. Sometimes, with the help of Mummy, we provided something to eat as well.

My dad had a surgery in town, close to where all the Indian cinemas were located, and he would often treat us to movies on Saturday mornings and, during the holidays, on Wednesday afternoons. He would see us to the cinemas and buy our tickets (19 cents each) to watch a double feature, two films back-to-back, while he worked, tending his patients. By the time we were done, Dad would have finished too and we would head back home together. Often our friends would tag along and together we experienced joy, anger and fear and all the other emotions the big screen can invoke.

Sanjeev and I both inherited our family's passion for swimming, and during the summer school holidays we spent entire days at the public pool in Asherville, the only one for people of colour in all of Durban. We would purchase, for no more than a couple of cents, samoosas, nuts and vadas – a savoury delicacy – for lunch. These would inevitably be courtesy of the entrepreneurship of one of the neighbourhood mothers or grandmothers, hovering at the entrance, peddling their wares to youngsters out for the day, lunch money jangling in their pockets handed over by their own mothers. Very often, this was how communities put those same children through school.

Diwali – the Hindu Festival of Lights – and Guy Fawkes were special times in Reservoir Hills, Guy Fawkes particularly for us because Daddy's birthday was on 5 November. A double celebration. We loved the firecrackers and the street celebrations and, as young boys, we lived dangerously, lighting up soorbans whenever we could. A soorban is made from a firework that hasn't gone off. We would crack it in half and light the open ends, watching with delight as the gunpowder blazed in a fiery blur, much to our parents' horror whenever they caught us. On occasion, the fireworks would go off in our hands – not a pleasant experience. I explored making a larger version by opening up the fireworks and assembling all the gunpowder together to make one big firecracker!

The children were also the ones saddled with the task of delivering Diwali parcels to all the neighbours, a chore we loathed because it took us away from our friends and our games. When I look back now, though,

I realise they were some of the best times of our childhood. Diwali is still celebrated across the world but it has been scaled down in South Africa since I was a youngster, the only exceptions perhaps in the historically Indian areas of the country where Diwali is still celebrated in the traditional way with prayers, new clothes and the customary exchanges of food parcels, sweetmeats and gifts.

Children in South Africa today rarely hang out in their neighbourhoods. Now, it's all high walls within secure estates or apartment living. Back in the day, in the close-knit Indian communities in which I grew up, there was a greater sense of community and we benefited enormously. It gave us grounding, but also opportunities for innovation and creativity. I experimented with many things: I was forever opening up batteries, dismantling old radios, learning to fix things using my intuition, or just acting on a natural sense of curiosity. For the Singhs, however, tragedy was lurking around the corner and on 30 December 1969 it hit us right in our home in Reservoir Hills.

3

Early days

In November 1954 more than 3 000 people are said to have attended the wedding of my parents, both of whom were from families well known among the community. Held in the full tradition of our Hindu religion and a ceremony that lasted an entire day, large parts of the suburb of Sydenham apparently came to a standstill amid the pomp and ceremony. It must have been the wedding of the year in Durban. Think Grace Kelly and Prince Rainier of Monaco, in our own Durban style. The thrill of the pageantry, the excitement, the interest – for an otherwise ordinary Indian couple on the southernmost tip of Africa.

An article in the daily newspaper, the *Natal Mercury*, the pages yellowed from time, remains in the family's possession. It describes my father Hareebrun as dressed in an 'impeccable English suit along with a turban and sash of the finest Indian silk and gold thread' and states that the beauty of my mother Bhindoo's wedding gown was 'overpowering'. The saris worn by my mother and her attendants were straight out of Bollywood.

On arrival each guest was presented with a carnation and then ushered into a marquee where places had been laid for 2 000 guests. Here there was an explosion of beautiful colours, guests resplendent in elegant, brightly hued robes and saris with jewellery to match, and the women with their hair knotted low on the neck. There were tables loaded with coloured drinks and Eastern sweetmeats and in the centre of the marquee a bridal bower, trellised and hung with fresh flowers and coloured lights. Added to this was the scent of burning camphor chips and incense. The ceremony was conducted in the millennia-old and traditional Sanskrit language but translated over a speaker for the benefit of guests of other ethnicities.

The traffic jam in Randles Road, in my mother's neighbourhood of Sydenham, in the heart of Durban, must have been memorable, with guests spilling out of the marquee. It was an occasion that would be remembered for decades to come.

Decades before, however, it was an entirely different story. One of poverty and desperation, of greener pastures offered by strange new worlds.

If it weren't for sugar and the world's insatiable demand for it, the Singh family would in all likelihood never have ended up in South Africa and Durban would not have become the global city it is today. It all started when the early British colonialists in South Africa discovered that the fertile hills of Natal were ideal for growing sugar-cane. This, in turn, led to something of an economic sugar rush and, as the sugar industry boomed, there was an increasing need for a labour force.

But because slavery had officially been abolished in 1834, the demand for labour to work the cane fields became a growing challenge. At the time, the British government for some reason elected not to use locals. As India was also a British colony and many Indians were living lives of extreme poverty under oppressive colonial rule, in 1859 legislation was passed that enabled the British to ship Indian workers to Natal – and other British colonies – on five-year contracts. Over time, nearly 1.25 million Indians migrated to destinations around the world as indentured labourers, essentially entering a life of debt servitude.

My great-grandfather Tikaram was subsequently indentured to a sugar-cane farmer for a number of years. For many, a future in South Africa was considered a better prospect than the day-to-day struggle that was life back in India; it was a means of escaping poverty and deprivation, perhaps even an opportunity to make a better life for oneself, or at least try for the five years of indenture. The choice of leaving India for Natal was thus not one of adventure but of necessity. While this form of servitude was different from slavery, conditions could be similarly atrocious and the promises made to entice people to Natal were often broken.

The first ship, the *Belvedere*, departed from Calcutta on 4 October 1860, carrying 342 passengers. A week later the *Truro* followed from Madras, and over the next half-century a further 382 ships made the voyage. In total, 152 184 Indians were despatched to Natal as indentured labourers. It was only in 1911 that the Indian government finally prohibited the arrangement because of the continued ill-treatment of its citizens abroad.

Central to the ethics of these immigrants was hard work, perseverance and an unreserved commitment to family and community – a work ethic that I saw every day in the subsequent generation of my father and uncles. It was this moral compass that became the driving force behind their endeavours, a determination to create a better life for their children and future generations.

The experience of indenture was abhorrent, and when their contracts expired Indians faced debilitating pressure from their white 'employers' to stay on, in the same dreadful conditions. Many could not escape what was essentially servitude. However, when he reached adulthood, Tika's son Bunsee was spared from toiling in the fields. Education for Indians in South Africa was limited, but my grandfather found work as a law clerk at the firm Burne & Burne.

My father was even more fortunate and managed to secure a very good education. It was his dream to be a doctor, a challenge for someone of colour. After he completed his schooling, he studied at Fort Hare in the Eastern Cape before enrolling at the University of the Witwatersrand in Johannesburg. Eventually he was afforded an opportunity to complete his studies towards a medical degree at the University of Edinburgh in Scotland, a feat already challenging enough financially, but almost unheard of given the racial restrictions imposed on South African society at the time.

His studies, for the most part, were funded by his father, his brothers and other close family benefactors who made modest contributions. Within the Indian community, however, there were further offers of help, but his father respectfully refused. Far too often these offers came with strings attached, not least of which was a commitment of marriage to their daughters after qualification. Instead, the family shouldered the burden alone, often with great sacrifice, cutting all expenses to the bone. His father, however, never compromised on food, always maintaining that the family should have the best quality food.

In those days in South Africa, only white people were allowed to study medicine. There were very few exceptions. Indians who were determined to be doctors – and grit and determination were what were needed to run the daunting gauntlet of red tape and withheld opportunity – had to do so in England, Ireland or Scotland (and, much later, in India). Those choices all came with severe challenges of their own, particularly in terms of finances. The result was that very few Indians ever had the opportunity to study towards a medical degree of any kind. And even when they were able to study medicine abroad, the South African authorities refused them permission to practise back home without first completing a series of additional courses. And then they were able to serve only their own communities – yet another draconian system that enforced segregation in every single sphere of everyday life for people of colour. As a result, many who left to study abroad simply never returned, even though their entire family had settled here, very often making inordinate sacrifices in order to ensure that their loved ones had opportunities denied to them back home.

Although more than a little intimidated by the prospect of leaving behind all that was familiar and finding himself alone in a foreign land, my father left South Africa at his parents' insistence. And so he persevered and became the only doctor in the family. Like so many of us, as a child I would look at my dad with pride, but perhaps more so as I grew older, when I could more fully appreciate the hoops he had had to jump through and the odds he had been forced to overcome. He – like his father and grandfather before him – rose above his circumstances and way above anything expected from a person of colour in apartheid South Africa. He overcame many odds and made many sacrifices to qualify as a medical doctor. He was also one of only a handful of practitioners in South Africa at the time with special qualifications to treat tropical diseases.

Old family letters highlight how my father kept in touch with his parents and siblings while he was overseas, often guiding and advising his parents, who struggled at times with the other children.

27 Rosslyn Crescent
Edinburgh
24th April 1950

Dear Dad

The last time I wrote to you was about two months ago when I asked you for some extra cash – since then I haven't heard from you.

We started the summer term last week on the 18th – Tuesday. This is the final term when we do Obstetrics, Gynaecology, Paediatrics and Therapeutics. Our final exams commence on the 5th of July – so first another two months of hard work & the long struggle will be at last over.

I am in the best of health and hope the same applies to you all at home. From the letters that I receive from home I note that you're a source of constant worry to all at home – your coming home late in the evenings, which seems to be a daily occurrence, must be upsetting to all at home – surely you must realise that the roads, in view of the [1949] riots, must be dangerous to travel by at night and alone. One is never sure when an attack might take place, and I think that it's unfair on your part to worry them at home – particularly since it can be so easily avoided. I sincerely hope you take this seriously and go home at a safer period.

The weather here has been very fine, as we are approaching summer.

Closing with love to all at home.
Yours lovingly,
HB Singh

My father was abroad for five years. During this period, the family didn't have a telephone to call him and all correspondence was through letters. This was a long time to be away and many felt he might not return to South Africa. But his roots ran deep and his devotion and loyalty to family even deeper. Following graduation, he felt compelled to return.

While the story of my father's family's trail – from India to Durban to Scotland and back to South Africa – is hardly one of rags to riches, it stands in contrast, on the surface at least, with that of my mother. Whereas my father was raised with some understanding of hardship and sacrifice, my mother and her family's experience was one of less angst, less fear. In a sense, it was more privileged.

My mother, Bhindoo Moonilal, and her family were from Sydenham. Her dad Mothilal (Morty) was initially a school teacher. Then he became a transport merchant, running a successful business that saw to it that he was relatively well off, given the circumstances. Morty was considered the patriarch of the Moonilal family, often described as a man born before his time. He was a Renaissance man, and well travelled, despite the apartheid-era restrictions. From his travels he would bring scores of new ideas and news and hold court at his home, where he would regale the family with stories of life outside South Africa, a world perhaps less constricted by issues of race and deprivation.

Morty and his wife Rajpali would host large and extravagant dinner parties where the children would eat at the main table with the adult guests. My grandfather had a passion for playing the horses, as did his father before him, and one that I share to this day, which tells perhaps of a generation and a class less confined by rigid social norms. The home in which my mother grew up boasted a tennis court and large vegetable and flower gardens. She led a life quite different from those of everyday Indians struggling from sunrise to sunset. This all changed in the 1960s, however, when apartheid legislation removed the family from their property as part of the plan to relocate Indians to designated Indian-only areas – out of sight and out of mind.

My parents' courtship and marriage were what would probably be described today in the modern world as an arranged affair between the Singhs and the Moonilals. The families got together and at the end of it all there was a union of souls. Of course, it is much deeper and more intricate than that and, suffice to say, theirs became a true love story in all its magical glory. In a world of arranged marriages where a doctor is considered a good catch, my parents were indeed the perfect match in every way.

Traditionally, in Hindu families, particularly in those days, the bride would move into the groom's family home, often sharing that space with up to three or four family groupings within the same household. So it was that, following their wedding, my parents moved to the Singh family home in Springfield. Every morning in season, my grandfather Bunsee would pick a rose and present it to his daughter-in-law in his humble and ongoing effort to welcome her and show her his family's affection.

Two years into the marriage their eldest child was born. Me. Three years after that, we welcomed my younger brother Sanjeev.

Like all parents, I suppose, my parents, especially my father, loved his sons and would do anything for us. Sanjeev and I always felt that love keenly and we loved him in return. He also knew, however, how to deal with excitable young boys whose heads were filled with grandiose schemes and far-fetched ideas. He was encouraging and, even at times when he was clearly in disagreement, he would not try to stop us from striving for certain goals. Instead, he would help. I, in particular, had a strong and wilful character and my father was quick to observe it – and then to accept it and work with it. He allowed me to chase my dreams, cultivating in me a sense of independence and self-belief that has carried me all my life.

He had a heart of gold, his kindness not limited to his family, and he regularly treated people without any charge. There were times that I went with him to poorer communities, including Black townships around Durban where doctors were rarer still, and waited while he consulted with patients in need of medical care. As a result he became a much-loved member of society.

Not that Dad was always such a saint in our eyes – he was often, to our minds, too strict for that. He certainly didn't allow us boys to get away with ill-discipline or disobedience.

This was a time when parents believed that errant kids had to be physically punished and, when it came to discipline, Dad ruled his home with a sjambok (a whip traditionally made from strings of leather braided together, ours being of firm plastic). Often punishment was little more than a simple smack, but when he was serious, out came the sjambok. It hurt like hell. In those days if you did something wrong, you'd get it. And, boy, we got it.

But Dad also gave us freedom. Although a smoker and drinker himself, as a doctor he knew full well the dangers of cigarettes and alcohol, and warned us against both. But, having put his views across, he allowed us boys to come to our own decisions and to make our own informed choices. When I was 11 or 12, he gave me his box of State Express cigarettes and opened the cabinet which had Mainstay cane spirits and brandy, and said that if I wanted any of these things, they were there for me to try. I did, and I never smoked again, and only started drinking beer when I was 16, with the group at the back of the shop.

At his surgery on Saturdays, Sanjeev and I saw first-hand the deep respect and enduring admiration my father enjoyed among his patients, an insight that allowed us both to appreciate and understand more about the human being that was Daddy. Many people have told me, and I was also witness to this, that he willingly treated those who could not afford to pay, and they would sometimes gift him their home-grown produce or bring him fish that they had caught.

Dad would perhaps have wanted his sons to follow in his footsteps and become doctors. But we never got to know for sure. What's that quote heavyweight boxer Mike Tyson is famous for? 'Everyone has a plan until they get punched in the mouth.' Well, that came for us on 30 December 1969, when my father Hareebrun – suddenly and without warning – died at the young age of 47. A massive heart attack in our home in Reservoir Hills. My mother found him in the bathroom where he had collapsed. I remember walking into the bathroom and seeing him lying there, not quite comprehending the loss.

I was 13 years old.

4

Sink or swim

Dad's death hit us hard. It was so sudden, so surreal, and so unexpected.

It affected the entire community. Everyone grieved for him. As for me? Indian tradition and customary norms for an eldest son meant that I immediately had to become the man of the house. At this young age you don't really comprehend the significance this has on your life. It is a frightening and lonely prospect at the age of 13, but we were blessed to be part of a large Indian family, where the family supported and loved each other.

Despite this support, I had to grow up very quickly. I knew so little. But taking up that new responsibility became a necessary reality. Dad's passing, when I look back on it now, was probably a foundation of sorts for me, compelling me to develop a strength and understanding of life that would stand me in good stead in navigating my own life. Our father had already entrenched his legacy in our lives, one that still serves us well. We try to follow in his footsteps, taking lessons from those foundations, heeding his simple rules, sticking to principles and following our instincts on right and wrong, based on our own judgement and not that of others.

Mummy never remarried after my dad's death and nor did she let others know of her struggles. Instead, she was always the one helping others with theirs. She spent the rest of her life as a single parent, raising two headstrong and determined young boys, which can be difficult at the best of times. Hers was the iron fist in the velvet glove. From those early days, we boys had little option but to pull our weight at home, which meant helping Mummy out wherever and whenever we could. Only later in life did it dawn on me how significant this contribution was; she gave all for us, for our upbringing and well-being. She took on the roles of both mother and father.

While Mummy still cooked and attended to most of the household chores, we not only had to continue with our existing responsibilities but also take on new ones: water the garden, pull weeds, wash cars (something we did even when Daddy was around) – not so much the tasks that my father ever did, but rather to teach us responsibility and free up our mother to tackle some of the responsibilities that previously had been his. Occasionally, we'd be rewarded with a day at the public pool or an afternoon at the movies, always with the understanding that this was a reward for meeting our responsibilities – Mummy never saw them as chores – rather than a handout.

After school, it was my task to make my way to the law firm in town dealing with my father's estate to collect the monthly cheque of R100. It's hard to imagine living on R100 per month today, but we managed. From there I made my way to the bank, waited in the queue to cash the cheque and then set off to pay the utilities: the electricity bill at the Martin West Building in Smith Street and the telephone account at the post office. My instructions were very specific: I was to wait for a receipt each time and then head directly home with the balance, which would then have to last the rest of the month, to be spent on food and everyday household expenses. It was a tall order for a boy just into his teens. I don't really remember how we got our clothing, other than school uniforms, but somehow these were always there.

Fortunately, the house was already paid off, as was the R2 727 Valiant Dad had bought two years before he died. Although Mummy did have her driver's licence, she hadn't driven much. Now, however, she had to master the art of driving this big American car – quite a feat, but she conquered it almost immediately. She would only drive when necessary, however, and so we generally used public transport, like the bus, or walked. We did a lot of walking in those days – it was sometimes the only way we were able to get to places and do what we needed to do. This included walking the several kilometres from school to the bus stop every day, which meant that we only got home around five; in winter it would be almost dark by then, and on the days I had Speech and Drama classes with Mrs Shepherd at ML Sultan Technikon after school, it would be later. My route took me past the Victory Lounge, from which a taxi-type service operated. The owners, an Indian family, had a 'fleet' of cars (three or four) and they charged 2 cents per kilometre. Occasionally, if I were lucky, one of their drivers, who was a family friend, would offer me a lift if he was heading my way. People were kind and generous like that back then.

My friends Larry Kulpath and Vinod 'Wally' Mistri used to give me driving lessons in their own cars. I remember misjudging a turn on one of those early expeditions in the driver's seat and promptly mounting the pavement. Out of necessity, and without a licence, I started to learn to drive the Valiant. It was a large car, but an automatic. Initially, I took the car for drives only secretly, but later, with my mother's permission, I got Michael, who worked at the film rental store where I had a part-time job, and who was licensed, to sit with me while I drove. Finally, after I felt I had mastered driving, I went for my licence and took my test in the Valiant. I failed at the first attempt – parallel parking with that huge car was insane – but I was successful in my next attempt.

Looking back, while it was my father who introduced me to the thrill of the moving image and instilled in us a sense of direction, it was my mother who, through her unstinting love and unwavering care, stepped up to the plate and reared us as a single parent through the most difficult period of our lonely lives.

But Mummy was no pushover. When we were naughty, she would try to use my father's old sjambok on us, but by the time we were 14 or 15 we had become sturdy young lads, and proved too wily for her and too strong. With our long, gangly arms, we would grab her hand – the one tightly gripping the sjambok – and hold it away, out of reach. Poor Mummy soon had to abandon the idea of any kind of corporal punishment when it came to her ever-growing boys, although that never stopped her from her goal of raising honest, respectful and hardworking young men.

After my father's death, we continued living in Stanton Street. Most of the family were some distance away, but they would visit often at first; later, however, they came by less and less as they got on with their lives.

Memories flood in of us youngsters – me, Sanjeev and our best friend Raj Naidoo and his sisters, Snowy and Neri (who became sort of sisters to us too) and Anthony Naicker, who lived up the road, and Nalin and Reshma Sathiparsad who lived around the corner – haring down the street, laughing.

Me, Sanjeev and Raj were like The Three Stooges, causing trouble where we could, much like young boys do across the world. Long-suffering Raj was the ever-patient sidekick. I was the quiet one; I guess, being the oldest, the others looked to me for guidance. Sanjeev was the hellraiser. He and I had many arguments, but most times I was wise enough never to pick a fistfight with my brother. Through thick and thin, one thing was always understood: we had each other's backs. The Three Stooges did practically everything together and we also attended the same school.

Because there were no high schools in Reservoir Hills we had to travel by bus, which was in itself an exercise in patience, sometimes taking about two hours all told. There was no such thing as a bus timetable; you simply had to wait it out, with someone keeping a lookout to alert us when the bus was heading down the hill. Then we'd run out of the house and dash down to catch it. Many times we'd forget our bus fare, but the drivers knew who we were and allowed us to pay the next day. The fare to school was about 5 cents but only 3 cents to the bus stop two stops before school, so often we'd get off there and walk the rest of the way. Naturally, the pocket-money was used to feed our movie addiction or to buy ice-cream.

In those early years, neighbours would perhaps hold a party, sometimes even with a local group of young musicians who'd started up a band, and have about 20 guests sitting around in the garage. Only a handful of teens were brave enough to dance.

In my last years of primary school, Standards 5 and 6 (Grades 7 and 8), I was especially in awe of our art teacher at Springfield Flats. Both talented and enthusiastic, he introduced us to the world of creativity. He encouraged us to work on crafts such as pewter, painting, sculpture, pottery and mosaic, and also to use practical woodworking tools, a hacksaw, for example, to create templates for design. These skills I picked up helped throughout my life. Handwork skills seemed to be the one area in which our school was relatively well resourced, perhaps because white education authorities felt it safer and, in the long run, more beneficial for the apartheid cause to promote trade and other labour-intensive skills among 'non-white' communities. Whatever the reason, these tools were made available for schoolwork and after school we had additional opportunities to work with them. We also had Woodwork as a subject. I remember making a relief map of South Africa using masonite plaster of Paris moulds and then painting them based on the vegetation. So 'Arid Lands' would be a dirty sand colour and 'Subtropical Natal' a bright emerald green. These explorations into the world of creativity as young boys provide solid foundations for the future, and the benefits shouldn't be underestimated.

Later – when The Three Stooges were no more – I attended Sastri College, a public school on Winterton Walk in Durban. In the early 1970s, all schools were of course still segregated and our school, Sastri, was for Indians only. Established in 1929 and situated in the heart of Durban's CBD, it was an icon of education for pupils in the greater KwaZulu-Natal area. One of my uncles was among the first batch of pupils, followed by my father in 1941 and his younger brother in 1943. Notable alumni include Pravin Gordhan, who went on to become the South African Minister of Finance, and lawyers and struggle stalwarts Ismail Meer and JN Singh – friends of Nelson Mandela – as well as Sam

Ramsamy, the exiled anti-apartheid activist who spearheaded the international sports boycott against the apartheid state.

Like all children, we revelled in being outdoors and occasionally attended sporting events, often with Uncle Jonsy, who took me to cricket matches at Kingsmead, where spectator areas were segregated. The Indian section had no stands and so we watched the matches sitting on a grass bank, while braaing on a 'suitcase' braai stand. The only other spectator sports were rugby and hockey, which subscribed to the racist laws and were exclusively for whites. Uncle Jonsy also took us to watch legendary Indian golfer Papwa Sewgolum play at the Durban Country Club and the Royal Durban Golf Course. In 1963, when I was seven years old, Papwa was subjected to the horror of the discrimination that came with racist laws when, after winning the Natal Open, he was not allowed to enter the clubhouse of the Durban Country Club for the prize-giving ceremony. He was handed his trophy through the window while he stood outside in the rain. And when he beat South Africa's greatest golfer, Gary Player, in the Natal Open in 1965, again he was not allowed into the clubhouse to receive his prize. What humiliation for such remarkable achievements for one who learned the skill of golf by watching as a caddy.

Despite not being a particularly good scholar, I enjoyed school. It was there that I developed a love of reading, storytelling and the arts. There were always books and magazines around, which I began accumulating from people who discarded them. In the process of working through everything I could lay my hands on, I came to understand a little about film.

While I was at high school, it became my task to arrange film screenings for fellow pupils at the end of each school term, just as I had done for the neighbourhood kids. I continued to be mesmerised by the magic of film, but I never really imagined back then that one day I'd be the one making those movies. I just wanted to be with film. Or involved with it somehow. Those strips of celluloid that we used to watch with my dad, those were the greatest inspiration I carried from my father.

My continued enthusiasm, my immersion into that extraordinary dream-like world, led me in 1970 to give up my Saturday job at Freed's, a furniture store on Field Street that was later assimilated into Morkels. Freed's, to its credit, had an 8mm and 16mm film rental library to supply content for the projectors they sold, but even that was not enough for me. I needed to be more hands on. And so I found a new holiday job: rewinding movies at a film rental store. Humble, yes, and hardly captivating or financially rewarding, but it was a job. And a job 'in film'. It also meant that I had to take the bus from Reservoir Hills, a trip that was perfectly safe but, with all the stops, took about an hour on a good day – not that that bothered me in the slightest now that I had landed the dream job. For one, the quiet time alone meant that I could think, or sleep, or daydream, or read comics; on the bus home I'd sometimes fall asleep and have to be woken by the conductor at my stop, although occasionally I missed it and had to walk all the way back.

Initially, the job paid next to nothing, the real remuneration being the opportunity to borrow movies free of charge – how lucky can a boy be? Eventually, though, I was offered R1 per day, but still the benefits continued to far outweigh the miserly remuneration: I was able to take movies home to watch and that, of course, meant that I could keep charging the neighbourhood kids to watch films in our garage. That darkened garage with its miraculous flicker of 16mm film opened up a magical world for me, Sanjeev and the neighbourhood kids. And also provided a handy income.

But, away from the magic of the movies, from the distraction of make-believe and far-fetched fantasy, there waited the reality of 1970s South

Africa, a world far removed from the dreams, drive and ambition of an
Indian youngster in Durban. The country was changing. We were becoming politically aware, apartheid atrocities becoming more and more
prevalent. There was no mistaking that the watershed years were fast
approaching, and most South Africans who were simply struggling with
their day-to-day lives, head down, avoiding conflict, just getting on with
the business of life as inconspicuously as possible, could not look away
and pretend that things were as they had always been. So it was then, as
I trudged my way through high school, that I, too, began to ask more
questions. I became more active, more conscious, and more involved.

A triggering moment for me was when I got involved in the screening
of a film on the last Thursday of the school term. The school had its own
projector – generally reserved for the occasional educational film – and
we were able to make use of it in our unofficial 'screening programme',
making the most of the opportunity and, for me at least, a lesson in
responsibility, as I was tasked with sourcing the movies. I'd head off to
MGM in West Street and select the longest movie I could lay my hands
on, at least two to three hours (which usually meant a minimum of five
reels): *Lawrence of Arabia*, *Gone with the Wind*, *The Dirty Dozen* and
Boris Pasternak's *Doctor Zhivago*. These films showed me the power of
the moving image to transport us to faraway lands, all against the backdrop of survival, and the ability of film to influence the lives of someone
like me, thousands of miles away.

While renting these films for school, I was confronted by the fact that
there were films that could only be seen by white people, films that were
restricted from a Black viewership. I had had first-hand experience with
this working in the film rental shop, but still I struggled to fathom the
rationale. How could anything so outrageous be even marginally accept-
able? I was so enraged that I borrowed some of these provocative films

from the shop and deliberately screened them at school or at home for the very audiences forbidden to see them. Naturally, this did not go unnoticed, but the trouble that came with it was worth it for me. It afforded me the opportunity to take a stand – nominal, some would feel, but a stand nevertheless – and to take action rather than observe from the sidelines.

I was 16 in 1973, still working part-time in the store – a whites-only store in the whites-only inner city of Durban. Working there and having a job gave me a sense of what entrepreneurship was and what independence was like. And I learned a lot, not only by working hard but also by observing. These were realisations I made only later, as you live your life on a day-to-day basis, but appreciate it later in life. There was the store at 136 West Street, Durban, near the beach, owned by the Greek Dimitri Thomopoulos, whom we called Jimmy. Jimmy was a champion hustler, always hustling everyone. And I mean everyone. Constantly making a deal of one kind or another.

Across the street was an auction house – owned by another Greek family, whose daughter Jimmy had married – dealing in paintings, Persian rugs, French bronzes, sculptures and other art of value, mostly sourced from deceased or bankrupt estates. It was here that I first began to appreciate great art, the property of wealthy white families, or imported pieces: sought-after Persian rugs of the finest quality, the work of great South African painters: Pierneef, Irma Stern, even Tretchikoff. It was not unusual to see valuable pieces of art and other collectibles being auctioned off from that place. It was here, too, that I learned how people got hustled. For instance, stooges in suits would be planted among legitimate bidders to chase up the price on certain items, higher and higher until someone in the audience placed a bid high enough to meet the expectations of the auction house. It was ruthless manipulation. Being an observant youngster, I learned one important lesson: that it is good to be clever, but you don't have to be dishonest to be a success.

It was in Jimmy's shop that I learned to gamble. Most days, it would be me and four or five Black guys also employed in the area, including David and Louch, while Aaron Ndwandwe, who worked at the auction house, would simply watch us. To while away the hours, we would play cards or a version of craps in the backroom where we did the rewinding, and sometimes outside on the pavement, like in the movie *Green Book*, where the white chauffeur, played by Viggo Mortensen, gambles with the Black drivers and takes their money. Like that.

Except this time it was my money that was being taken and I had very little. These guys knew all the tricks and for a long time they hustled me, the youngster. But I watched and I learned and eventually they relented, realising that I was one of them, willing and eager to learn, and showed me the tricks, revealing some of their insights. For me this was a period of schooling in which I learned about the real world, one beyond the confines of a reserved lifestyle in Reservoir Hills. I would later use the tricks I picked up here to my advantage when, some two years later, I started buying films to distribute on my own. Even at the young age of 18, there was little that intimidated me – I'd learned to hustle, as part of survival, in a good way.

My schoolwork and part-time job at the shop kept me busy, focused even, but I knew there would come a day when this, too, would come to an end. What then?

5

The path less travelled

I wanted to go to university, in particular to film school, which was where my passion lay. I never even considered making movies; as long as I was simply around film I'd be happy – that much I knew. One far-fetched idea was London Film School but, with my father no longer around, that was never going to happen. Unbeknown to me, however, my mother – hopeful that I would be able to follow in the footsteps of my father – applied on my behalf to the University of Edinburgh. Blissfully unaware that it had even been a consideration for my mother, the application was declined. The only remaining option in South Africa was the Pretoria Film School, later part of the Pretoria Technikon, in the very heart of Afrikaner nationalism and a whites-only institution.

There was no way that I would get permission to attend. My dream was beyond reach, and I knew it. As a Black person in an oppressed community under apartheid, following your passion was not an option and the few tertiary education alternatives available to Blacks were severely limited. Indians in Durban could only attend the University College for Indians, which had been established on Salisbury Island in the middle of Durban bay.

The whole place stank of rotting fish and, to add insult to injury, also served as soldiers' barracks. I know this because it was where I went by ferry to play my role as the page boy in *Antigone*. At one point, the university was shut down due to a boycott from the community who demanded better facilities. It finally shut its doors in 1971 when it was replaced by the University of Durban-Westville. For most South Africans freedom was the only dream that seemed real; I, by contrast, was very privileged to be able to study at the new university, which was a stone's throw from my home in Reservoir Hills.

In those days, apart from the possibilities of teaching, accounting or science, there were two options for 'good' Indian boys: medicine or law, both careers the family were pushing my way, trying to guide me towards a better future. Despite my father having been a doctor, medicine held no appeal for me. I didn't like the idea of surgery (and had squirmed in my Biology class in high school when we had to dissect small animals). I opted for engineering. I applied for and was awarded a bursary to study engineering at the University of Durban-Westville. At the time, it was still an Indians-only tertiary institution. It finally merged with the whites-only University of Natal in the post-apartheid era and is today known as the University of KwaZulu-Natal. They kindly bestowed upon me an honorary doctorate in May 2000.

But second best is never good enough. Although intellectually I knew a degree in engineering was a good thing – a solid investment that would secure not only my own future but also that of my family – emotionally I felt that I had sold out, sacrificed my ambition, abandoned the only dream I'd ever cared about.

I hated university, or maybe it was just engineering; I really hated it. It was not the creative, exciting storytelling industry I craved. It was cold and clinical and numbers oriented. It left me drained, frustrated, bored and even a little angry.

And so, to distract myself from the tedium of a field in which I had no real interest, I started running a card game gambling book in the university's cafeteria. That pastime became a modest money-spinner for me. I received a tiny commission for each bet placed through me; although pitifully little, those commissions added up and, in the end, paid quite handsomely. All the tricks I had learned at the back of Jimmy's shop were finally delivering dividends.

At the time, the Greyville Racecourse in Durban was hiring university students, one of a limited number of jobs available to Indian students. Needing some additional income, I applied and got a job working on the tote machines at the track, mostly on Wednesdays but sometimes also on Saturdays. The job paid R7 per day, good money then, but it wasn't long before the great torment of apartheid raised its ugly head yet again.

Like all places in South Africa, Greyville Racecourse was racially segregated. I worked in the Indian section of the Turf Club. The racism I experienced on and around the track was a revelation. For one, they had separate stands and tote spaces for different race groups: Africans, Indians and whites, the last mentioned boasting the best facilities. The white people who worked there were racist, unsophisticated, blue-collar workers with limited skills and even more limited education. Yet here they were, barking out instructions to anyone of another race, purely because their skin tone gave them authority to do so. They were demeaning and petty. If, for example, I wanted to place a bet with the bookmakers, I had to walk all the way over to the white section of the course – and that made my blood boil. Despite the colour of our skin, our money was good enough when they needed it. They took our money from the rear side of their betting posts, but still treated us like dogs.

I didn't work at the track very long before I'd had enough and resigned in protest. I lasted a little longer as a student, sticking it out for two years before a huge opportunity arrived, one that meant I could finally follow my real passion. Movies.

During this period, I still worked part time in Jimmy's shop, International Films. Jimmy had his flaws, but it was the one place where my race never counted against me, certainly not with Jimmy and my colleagues. Yes, Jimmy was white. And, yes, he had been raised in a culture entirely different to mine. But, to Jimmy, I was becoming a budding entrepreneur, a young man determined to make something of himself, and our relationship was always business driven; not once did I ever have a sense of the racial tensions I encountered later in my life and career. I did what I had to do, working 18-hour days, seven days a week, including holidays and weekends. I did not have a grandiose plan but I knew that I had to make every effort to succeed in business.

Jimmy's shop was in West Street, in the Durban CBD, and for me, working there was the next best thing to film school. One of the rewards was being able to take films home, watch them and learn from the best filmmakers. And so it was that I fell in love with the work of Cicely Tyson, Bill Cosby and Sidney Poitier. To see Black people on screen commanding dignity was incredible. Sidney's presence in particular was profound, but then to see him take on authoritative roles? That was transformational for a Black kid in apartheid South Africa, especially as the law at the time did not allow these films to be seen by us because they had racial connotations. My unofficial film school also allowed me to fall in love with every avant-garde flick – Michelangelo Antonioni's *The Passenger* and *The Last Detail*, both with Jack Nicholson, as well such classics as Sam Peckinpah's *Straw Dogs*, *Soldier Blue*, *The St Valentine's Day Massacre* and *The Wild Bunch* and so many more.

Sanjeev and Rajan Pather, who had moved next door to us in Reservoir Hills in 1970, and many other guys over the years – among them Rajesh Rajkumar, who was the son of a family friend – would help out in the shop during holidays and on weekends. Many of these friendships, going back 50 years, continue today. Rajan, in particular, became well known for his pleasant nature and his ability to sell a story and recommend movies; in fact, customers were so impressed by his reviews that they would bring him cakes for Christmas.

The year 1974 was an especially significant one for me because of two key developments in my life. I was 18 years old and just into my second year at university.

The first key moment in 1974 came when I attended a political rally in a community hall in Durban. Steve Biko, the activist who was later brutally murdered by the police – and whose story was told by Richard Attenborough in the unforgettable *Cry Freedom* many years later – addressed the crowd. He was a young man, not much older than me, and I found him inspiring. Back then, I didn't really grasp it all properly, what he was saying about Black Consciousness, but I knew about apartheid and, of course, the harshness of racism. But his eloquence, his honesty, his deep understanding of the fragility of the status quo, his unravelling of the complexities we all faced captured the ears and minds and hearts of every individual sitting and standing spellbound in the audience that day. I remember thinking about how young this man was and how powerful he seemed. Biko became an early influence on my political awakening.

The second significant development was one that allowed me to shut one door and open another.

I had been working at International Films since I was a schoolboy, on holidays and weekends; often I'd be called in to lend a hand after school. But all good things must come to an end, and one day the owner, Eddie Falconer, and his partner – who had since bought the place from Jimmy – decided to sell up. Eddie felt that the business was too small for them and he asked me if I wanted to buy it. I remain hugely indebted to Eddie, not only for the opportunity he offered me, but for his guidance and mentorship going forward. While I worked there, he allowed me to use his office, lent me his car and when I was out of line, he shouted at me! He was in his 60s then.

The first thing I did was head off to the dean of the Faculty of Engineering at the university; we discussed my options and he offered some advice. He explained that when I finished my course in five years, I would – as a Black engineer – be lucky to earn R2 000 a month, and that was only if there were any vacancies at all for non-white engineers in South Africa. The apartheid policy of job reservation for whites would make that near impossible. So, if we had equal or better qualifications than a white candidate, the white person would get the job. After that conversation the decision was easy. I decided to take my chances in the film business.

Unsurprisingly, my mother did not approve of this bold move into business. Like the rest of the Indian community, she had an unshakeable faith in the power of education, and careers in engineering or medicine especially were regarded as the key to a good future. She believed without a shadow of a doubt that I was making a big mistake. She tried to get every-one who had any influence over me to talk me out of this insane move into an industry nobody had even heard about, let alone made a career of. The very notion was absurd to her. She felt I was headed for ruin and poverty. But I was immovable, motivated by the mantra impressed on me by my dad: if you believe something is right, pursue it. And I did, paying off Eddie's loan in full from the store's profits within nine months.

Eddie wanted R10 000 for the business. I, of course, had not a cent to my name – I didn't even have a chequebook – but I decided to chance it nevertheless. If it didn't work out, at least I'd know I'd tried. I could always go back to university.

So it was that I negotiated the purchase on an instalment basis through monthly promissory notes which would be exchanged for cash on the day they were due. They said they trusted my work ethic and ability and agreed that I could pay them out of the profits over two years, with a monthly payment of R800.

Since non-whites could not own businesses in this part of the CBD, the shop remained in the name of its previous owner for a while, and later another white friend, Ian van Rooyen, put his name on the lease. Ian and I were the same age. He was a surfer who came into the shop one day to rent a movie. We hit it off right away and he became a regular customer. His day job was working for South African Airways freight depart-ment. I would meet up with him at the airport when I was freighting films to Johannesburg to swap with my associates in Johannesburg. The Johannesburg guy would send his movies to me and I, in return, would go to SAA freight with Ian to send off my own batch of about 20 movies. It was an easy and convenient way to keep stock fresh and circulating, and Ian became my go-to guy. We used late-night flights as costs were lower and on weekdays so that we didn't lose valuable weekend revenue.

I suppose that, in many ways, I've always been a gambler, be it making movies or playing cards or working at the track.

My interest in gambling was almost certainly ignited by Jimmy while I was working in the film shop. Both he and his father-in-law, the Greek auctioneer across the road, were quite involved in horseracing, boasting a slew of contacts in that world, from trainers and owners to grooms and bookmakers, many of the more well-heeled regular bidders at the auction house.

In 1975, word had it that the Durban July – one of the country's fore-most horse races – was set to be a foregone conclusion that year, with Gatecrasher taking it all the way home. Jimmy and his cronies had bet heavily early on when betting opened at generous odds, with hundreds of thousands on his win. At that time, I was earning no more than about R25 a week and, brazenly – perhaps buoyed by their bravado – I put R100 on it to win R1 000. And, as fate would have it, Gatecrasher did indeed win – only to lose out on an objection that saw the second placed Principal Boy (owned by Bridget and Harry Oppenheimer) take the hon-ours. The loss was catastrophic, for me as well as everyone else at the shop.

But the field was set, right there and then. The tension of the build-up, the excitement of the race and the unbridled joy – perhaps even the disappointment of defeat – kindled in me an interest that grew over the years and become a lifelong passion. As a youngster, I took jackpots and the like, and in time gathered around me friends and acquaintances who had contacts in horseracing, grooms at Summerveld stables, for instance, who occasionally gave us tips. Of course, as novices we'd win some and lose some, but always there was the thrill of the race. Once we even scored what was considered something of a coup when, with inside intelligence from the groom at the stable, we made a bold decision. We knew that the horse was a good one and had the potential to win. Betting opened with the bookies at 7-1. We placed our bets. I was bravest, I think, but my friends Lionel Calvert and Vicky Jacobs, who were regulars at the stable, put up R100 each. Finally, with starting odds of 4-10, first-time runner Himself went on to just win. We pocketed about R7 000 between us, with me walking away with no less than R5 000. The jubilation!

My interest in horses and the sport of kings was there from early on. Years later, when I could eventually afford it, in 1989 I bought my first horses – Sacred Pool and Hawkstone. It was very exciting to enter the segregated environment of the horseracing industry, which by that time was slowly starting to open up. It was a thrilling feeling to share with friends and colleagues the joy of owning racehorses, an experience that people of colour had previously been denied, and also to make some modest profit at the same time. As I had learned, however, for a South African person of colour venturing into a lily-white world – in this case, the arena of horseracing and wealth and endless contacts and connections – this did not prove easy. It was a long, hard and onerous process, one reserved for white folk – perhaps the very reason I clung to it. No one was going to tell me that I wasn't allowed, that this was For Whites Only.

In 1994, there was an interesting battle that I had with the Racing Association as I proposed that our racing colours (each owner has their own unique colours worn by the jockey) be in the colours of the South African flag. They rejected my proposal as it had one colour too many. I fought them on their flawed logic and my valued pride and finally acquiesced.

Eventually, my perseverance and passion saw me appointed, in 2001, a board member of Gold Circle, the racing authority of my home province, KwaZulu-Natal. I was one of the first persons of colour to step over the threshold into the otherwise white world of rules and regulations, of white mores and white morality and, most especially in this context, of silk and chiffon, of shirts and ties and hats. And yet, here I was, in my trademark uniform of jeans and T-shirt. I have always been at my most comfortable in casual attire, and I saw no reason to change my ways, even as I picked up on the startled looks and the arched eyebrows. I stuck to my guns. I am who I am, and I didn't get here by grace and favour. I worked hard to get where I was, even there among the well dressed and well heeled of the hypocritical white elite. Unsurprisingly, at one point, there was talk about adopting a more appropriate dress code; at the racecourse, for instance, if you were in the parade ring or dining at certain restaurants, you were required to wear a jacket and tie. Needless to say, I regularly ignored those conventions, although I did give in when it came to big race days, such as the Durban July. Then I would dress up, usually in a suit but not always with a tie. These habits prevail even at black tie events in the film world, including the Oscars.

In 2006 I entered into a partnership with Barry Irwin's Team Valor, which bought South African horses and managed them. It has been a fruitful and enjoyable partnership, having some success and seeing some of our South African horses progress in Europe and the States.

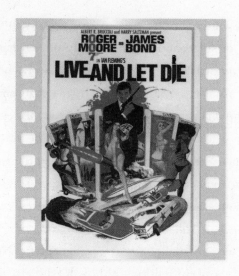

6

James Bond, Basie Smit and the Durban Vice Squad

In the mid-1970s, I found myself the owner of a modestly successful film rental business. We had moved to Smith Street, but were still in the whites-only area of the Durban CBD. Most of my customers had no idea I was the owner; many simply assumed I was the hired help. My day-to-day business was simple – renting out films and projectors – but I gave it everything I had. By 1975, having relinquished my studies and boldly gone where no one had gone before, I was working 16- to 18-hour days. This is okay if you love what you're doing. And I did. I was soaking it all up, taking it all in my stride.

In those days I was an avid reader of international magazines, for which I would place an order at Avalon Tearoom, the local newsagent on Victoria Street alongside the Avalon Cinema. Then I'd sit it out, waiting for the next shipment of international stock to dock a month or two later, bringing with it a bunch of magazines for me – *Popular Mechanics*, *Variety*, *British Screen* and *Film Comment*, among others – which provided me with two to three months of reading. Much of what I learned about the movie business came from some of the articles I read in those movie magazines. I learned about different film styles, took note of the reviews of the latest international releases, and read all the interviews I could find with prominent individuals in the industry. These magazines also provided me with rich source material: the names and addresses of overseas studios with whom I could potentially strike distribution deals. During the day while in the shop I had the time so I started writing letters. Hundreds of letters.

At one point, when I was struggling to keep the momentum going, Eddie Falconer offered the services of his assistant at Central Agencies. The poor woman had no idea what she was in for. I kept her really busy, churning out correspondence day and night. These letters she diligently typed on her typewriter for me, using carbon paper so that I had duplicates and a paper trail. Alternatively, we would send a telex, which – theoretically anyway, given the time differences – would be responded to within a day or two.

I was still living in Reservoir Hills with my mother, writing to people in Beverly Hills and Manhattan, trying to secure deals with everyone and anyone. I often wondered what the Americans must have thought when they saw Reservoir Hills as an address, whether they imagined it to be the equivalent in South Africa of Beverly Hills in California. That possibility and the anonymity of my situation gave me something of a thrill. Given the boldness of my approach, I was sure people must have thought I was from some fancy, lively place. There was no Google to consult back then and mail was delivered the old-fashioned way – on foot, by a postman lugging a big brown leather bag, sometimes months later.

Most people would generally get a letter or two per week, seldom more. But things were about to change for the postman and the Singhs of No 11 Stanton Street. Almost overnight I started getting loads of letters, large envelopes full of glossy brochures. I was getting more mail than the rest of the block put together. Our tiny postbox was no match for the volume: the postman would shove the bulky envelopes into it and half of them would spill out onto the street. It frustrated that postman no end. Often I'd have to pick up thick brochures directly from the post office, many times taking Mummy with me to help carry them. For me, it was hugely exhilarating – each letter, each piece of correspondence. It became so much that Rajan's dad, who had a box at the main post office – PO Box 3253, Durban – allowed me to use that; in return I would pick up his mail and deliver it to him the next day.

While apartheid restricted the ambitions of many South Africans, I saw the status quo as a challenge to succeed, to beat it. I learned that there are no short cuts, that if you want to succeed you need to be both passionate and hardworking. And there's always a way. It helped that South Africans were starved of entertainment. The country still had no television – that would only be rolled out in 1976 – so 16mm film was the only home entertainment available.

Segregation in every aspect of my life continued to be unsettling – that was simply a reality I had to deal with – but it was James Bond who landed me in trouble with the law.

Many of the movies craved by consumers in South Africa (and certainly my customers) were banned by the state. The Directorate of Publications was the statutory body that controlled books, films, plays and other means of entertainment. It had the power to either ban them outright or restrict their publication on political or moral grounds. Books that were banned under apartheid included Steve Biko's *I Write What I Like* and, bizarrely, the classic Anne Sewell novel *Black Beauty*. (Rumour had it that the censor board had not even bothered to read the book, but was convinced by the title alone that it had something to do with the 'black is beautiful' slogan; they promptly banned it, never realising it was a book about a horse.)

Of course, a number of films were banned, and many more had to undergo extensive cuts and editing to the footage before they could be shown. Banned films deemed 'undesirable' for white audiences included *Super Fly*, *Guess Who's Coming to Dinner* and *Soldier Blue*. A film that could be watched by whites but not by Blacks was the acclaimed Mob drama *The Godfather*. The state apparently believed that it might spur Black people on to some sort of rebellion. It seemed that the less Black people knew, the better.

Distributors sometimes appealed the bans and orders for cuts or censorship, but these appeals rarely resulted in the original decision being overturned. The censor board, which was based in Pretoria, was comprised of six white right-wing Afrikaners. The Broederbond, the secret Afrikaner 'brotherhood' that seemed to have a hand in everything and whose agenda was to further Afrikaner interests, was no doubt well represented on it. It was therefore hardly surprising that their views were ultra-conservative and their decisions in accordance with apartheid's strict legislation.

Often in those early years as a business renting out films, I chose to break the law – a law I refused to recognise anyway – and brazenly showed or rented movies I wasn't supposed to. I simply followed my instincts. It was the right thing to do.

In 1973 the eighth James Bond film, *Live and Let Die*, was released. The uncut version was banned for Black audiences in South Africa because Roger Moore's James Bond was in bed with a Black woman. Rosie Carver was the character's name, and she was played by actress Gloria Hendry. That wasn't the only 'sin', however. The ubiquitous baddie in the movie was a giant Black man by the name of Mr Big, a corrupt Caribbean prime minister who doubles as a drug kingpin. He was played by Yaphet Kotto, 6ft 4in tall and the first Black actor to play a major Bond villain. Jane Seymour was the other Bond girl and in the movie Mr Big slaps her around. This was something, the censor board decided, that Black people in South Africa should not see. Non-whites could not only be inspired to become gangsters, but perhaps even be encouraged to treat white women with similar disdain. Or some such nonsense.

As a distributor, I was required to cut both those scenes before I could rent out the film. Needless to say, I didn't cut either. Legally I was in a double-bind: as the business owner I was prohibited from distributing the uncut version, and, as a 'non-white' person myself, I was one of those who weren't allowed to view the film uncut. Needless to say, it was a dilemma I decided to ignore. I continued to rent the movie out, uncut, to anyone who wanted to watch it.

The thing about films such as these, with heroes and strong characters who are not white, is that people learn about a culture. Great filmmakers use their medium to tell stories that need to be told – precisely what artists like Costa-Gavras did – making overt political statements through their work. Films such as *Z* and *State of Siege* were hugely inspiring in our racist world, and showcased for me the power of cinema. It became clearer and clearer to me that movies were one of the few tools available to us. If defying the law was the only way to see films with Black heroes, then so be it. That was the programme we needed to follow if we were to understand the world of oppression, freedom and rebellion. Every movie that we saw made us even more determined to take the necessary ethical, moral stand. As part of this process, I went on my own civil disobedience campaign, and wilfully defied apartheid laws, and not only in making a stand on the movies I rented out, uncut, and to whom. I would deliberately use the whites-only entrance at the post office and liquor store and walk into whites-only restaurants, and some were happy to have us. I got noticed. Eventually, inevitably, the police came for me. I had apparently been on their radar for a while so when they came, they came with a vengeance in the form of the notorious Durban Vice Squad.

The man in charge was a small giant of an Afrikaner, Captain Basie Smit, who was known for being ambitious. He was desperate to climb the ranks and in Durban – a city decidedly more liberal than most in the country – he found the ideal playground in which to unleash himself. Whether it was clamping down on marijuana smokers on the beaches or tackling interracial and homosexual liaisons, Smit and his team were on it like a bad rash. We, at the shop, made the list too, given that we were contravening the Publications Act and daring to rent out banned and uncut films to Black customers. And so one day Basie Smit and his lackeys pulled up outside the shop on Smith Street. I was arrested, manhandled into a police car and whisked off to Point police station.

My family and friends immediately sprang into action. Rajan's dad fetched my mother and drove her to the cells at Point Prison. My Uncle Jonsy and Aunty Prem met them there. Larry Kulpath brought me Kentucky Fried Chicken, which I shared with my fellow inmates. I spent two nights in jail before I was required to pay an admission of guilt fine, and was finally released – a not uncommon response from the authorities when a prisoner engaged legal representation. The authorities generally chose to let the matter slide rather than become embroiled in extended (and embarrassing) legal wrangling.

The harassment did not end there though. Nothing was ever that simple for an Indian, nor was it for any other people of colour in South Africa in these times. Although my first arrest ended with me walking out of that cell a free man, the second was not quite as trouble free. When I was arrested again following yet another contravention of the senseless censorship laws, I actually went to court – and was promptly convicted. The junior advocate who represented me this time was Philip Levinson, who later went on to become Deputy Judge President of KwaZulu-Natal. Again I was fined, which of course meant that I could leave, but I now had a criminal record, simply for screening an uncut movie of James Bond to a Black audience. For me, my actions were acts of defiance against highly unjust laws that were based purely on race. It was my way of taking a stand against the apartheid system and making a political statement of sorts – and it felt good!

When I travelled to Canada years later, I was asked at Immigration whether I had a criminal record. And because I indeed did, I was ushered into an interview room for interrogation. But when I explained the nature of my crime, the authorities saw it more as a badge of honour than a blight on my character and waved me through. Later, too, I made a film with Yaphet Kotto. I gave him a copy of the original censor board certificate that stated *Live and Let Die* had to be cut. He found it hilarious. As did Roger Moore when we lunched together at the Hilton Hotel in London one day and I repeated the story to him. It was mind-boggling to both of them.

The *Live and Let Die* episode and my subsequent incarceration, no matter that it was brief, was not the last time I found myself behind bars. Just six months later, I was in an equally anxious predicament – perhaps even more so, considering the context and the time.

It so happened that a projector and some films I had bought turned out to be stolen items – not by me, I hasten to add. It was only when the police came knocking that I realised that they were. And because they had been stolen from a company in Johannesburg, I was bundled into a police vehicle and, in an eight-hour car ride, carted off to Johannesburg and taken to the dreaded John Vorster Square. As a Black South African in custody in one of the most tumultuous times in the country's history, I was under no illusion about what could happen to me at John Vorster. Walking in, there was a very real fear that I would never walk out. The horror stories of Ahmed Timol and others – outspoken activists who had died under very suspicious circumstances while in custody there – were foremost in my mind and I was terrified. In the end, thankfully, mine was a less eventful story. The officers received a reprimand for having made a wrongful arrest, and I was released, although I had to make my own way back to Durban. On reflection now, my blood still runs cold at the thought of having been in such close proximity to that house of horror. Timol had been pushed to his death from the 10th floor of the building on 27 October 1971, and the inquest into his death continues today.

And as for Basie Smit? He succeeded in climbing the rungs in the South African Police. By the early 1980s, Smit was a lieutenant-colonel, having made his name as the head of the police's Narcotics Bureau in Durban. Following that, he was promoted to brigadier and then went on to become Northern Transvaal divisional commander of the Security Branch, the notorious South African government unit that ran alleged death squads and the Vlakplaas operation. He headed up the Security Branch from 1988 and was, among other incriminations, identified by the Goldstone Commission in 1994 for fomenting violence during the 'transitional' years from 1989 onwards. He was later also implicated at the Truth and Reconciliation Commission on a charge of attempted murder of the prominent anti-apartheid cleric Frank Chikane in 1989. In 1994, at the turn of democracy, Basie Smit was one of the most powerful policemen in South Africa, second only to General Johan van der Merwe. Van der Merwe had told Nelson Mandela before the 1994 election that he intended to retire early and he nominated Smit as his successor. Mandela refused. The buck had finally stopped.

My encounter with Smit and other menacing characters, especially within the apartheid security forces, meant that I was able to experience at dangerously close quarters the power and drive behind the regime. But whereas their attempts – as it was for all those who fell foul of their draconian measures – were intended to steer me from the path I and many others had chosen, it accomplished quite the opposite, serving only to reinforce our beliefs and determination to challenge the status quo at every opportunity.

Those early days in business were tough but I was ambitious and motivated to work hard. Apartheid effectively forced me to become creative and streetwise. If I wanted to make money, I had to outwit the system. But I persevered and the breakthroughs came.

7

The arts of persuasion and distribution

At this point, I was taking one day at a time, not looking back but not really looking too far ahead either. I continued to rent out films, saving and building up capital. And then one day, quite out of the blue, I made a big decision. Apartheid and all its rules were constantly disruptive – one of the reasons perhaps I was so driven to succeed – and I wanted to do more, to make a real mark. Something that had been fluttering at the back of my mind for a while was the idea of somehow getting into the distribution side of the film business. It seemed to me to be the next logical step. Setting my sights on buying exclusive rights for the distribution of films in South Africa, to Black theatres in particular, I began to make cautious inroads. I renamed my business Movie Place and it became the conduit for my new international distribution enterprise.

During this period I met Sudhir Pragjee. A chartered accountant at the time, Sudhir would visit the store and just hang around as youngsters do, renting or talking movies and shooting the breeze. Many friends would gather at the shop as it was more exciting than the other options, which were considered to be dull. When I realised that I needed to start doing grown-up things like tax returns, I asked Sudhir to help out, which he did, on the side, for a few years – and then with his firm Mahomedy and Manjee CA (SA) as my accountant. The first non-white Wimpy in Durban was downstairs from Sudhir's office and I would pop in there, buy us a couple of milkshakes, and take them up to his office where we'd discuss the books or my tax affairs.

When I first started out, funding was a major constraint. I needed money to buy the films I wanted to distribute but South African banks weren't dishing out loans to a Black-owned film business. I couldn't even get a credit line with a bank, even though I was doing well enough financially – and whether I wore a suit or not wasn't the issue. It became clear to me that I was dealing with managers and officials who were essentially racist, who looked no further than the colour of my skin. They didn't even want to see the potential in what I had to offer. There was simply no other explanation for the way they treated me.

Hurdles were deliberately placed in my path, but this only spurred me on to try harder, work harder, find a way to succeed. In fact, even though it was often an uphill battle, it made me even more determined. I developed a tenacity that would stand me in good stead through the years to come and I called out racism and prejudice in business dealings wherever I saw it.

When, in 1982, Standard Bank bounced a R700 cheque at a particularly sensitive time for me, I was livid. I wrote a letter to the manager of the branch, Mr Slabbert – a white Afrikaner – telling him in no uncertain terms how I felt about this as well as what I was going to do about it.

> … As you may or may not recall, I have been operating my account with your bank for over four years. In the span of these four years even you will admit there has been a rise in the account turnover from a mere R20 000 to R500 000 for the nine-month period 1982/3 financial year. Also I have honoured every commitment I have made to the bank and done considerable business in the form of Letters of Credit etc.
>
> I feel that in the years of banking with you, you have not afforded my account the respect and interest expected.
>
> In light of the above, I feel it will be to the best of my interest to close my account on the 30th of this month, at which time I will inform you of my new bankers to whom you can submit any remaining transactions.

I held true on my threat. I closed my account immediately and opened one at Nedbank, at the Albert Street branch in an essentially Indian neighbourhood. There I was treated differently, with respect, and I continue to bank with them to this day.

Another direct experience of racial profiling in the early 80s turned into a costly victory for me. I did not yet have my own car so travelling to and from work was generally by public transport. On nights when I worked late, finishing only after dark, I relied on friends for a lift home. To get to work in the morning I took the bus into Durban. I'd get off at Beatrice Street, some distance from the shop on the outskirts of the whites-only area and walk the rest of the way. My route took me past a branch of American Swiss, the jewellery store. At the time, my take-home pay was still no more than about R200 a month. One morning, something glinting in the display window caught my eye: a gold Rolex watch. AK Rajab, the patriarch of the Rajab family, who owned the 2 000-seater Shah Jehan cinema, wore one, and I knew it. I thought, Let me take a look. I stepped inside the cool, air-conditioned domain of white upper- and middle-class suburbia and marched over to the counter.

The assistant, a white middle-aged woman, looked a little startled. I saw her eyes flit nervously behind me to check what this jeans and T-shirt wearing Indian person wanted. She was alone at the counter, her manager ensconced in the back office, and here she was being brazenly confronted by a man of colour. I asked to see the gold Rolex. As perhaps can be expected, considering the times, the woman seemed reluctant to show me the watch, assuming – simply by virtue of the colour of my skin or the way I was dressed – that I couldn't possibly afford it. Insultingly, she tried to sell me a cheaper one, which only got me more exasperated. I insisted on seeing the watch that was displayed in the window but she refused to bring it to the counter. After much toing and froing, I asked to speak to the manager.

This was a young white man and he was at the counter in an instant. He gave me a wan, almost apologetic smile. Looking him straight in the eye, I told him how the shop assistant had treated me, then threw down a challenge. 'Is this how you treat all your customers?' I demanded. Before he could open his mouth to reply, I asked to see the watch. The assistant was forced to take it from the window after the manager instructed her to do so. I looked at it carefully as I pondered over it. I hadn't used my brand-new Diners card yet, and I had no idea whether I'd ever be able to afford to pay the watch off, considering the salary I was currently earning. Credit card transactions were not electronic then, and I remember the moment the assistant brought out the franking machine. I took the budget option, which would allow me to pay over six months. But I was also in luck as they were offering a 20 per cent discount for cash, and a credit card transaction was considered to be cash.

R6 000 later – a ton of money for me, for anyone, back then – I walked out of American Swiss with a gold Rolex in the bag and a fury rising in my chest. I had done it, I'd bought the thing, not because I needed it, but because I wanted to make a point. It was a costly exercise in education, in levelling the playing field, and it meant a lot of extra effort and sweating of blood to pay off that gold watch, but I did. I still have the watch, which now retails for lots more. The insurance alone is more than the original retail price. I look at that Rolex sometimes and it still provides me with a sense of pride and accomplishment.

One early breakthrough for me was meeting Jimmy Pereira. Yes, another Jimmy! My pursuit of scouring the world for films for local cinemas was simultaneously making me a number of key contacts, and Jimmy was one of them. At the time Jimmy was the only independent film distributor in Zimbabwe (then Rhodesia) and he and I became good friends. If I remember rightly, my very first business trip was when he invited me to one of his cinema openings in Harare, and whenever he came to Durban he would visit us and come home for lunch cooked by Mummy. I think Jimmy saw in me someone he wanted to teach and I learned a lot from him, both personally and professionally. He had a *joie de vivre* and was an amazing mentor and friend. It was through Jimmy I was able to make other contacts on the African continent, among them Mr Njoroge Njoroge in Kenya and then Indian cinema owners in Bujumbura and Tanzania, while he would distribute in Zimbabwe.

It was Jimmy who encouraged me, in 1978, to travel abroad to Cannes and Milan, to buy what the highbrow critics called 'exploitation films'. These were for the most part B-rated movies aimed at exploiting the latest social trends or genres at the time of release.

My one and only venture abroad without my parents until then had been a vacation to Las Palmas, Gran Canaria, with a group of friends, including Babs Naidoo and the Dass brothers, Pickey and Kuben. That visit was my introduction to what a truly non-racial society might look like, with individuals of all races and colours simply getting along, living their lives alongside one another. It wasn't all smooth sailing, but it was still a world away from my experiences back home in a society that was deeply segregated in all spheres and in every way. The region was pretty much a British outpost at the time, full of visitors on a tight budget and UK football thugs, and there were one or two incidents that threatened to topple my otherwise idealised view of a fully integrated society. Perhaps I was bolstered by both my youth and the fact that I had the back-up of friends, but I was having none of it. I quickly put an end to anything that felt even remotely racist to me. It was a surprise at the time but, on reflection, I quickly understood the various levels of division and class in society.

Now, at the age of 22, I embarked on my first buying trip abroad, where I set about making business contacts in person. I travelled to London, Rome and, of course, Cannes, which was top of the list and it has remained one of my favourite places, but for a youngster from apartheid-segregated Durban, my first experience of the Cannes Film Festival turned out to be a steep learning curve. I was starting out as a new kid on the block. This was the late 1970s. There was no internet, no email, and no way of checking ahead of time what to do or even where to stay. I booked a room via long-distance telephone, believing the hotel's promise that it was well located, right where all the action was. It turned out it was way on the other side of town ... Despite staying in a bad hotel, I worked long hours in Cannes nevertheless, viewing many films and attending many parties.

My venturing into securing distribution rights abroad would bear fruit before too long, but first I had to master the art of negotiation and persuasion – with the emphasis on persuasion. Movies are abstract things, and the rights to them even more ethereal. It can cost anything from hundreds of dollars to millions to bring a film into South Africa. When I started buying the South African rights to foreign films, to my own astonishment I found I was able to haggle Hollywood studios down from $50 000 to $1 000 and I got increasingly better at it as I went along. They didn't need to know how little money I had to bargain with and that I had no choice but to low ball. But I stayed the course and it worked – not always, of course, but often enough. I never resorted to using the oppression in South Africa as a tool to gain sympathy from my suppliers, which was a ploy used by many others. When you're a Black South African without a vote, one of an oppressed majority, you're politically active whatever you do.

But back at home there was always that tired old cliché – the Black man on his high horse. It continued to irk many both within and beyond the industry that I was making inroads. The movie business in South Africa was still dominated by whites, and at every turn racism in one guise or another confronted me. Buying the films was only half the battle. Once I got back home, I had to find outlets that were willing to distribute these movies (many of which contained scenes of sex, violence and cheap thrills) as well as run the censorship gauntlet. It was very tough persuading theatres to show my films and tougher still to make money. For a long time, the only audiences and cinemas I was allowed to deal with were Black and Indian owned.

The white cinema chains simply refused to do business with me. At the time, 90 per cent of the whites-only cinemas were dominated by Ster and Kinekor (they merged in 1976 under a single banner, Ster-Kinekor, owned by Sanlam) and the international company owned by the studios, CIC-Warner, both of which had their own movie distribution businesses that fed their cinemas with product. The duopoly was tight, locked down, and I struggled every step of the way. I don't know whether it was because they feared me as a competitor or whether it was simple racism at play, but they just wouldn't take my films. And when it came to making money as a distributor, white cinemas were where the money was. Not only were there way more white cinemas than Black ones, but white cinemas also charged much higher ticket prices. If you didn't get a share of that, you were wasting your time.

Looking back now, I realise that, despite the successes, staying motivated was tough at times. There were many obstacles to overcome and challenges to face. Very often that meant pioneering new ways of thinking, of hacking my own path through the jungle rather than following those set by others. But through all of this I remained passionate – passionate about film, about what I was doing and where I was going. I was determined to succeed. I continued to learn everything that I could about the industry. I also learned to be clever with money. When you are still learning – and learning from the street – every new revenue stream is appreciated. At the start, whatever money I made, I reinvested in the business. I did not even take a salary. All my assets were in my films. It's like investing in expensive paintings and understanding that the value depends entirely on what the buyer is prepared to pay. I also realised that

I needed to grow the distribution business – the area where the greater potential lay – so I continued making the rounds at international film markets, buying up the rights to distribute low-budget pictures in South Africa. When contracting to secure these rights, I made sure that I was buying 'African' rights, allowing me to extend my reach into countries on the continent other than South Africa.

My recipe was simple: comedy, action and 'exploitation' pictures. If they had a bit of nudity in them, all the better. All the things South Africa was starved of. In my quest, I accumulated a substantial amount of knowledge about the industry and the content available around the world. I also had the foresight to buy the rights for films in all media formats, including future formats. This decision would prove to be the most fortuitous of all.

Jimmy Pereira was well versed in the challenges of squaring up to Ster and Kinekor, which at the time dominated the entire subregion. He gave me a great opportunity to expand beyond the South African border in distributing my films to his cinemas. He catered to a more diverse market, too, white and Black, and many of the films I was acquiring were suited to his more diverse audiences. From this initial access to the Zimbabwe market that Jimmy provided for me, other African markets followed. As a result I was no longer confined to a particular audience, or as restricted in the marketplace. I continued supplying 16mm films to Kenya, Tanzania, Bujumbura (Burundi) and Uganda.

My first distribution success was the movie *Secrets*, a largely forgettable film, resurrected only because it featured a naked Jacqueline Bisset in 1977. She had recently stepped into the spotlight thanks to the hit film *The Deep*, which was remarkable primarily for its shots of the actress in a wet T-shirt. *The Deep* was a huge hit in South Africa, mostly I think because local audiences were largely starved of material that treated them as adults. Understanding this issue early on would become a key advantage and I would go on to exploit it to its fullest. The American ad slogan for the movie was 'If you liked her in the wet T-shirt in *The Deep*, now see her without it.' Very gender insensitive.

A particular coup for me was acquiring the distribution rights to one of the Trinity series of Spaghetti Westerns, which starred Bud Spencer and Terence Hill, and were sold in Italy by Sergio Felicioli. These movies were phenomenally successful in the South African market, their particular mix of cowboy and comedy appealing to the country's very broad audience. CIC Distribution secured the big screens for me that I could not get on my own. Felicioli, who is now 94 years old, has remained a friend and I recently spoke to him and we reminisced about our many years of association.

8

The vision that was video

It was in the 1970s, especially after the Soweto uprising of 16 June 1976, when the country was volatile, with widespread resistance and unrest that sometimes turned violent and bloody, that things really changed for me. As the nation simmered and sputtered and PW Botha made the transition from prime minister to president, still ominously wagging his finger in warning and recrimination, matters were about to take a turn for the better for me personally, certainly from a business point of view. It may not have been earth shattering for the nation as a whole, but it would change things entirely – for me, for the film industry and for many ordinary, blue-collar South Africans simply trying to get by. That sea change was the replacement of 16mm film by video.

For the first time, anyone could rent or even buy a video machine and watch movies on a television set in the comfort of their own homes. Gone were the days of lugging projectors around and of tired reels looping on a machine whirring in the background, scratchy images flickering across Mummy's white sheet strung across the living room curtains or competing with paint peeling off the side of the garage in the back yard. This, in comparison, was hi-tech – and the move revolutionised home entertainment across the globe, turning everything we knew on its head. For at least some South Africans, then, video provided an escape from the turmoil that was their everyday lives. Like the rest of the world, we seemed to have a voracious appetite for this format (first the Philips format, followed by Sony Betamax and then the universal VHS format) and very quickly video became big business, with video stores opening on every street corner. It also helped that we only had one television channel at the time, the SABC.

My early decision to buy the rights to *all* formats of the movies I distributed paid off and the move to video immediately gave me access to a library – quite literally hundreds – of movies for which I already owned the distribution rights for South Africa. I was thus able to unlock real value from the library I had built up. Almost overnight, all those cheap films to which I had bought the rights over the years were suddenly worth a great deal. Right away I was able to licence almost 1 000 titles per year into the video market. And by then, of course, I also knew where to source additional films I could feed into the burgeoning video market. It was a big, bold move that could have sunk any budding entrepreneur, but experience had taught me that this was a chance worth taking. And my countrymen were proving me right, with the expansion into video catapulting the business to new heights. Video provided a huge advantage – and one I thoroughly exploited and enjoyed pursuing. I have thought of the global opportunity poised before me and with all the knowledge I gathered, whether I could have used it on the bigger stage. But I have always looked at my plate and have been satisfied.

So it was, then, in 1979 that Videovision Enterprises was born – in Smith Street, Durban. I had always had a presence in other cities, including Johannesburg, but deliberately chose to keep Durban as my base. One of the great advantages of sticking to Durban over Hollywood or Johannesburg or any other big city was being removed from those other environments. Being on my own, far from the bustle of other sprawling urban centres that were the breeding grounds of great movies, allowed me to focus on my own job and retain a much clearer perspective of the business as a whole. When you are caught up in the industry – and Hollywood is the perfect example – it is all too easy to become consumed by the business, living it 24/7. But if you are able to extricate yourself, give yourself some distance, you get to think about things more sensibly and, as a result, make better decisions. You are able to focus completely on a script or some aspect of the industry and not be caught up in the race to do whatever the herd is doing next. I have always made a conscious decision not to chase after what the herd is gathering around. Getting caught up in that mentality of trying to compete and compare will crush you, suck the soul from your work and distract you from your own vision.

Business boomed, with distribution rapidly becoming the major focus, but the hard work never stopped. High telephone call rates meant that it was only after midnight that I would start making calls, hundreds of them, staying up until all hours of the morning in an attempt to connect with people. And, of course, given the time difference between me in Durban and potential clients in the US, this suited me perfectly. I also continued scouring film festivals around the globe, snatching up cheap films and tying them up in deals as sole distributor in South Africa. My life essentially consisted of watching movies, buying rights and buying movies.

As an independent setting himself up against the big distributors, on the distribution front I continued to have a hard time back home. Every day was still a struggle, of having to scale obstacles, bang your head against brick walls. Little had changed on the political and socio-economic front in South Africa on that score. The white cinema circuit remained closed for me as a movie distributor, still locked up tight by the giant Ster-Kinekor, which was owned by Sanlam – at the time, a pro-National Party business with strong ties to the apartheid government. All their cinemas were whites-only.

I knew I stood no chance against Sanlam/Ster-Kinekor. My best hope, I realised, would be with the other entity in the duopoly, CIC-Warner. At the time, CIC was a partnership made up of entities that included Paramount Pictures, MGM, Universal Pictures and Warner Brothers. CIC had taken over the Metro chain of theatres in South Africa and was thus managing about 30 per cent of the screens in the country – so not the majority, but certainly a significant player in the local industry. I wrote to the managing director of CIC in South Africa, based in Johannesburg, explaining that I'd like to meet and get advice. Sure, he said, come. So I went and that was the start of a close and long relationship with the enterprise's representatives in South Africa.

My association with CIC opened significant doors for me. Again, it began with a letter to the MD, Wayne Duband, who was a foreigner and he immediately saw the racism that was rife in the industry. I was fortunate to maintain this relationship with his successors, Tim Ord and Peter Dignan, and they in turn introduced me to Michael Williams-Jones, a South African who headed operations in London. Soon it became possible for me to supply movies that I'd already acquired to CIC-owned cinemas that catered to mainly white cinemagoers, terrain that had previously been off-limits to me.

As is to be expected in the corporate world, CIC changed over the years, losing some of its partners along the way, including MGM and Warner Brothers. Today the business is known as United International Pictures (UIP), and no longer owns any cinemas in South Africa, but between 1982 and 1986 my film-distribution business generated approximately $8 million in box-office revenue for them. This grew even further in successive years, really taking off from 1986 onwards, and to this day UIP remains my main outlet in South Africa.

At this point, my team consisted of my brother Sanjeev, who had joined me in 1981, and my secretary Rosanna Oliva. Relatively confident that the business was growing sufficiently, we took on Aaron Ndwandwe in June 1983. Until then, Aaron had been working tirelessly at John's Auctioneers across the road but he used to help me after the auction house closed at 5 pm. He would remain with us until he retired in 2007.

That same year, my young cousin Nilesh started working part-time with us too. At the tender age of just 14, he would head off to movie houses in Durban and stand outside the doors to collect ticket stubs. To ensure that the cinema owners didn't cheat the distributor (in this case, me) we needed the stubs to check how many people went to watch the movie. I was handing out movies to show, but it was the cinemas that sold the tickets and collected the cash. We had to check how many people were actually showing up and when the returns came those numbers had to tally. If there was some short-changing going on, we needed to be extra vigilant in order to protect our revenue, especially in an industry that was small but growing so rapidly.

With my relationship with UIP set to blossom, the team in Durban grew to six people, overseen by Sanjeev. Two of those new members were Ronnie Govender and Teddy Ravjee, both of whom had been working for the chain of independent cinemas in Durban belonging to the Rajab family.

The Rajabs were a wealthy Indian family who had over many years cornered a large part of the independent cinema circuit in Durban. I would often go to their offices and negotiate to have my movies shown in their theatres. We had many tough conversations – those independent cinema owners were no pushovers and would try their best to intimidate you. Think Michael Douglas as Gordon Gekko in *Wall Street*. That was AK Rajab. And this, of course, meant that you would have to stand up and face them down, every second word an F and a B right along with them. And, naturally, I would use the words too, to prove I would not be intimidated by bully tactics. The result was that I got what I wanted, most of the time anyway.

In a message on the occasion of my 60th birthday, Mahmoud Rajab wrote that in the early days of my business career I had befriended older people who were already established in the industry, people from whom I could learn. Among them were his late brother, AK Rajab, Isa Stark and Eddie Falconer, who became mentors, and over the years as I ventured into new territory in the industry, I was fortunate to meet others who generously shared their knowledge.

Teddy Ravjee worked as a projectionist at the Rajab family's Shah Jehan Cinema. AK Rajab was a shrewd businessman and he ran a tight ship. His main cinema complex in Grey Street had two thousand seats and was always open to all races, although primarily Black and Indian cinemagoers were its patrons. The Shah Jehan was incredibly popular and played to full houses over weekends especially, generating a steady and impressive income. Often the tickets would be sold out, and you would then find black-market scalpers appearing, flogging tickets to patrons outside who were desperate to get in. When I had a meeting on a weekday, I would pay Teddy to watch my car, which was doubled parked, while I went inside to meet with his boss. One day he asked whether there were any vacancies at Videovision. That was Wednesday, 21 December 1983 – by Friday the 23rd, Teddy was working with me. His first task the following week was to transport new movies to Johannesburg, show them there, and then bring them back to Durban, sometimes with the cash from ticket sales. Often there was no more than a single copy of a film in South Africa and when that was in demand the price would be high enough to justify having Teddy either drive the 500 kilometres or fly to Johannesburg, show the film a few times and then return to Durban. One of those films that required such an excursion for Teddy was *Coolie*, starring Indian superstar Amitabh Bachchan. It was immensely popular.

At this point in my journey, life was pretty routine, following a predictable pattern of work, eat, sleep, work, eat, sleep, travel and, occasionally, party. I always tried to allow time for myself and the opportunity for play, but during much of this period it was more a matter of head down, making plans, setting goals, driving-driving-driving myself. I pushed myself, and was even, in retrospect, hard on myself. It was the stuff of movies really: *The Blind Side* meets *The Great Debaters*. It was all hard work, dedication and determination. Focus.

One of the few indulgences I allowed myself was good food and music, including live musicians on Sundays at a supper club. My tastes were very diverse and became even more so as I learned more and more about music in every form: from classical to pop, the soundtracks of *Woodstock*, the Bond movies, *Lawrence of Arabia*. It was my friend Larry Kulpath who introduced me to jazz, a genre I wholeheartedly embraced. Artists like

Quincy Jones, Nat King Cole, Glen Miller, George Gershwin, Nina Simone and Duke Ellington became favourites.

I was now in my 30s, and still living with my mother. I'd leave home early and return home late at night. She always had a delicious meal waiting for me and always wanted to get out of bed to serve me herself. Even at my age, she also tried to reprimand me for coming home in the wee hours of the morning. In any event, this suited me as I worked from home where I had three landlines to make calls to the US and Canada at 2 or 3 am every day.

In the movie business, relationships are critical. If you get that right, these become friendships and those links are like vines that produce better wine as the years tick on. In 1981 I was on the shuttle bus to screenings in Los Angeles when I met Mickey. We just happened to be sitting together. I was on my way to my first American film market; he was visiting from his home in the West Indies. I didn't know him or his films.

Later I learned that Mickey Kumar was born in India where he had started out at the 'lowest of rungs' as a tea boy at Filmistan Studios in Mumbai. He had steadily worked his way up until he finally found the momentum of his career in the film industry – in distribution. From India, he moved to the West Indies, where he became the pioneer of the motion picture industry in the Caribbean. But back then, on that bus in LA, Mickey and I simply chatted. In conversation I told him I was looking to buy up films to distribute in South Africa.

'Well, look, I made this movie,' he said. 'It's called *Girl from India.*'

Now, in this business, 'I made this movie …' is a line you hear all the time, but still, me liking Mickey and him being a nice enough fellow, I went to the screening somewhat reluctantly. I saw potential in this film for

South Africa, especially considering the Indian and African connection.

'Okay,' I said to him afterwards, 'I think there's something here.'

And so we made a deal – $5 000 – and I returned to South Africa determined to distribute it. Easier said than done, of course. I presented the film to AK Rajab, who promptly told me that no one would want to see this B-grade film. It was dead in the water. But when I hear no, I can be relentless, and I kept pressing him. Finally, we reached a deal with Mickey's movie which entailed me guaranteeing weekly revenue to the cinema owner. As it happened, my instincts proved correct. The film did so well that it ended up playing for about 14 weeks – a long time for a movie to be shown in a theatre in South Africa. *Girl from India* was a massive box-office success for Mickey and in South Africa it outgrossed a number of more mainstream films, including the Bond film *For Your Eyes Only*.

What *Girl from India* taught me was that audiences, no matter where in the world they are, identify with the emotion of a story, even one that might have enormous shortcomings. What Mickey did so well – having come from India to settle in Trinidad, which had a fair Indian population – was craft a film targeted at an Indian audience. He then skewed the same film in a slightly different manner, titling it *Man from Africa*; although the story was the same, he orchestrated a completely different campaign for each and this met with significant success on both circuits. For us in Africa, the exercise proved fascinating: in Zimbabwe I released the film under the title *Man from Africa*, and in South Africa as *Girl from India*, targeting the Indian diaspora. In Zimbabwe, the film played for two years.

At the time, demand for Indian films was high in South Africa, a country with a significant Indian community. In addition, it was very difficult to find quality Indian films for the local market. For one thing,

India itself had no trade links with South Africa. Back in the 1950s, due to apartheid, it had been the first country to cut ties. Of course, there was no shortage of illicit traders in Indian cinema who brought Indian movies into the country illegally, with no paperwork and no red tape, and ignoring the apartheid sanctions, but I refused to get involved in that. The entire situation was just too unregulated and uncertain, which meant that there was little protection of your investment. That was just too great a risk. And, as it turned out, my more orthodox way worked out in the end.

Girl from India, the first film I released for Indian audiences, was not only an enjoyable experience for me, but also a project of which I remain extremely proud. In those early days when I was just starting out I personally designed all the newspaper adverts we placed for the films we distributed. I did this at home, using Letraset letters and cut-outs of pictures, and I would go personally to various newspapers to book the space. One such newspaper was *The Graphic*, an Indian-focused tabloid. I had developed a friendship with one of the advertising representatives, Yogin Devan. He recently reminisced about those days: 'Anant would book 10cm x 2 columns weekly for advertisements for his fledgling film business. The cost was under R20. The instruction from the accountant at *The Graphic* was that only advertisers who had signed a long-term contract would enjoy a 30-day payment concession. Anant was a casual advertiser and must pay cash each week. Anant desperately needed the advertisement. I desperately needed the booking. In defiance of the accountant's rule, I would accept the copy for the ad – often accompanied by risqué photos – which were sometimes designed in my office with the printer's assistance, without any cash, on the promise that payment would be made by the Friday. And true to his word, before the accountant did his checks on a Saturday morning, Anant's payment of about

R20 would come through in bronze and silver coins in a plastic bank packet. It was that kind of honesty that formed the bedrock on which this media mogul built his thriving empire.'

9

Lights, camera, action

Even with all of the new developments and the overwhelming success Videovision was experiencing in the home entertainment market, when it came to the next logical step – the business of making movies – I was reticent. I'm not sure what was holding me back. Perhaps a fear of failure, the notion of new territory still unnervingly foreign to explore, the prospect of taking on more than I could chew, or an industry reserved for whites … My plate was already filled to overflowing, wasn't it? But, I was loving each moment.

But others were enjoying some success. South African films rarely made any impact abroad, but there was one notable exception: director Jamie Uys's *The Gods Must be Crazy*. Jamie was no amateur and his earlier film *Beautiful People* had won him a Golden Globe in the 1970s. It was *Gods*, however, that really rocketed him to stardom. It was produced by the Bloemfontein-based Boet Troskie, who headed up a studio by the name of Mimosa Films, and the project took them four and a half years to complete, costing some $5 million.

The Gods Must be Crazy is a comedy about what happens when a pilot drops an empty Coca-Cola bottle into the Kalahari Desert where it is found by a 'Bushman' who, oblivious to the modern world beyond the confines of the arid semi-desert that is his home, has never seen such a thing before. Intentional or not, in many ways the narrative was an allegory, a commentary on socio-political issues pervading the country. The plot centres around the discovery of the bottle, which soon becomes a much-coveted possession among a community that has until then always shared everything. Suddenly, it introduces into this pastoral milieu a tension that traditional folk have never encountered. Conflict breaks out and tempers flare as the family structure starts to unravel. One of the characters (the actor N!Xau) decides that the bottle – the source of the tension – must go, and he sets off to the end of the earth to toss it off the edge.

With its release in 1980, *The Gods Must be Crazy* shattered all local box-office records within the first week, and went on to win global acclaim, achieving enormous box-office success abroad, largely unheard of for South African-made films. In France it raked in more money than Steven Spielberg's *ET*, and rumour had it that Queen Elizabeth II went to see it twice. *Gods* eventually went on to make more than $200 million at the global box office, an astounding record for a South African film. In many countries at the time, *Gods* was sold as a film from Botswana, a country not affected by the global sanctions that were in place at the time against apartheid.

Boosted by my success with *Girl from India* and the Italian Westerns, and the rise of video, I started flirting with the idea of making movies. I knew it was a natural progression: from film rental, to distribution, to production, but, initially, the notion was no more than tentative, a resurgence of that dream I'd carried with me since I was a boy. A brief flicker: *I wonder what it'd be like to make a movie …* and then I'd continue with the day to day – which kept me extremely busy anyway. But one day the opportunity presented itself and I allowed the door to open a little wider.

I spotted a story in the local newspapers about a white Afrikaans schoolgirl who was intending to run – barefoot – in the 1984 Olympics Games, which were due to be held in Los Angeles that year. Her name was Zola Budd. Because of its apartheid policy, South Africa at the time was excluded from international athletics competition, including – naturally – the Olympic Games. The last time the country had taken part had been in 1960, and South Africans were desperate to compete globally again. There was no denying that Zola, at the age of 17, was an incredible talent and she was breaking records, even if they were not officially recognised because they had taken place in the pariah state that was South Africa. She was seven seconds faster over 5 000 metres than the current world record holder, the US athlete Mary Decker.

Here at home, while the waif-like Zola rapidly became the nation's darling, her father, Frank, who acted as her agent and coach, was fast gaining notoriety; he was widely considered as both ambitious and greedy. He had managed to facilitate an arrangement through a British newspaper, the *Daily Mail*, whereby Zola would move to England – the Budd family had ancestral links to the UK – and be eligible to compete at the 1984 Olympics in English colours. In April 1984, Budd's application for British citizenship was approved in record time and – having settled in Guildford – she was already preparing to claim her place in the British Olympic team.

A disillusioned Sam Ramsamy (who unbeknown to me was a family friend and a patient of my father), the exiled anti-apartheid activist who was spearheading the international sports boycott against South Africa at the time, felt equally angry and sad. Zola was a talented but innocent teenager who was being used: on the one hand by a British newspaper to boost its circulation figures, and on the other by the illegitimate apartheid regime to gain recognition for a country that had been banned from competing on the world athletics stage. 'I find myself in an awkward position,' he was quoted as saying. 'I feel that SANROC [South African Non-Racial Olympic Committee] must unequivocally condemn what amounts to a South African star athlete running under a flag of convenience, but I am also reluctant for us to look like bullies harassing a naive teenager who unfortunately was heeding the instructions of her handlers.'

The way I saw the controversy was a story seed waiting to unfold. A tale never told before. And one that I was being drawn to capture as each intriguing detail unveiled itself. The narrative intrigued me. I saw in Zola Budd's story perhaps a South African *Chariots of Fire*. So I reached out to Lord and Lady Rothermere, the owners of the *Daily Mail*. Because they had sponsored the drive to get Zola to compete for Great Britain, they owned the rights to the story.

'I know I'm just starting to make movies,' I said, 'but I think the Zola Budd story is a great one and I'd like to option it to see if I can make it into a film.'

I knew I was taking a gamble and I wasn't entirely convinced that my brazenness would bear any fruit, but no other South African producer had seized the opportunity and my speed paid off. To my astonishment, they agreed, and a deal was concluded. I immediately hopped back on a plane to South Africa to set the wheels in motion to make this film a reality.

Obviously, the *Daily Mail* is a newspaper and thus in the business of selling stories, and good stories like Zola's sell papers; so, unsurprisingly, they publicised the entire agreement. It was big news. Big. And then the mayor of Bloemfontein weighed in. He released a statement saying that should I – being Indian – plan to travel to Bloemfontein or anywhere else in what was then the Orange Free State province, where Zola's story plays out, I would first need to apply for a permit. Of course, the letter of the law was not new to me – one of those draconian apartheid laws particular to the white-dominated Free State that required Indians to apply for special permission to be in the province longer than 72 hours – but still I was stunned. I mean, it was astonishing to me that, with the magnitude of this story and the implications it would have for South Africa being exposed to a global market, such an archaic and mindless legality would be the automatic response. First I was in shock. Then I was outraged. But were we not in apartheid South Africa?

I made a statement to the press – 'I will never apply for this racist permit, and this movie will never get made' – and then I went right back to the *Daily Mail*. I spelled out the situation to them and explained that I could never bow to such discriminatory legislation and thus be party to any credence afforded it, especially at such a critical juncture in the development of the South African political landscape, which was already showing signs of rupture. Our deal with the *Daily Mail* had been for a few thousand pounds, but they stood firmly with me and immediately agreed to cancel it. In fact, they took it one step further – if Anant Singh was not making this movie, they announced, no one was. They would not entertain any further offers.

Coincidently, I was in Los Angeles on 10 August 1984 and I attended the Games of the XXIII Olympiad, my first Olympics. I bought a cheap ticket to watch Zola run. So I witnessed the drama first-hand – when US favourite, Mary Decker, tripped mid-race. The controversy that inevitably followed when Dekker blamed Zola for the fall resonated with Sam Ramsamy's earlier prediction. 'It ended in tears,' he said, 'for almost everyone.' The script was in effect writing itself, and had big-screen success written all over it – surely one of the most dramatic and bizarre Olympic stories ever. My interest in the Olympics and sport-themed stories has not diminished since.

But my Zola Budd/Free State story did not end there. In 1995, editor and MD of the weekly newspaper, *Mail & Guardian*, Anton Harber, called me to tell me that the state broadcaster, the SABC, and its shareholder – the government – had decided to dispose of several of their radio stations. I joined a consortium of business people and we bid for two of them: East Coast Radio in KwaZulu-Natal and Radio Oranje (since rebranded OFM), the station covering the Free State and based in Bloemfontein. We subsequently won both bids and Radio Oranje became the first state-owned station to be privatised.

Shortly afterwards, I paid my first visit to the Bloemfontein office with the premier of the Free State. I told the assembled all-white management and team my story about Zola Budd. 'You know,' I said, 'I'm here in the Free State as part of a new democratic South Africa and we've bought the radio station.'

You should have seen the faces. I'm sure they imagined we were going to fire the lot of them and kick them out on the street – sweet revenge for a lifetime of humiliation. But we didn't. We were never vindictive. Rather, we worked well together and did good business for a number of years.

Videovision Enterprises finally expanded into film production in 1984. At the time, as far as I'm aware, I was the only Black person in the country trying to make movies. The filmmaking expertise in South Africa was beyond reproach and the crews were both dedicated and enthusiastic, but they were, without exception, almost all white except for labour and other menial work. On the technical side, there were just a handful of equipment rental companies and only one film development lab, the Irene Film Lab in Pretoria. In terms of locations, South Africa had all you would ever wish for to make a spectacular film. Even back then, many international productions were shot in South Africa with no one really the wiser. A good example is *American Ninja II*, with Michael Dudikoff in the lead. The movie was filmed in South Africa, with Cape Town standing in as an anonymous colonial backwater of seedy bars, prostitutes and incompetent local officials and a number of scenes boasting picturesque ocean vistas. And most of the schmucks getting their butts kicked were locals.

Becoming a producer was a long, circuitous route. It took hard work and lots of research, and along with the successes there were some dismal failures. The genesis came towards the end of 1984 when I was roped into co-producing a movie called *Go for Gold* starring James Ryan, who achieved success in a local martial arts film, *Kill and Kill Again*. At the time, because of the lucrative tax breaks and subsidies available, lots of people were trying to make movies in South Africa. To boost the economy and encourage local investment, the state offered attractive subsidies for some industries. It was a strange set-up – people were making money even if there was no film at the end of the day. Often, once these filmmakers ran out of investors' money, the projects ground to a halt. *Go for Gold* was one such venture; when I became involved it had been abandoned by its financier and had yet to be completed. This meant that, although I knew next to nothing about that side of the business, I had to get into post-production quickly. It was an utter disaster. Not only did the project lose money, but it was, quite simply, a terrible movie and largely unwatchable. Everything I tried did not work. But what I took from the experience was some post-production skills. Even today I maintain that the best way to become a filmmaker is to make films – make mistakes, learn and move forward. It really is that simple. Film school is okay and definitely has its advantages, mostly from an aesthetics standpoint, but the best thing to do is to go out and make films.

For me, the filmmaking bug bit really hard.

One of my goals was to smash through the ceiling that kept people of colour out of the film industry by pioneering a focus on the international market. I knew there was an opportunity to produce films locally that would appeal to a much broader international audience and make money offshore. I had always known that the movie business is a crazy one, a high-risk field, where the odds are typically that one out of every three films isn't going to make any money. But I had also realised that if you do things right, the profits can be high. Motion picture investment in South Africa was by now becoming rather lucrative, thanks to the weakening value of the rand against the US dollar – and all international film sales were in US dollars.

I knew that I had a lot to learn. When I was just starting out, one of those rare individuals, the ones who step up to the plate to help guide a determined young hopeful in his formative years, came into my life. This was Tim Ord, the new MD of UIP, and a veteran of the industry. He and I spent many a late night unpacking the bumpy road ahead. Dinners together often spilled over into late-night conversations and went on into the early hours of the morning. Together we navigated a path through censorship and the apartheid regime's crazy laws. In many respects, I consider Tim a mentor and I learned an extraordinary amount from him, especially when it came to marketing, distribution and the positioning of films for success in the global market. Most important, however, was his kindness and generosity in allowing me to be a part of every aspect of marketing and distribution, which proved to be extremely helpful in the years that followed when my own production business began to grow. I remember vividly our meetings at the Total Office Tower in downtown Johannesburg, the long lunches at El Gaucho, The Three Ships at the Carlton Hotel and several other fine and exotic dining venues all around Johannesburg. It was thanks largely to Tim's largesse that I was able to experience and navigate some tricky paths.

In fact, it was at the urging of Tim Ord that I started looking into producing my own movie and almost immediately an opportunity came up that I couldn't resist. In 1984, *Deadly Passion* became my first film and an expensive experiment. Basically, it was a knock-off of a 1981 thriller called *Bodyheat*, which had made a killing at the box office despite its small budget. But I found out soon enough that I had jumped in at the deep end – a very deep end.

The first obstacle was funding. With any successful venture, there is always going to be an element of risk. If there wasn't any risk, everyone would be doing it. Much the same is true of making movies. We needed R1.5 million to make the film and, despite my success and track-record in the distribution business, there was no one prepared to climb on board.

When it came to funding for local projects, the biggest player was undoubtedly the state-owned broadcaster, the SABC. It had big budgets and commissioned a lot of work, but the SABC was interested only in material that would drive the National Party government's agenda, which meant that that avenue was not going to be one open to us. To exacerbate matters, none of the banks was prepared to give us a credit facility. I was essentially back to banging my head against the wall. Here I was, an established businessman, and no one was prepared to finance me. A lot of the people on whose doors I knocked were sceptical about closing a deal. I showed everyone meticulously detailed business plans, but there were no bites. What could be underlying all of this? Was race yet again the elephant in the room? Of course it was!

But I was determined. This movie was going to get made, come hell or high water. If, after everything I had already achieved, I was unable to engender trust in others, I would have to put that trust in myself. There was no other way around it. By this point I at least had some cash in the bank, so eventually I put up 85 per cent of the budget for the film, with other small investors pitching in for the rest. Sudhir Pragjee and Len Konar were some of those early investors. He was still an auditor at the time, but we were close and he understood the numbers. And, before he realised it, he had been dragged into movie production and was now also an executive producer.

So it was that I, not quite knowing how to swim, jumped into the deep end and launched into the making of *Deadly Passion*. At last.

The experience provided me with the opportunity to learn the process of film production and it was definitely a case of sink or swim! I had to quickly learn the intricacies of production – the protocols of working on set, why key crew had to be specialists, the editing and post-production process and getting the film ready for delivery to distributors, not to mention all the challenges that one inevitably encounters on a movie set. It was daunting yet very exciting because I was taking my passion for film in an entirely new direction.

The setting and storyline of the film got me thinking more and more about making films in South Africa that looked like they were produced abroad. This led to the development of a strategy I called the International Look formula. The trick behind making successful films in South Africa, I believed, was to bring in at least some overseas talent – the screenwriter or director and one or two international stars. This gave the project an international feel that would sell well overseas. We could also shoot very cheaply in incredible locations: many South African settings made brilliant substitutes for foreign destinations.

Deadly Passion was a formulaic movie, described at the time as an 'international detective thriller with sensuous undertones'. From the start I concentrated on creating a small, streamlined operation I could oversee while still moving into the new territory that was production. *Deadly Passion* focused on the rich and beautiful living in the Bahamas and Beverly Hills, but it was shot entirely on location in Durban and Johannesburg. The headline stars were two international actors: Ingrid Boulting – who had appeared opposite Robert De Niro in *The Last Tycoon* – and Brent Huff. They gave the production the international flavour I was looking for. The local cast was headed up by John Maytham and John Berks, both of whom went on to become well-known radio personalities in South Africa, as well as Lynn Maree. The art director on *Deadly Passion* was a relatively unknown artist by the name of William Kentridge, whom I commissioned to do three black-and-white drawings incorporating movies as a theme. They remain very special to me, and hang on my wall at home. William has since gone on to claim his own space and is now considered one of the country's finest artists.

His father Sydney Kentridge was the leading lawyer for the defence in the Treason Trial in the 1950s, the precursor to the Rivonia Trial that saw Nelson Mandela jailed for 27 years. In fact, during his illustrious career, Sydney represented no fewer than three Nobel Peace Prize winners – Nelson Mandela, Desmond Tutu and Albert Luthuli – as well as the family of Steve Biko in their action against the state following Steve's death. The inquest into Steve's death was a sham. The presiding magistrate accepted the evidence of the Security Police who said that Steve was aggressive towards them and was injured in the scuffle that ensued. He refused to prosecute any of those involved, including the doctors who tended to Steve. In 1985 world-renowned palaeontologist Professor Phillip Tobias, who was dean of the Wits Medical School at the time, along with five other doctors pursued the matter with the SA Medical and Dental Council, which had refused to take action against the doctors who were negligent, by mounting a Supreme Court action against the council. I read about this action in the press and that it needed to be funded and, having been inspired by Steve Biko as one of my early political influences, I made a contribution to the cause. Interestingly, I would later become friends with Professor Tobias, who was a true inspiration. Steve's contribution to our liberation was acknowledged by Madiba on the 20th anniversary of his death when Madiba said, 'History called upon Steve Biko at a time when the political pulse of our people had been rendered faint by banning, imprisonment, exile, murder and banishment.'

Deadly Passion was eventually released in April 1985. Although it was not a critical success by any means and was a highly flawed film, it did make money, just as we had predicted. Knowing what I know now, this film could have been made for a third of the budget. So many people took advantage of my naivety, and today I don't think any of them are still in the business.

If it wasn't already, frenetic activity had become the norm at Videovision. Early in 1984 I had recognised that the next addition to our staff needed to be a high-quality PR person. We wanted someone fresh and energetic and who wasn't afraid of hard work. This turned out to be Dezi Rorich who, before she came to join us, was still at college, where she was studying marketing management. She remembers that she had no idea what she might be getting into, only that I was 40 minutes late for the inter-view, sat with my boots on my desk and kept my Ray-Bans on the whole time we talked. I'm sure she is correct, but maybe I had a hangover.

'We discussed movies, and squash, and everything except the job,' she reminded me years later. 'I left with R40 to do some homework: go and rent any video and rework the cover to "make it jump off the shelf".'

Dezi's first official task with us was to publicise *Deadly Passion* and it wasn't long before this newcomer to the movie business had caught the bug too. A huge amount of very hard work went into that first project. Dezi still talks about how she was caught up in the pure thrill of movie-making she saw in me, how I shared that excitement with her – 'it was contagious,' she said. What I remember is that it was such a crazy time that we spoke more on the phone than in person, and my monthly phone bill rocketed to R5 000, an eye-watering figure back in the 80s.

By now it was as clear as daylight to me that the key to making suc-cessful movies was selling and distributing them properly, so I went on a month-long sales trip abroad, including Cannes, where I took a front cover ad in *Screen International*. This culminated in an international cin-ema and TV deal for *Deadly Passion* with New World Pictures, a major American distributor. In addition, a worldwide video deal for all mar-kets was signed with Vestron Video – then the biggest in the world, and where I would cement strong friendships with Marco Colombo and Ruth Vitale – thus securing video distribution. It helped that the movie poster showed the stars in a naked embrace, which was quite provocative for 1985. One critic described the movie as '*Bodyheat*, with the bodies but without the heat'. Another suggested that *Deadly Passion* was nothing but soft porn – which was of course ridiculous, but it was precisely these comments that boosted sales. The film brought in nearly R2 million, securing a profit, and went on to perform well on the domestic circuit in

South Africa too – an added bonus.

Concluding a deal like that in such a short period was unprecedented for a South African production, but was confirmation of my belief that to be really successful, local films had to be made with the international market in mind. South Africa was simply too small to focus on making films for the domestic market only.

The wrap party for *Deadly Passion* marked the completion of our first film, and what a party it was. Our entire Durban team and a huge number of friends travelled to Johannesburg to join the celebration. It was an elaborate and lavish event (I don't think we ever had a wrap party quite like it for any of our subsequent films) and people still talk about today. It might have been an unnecessary extravagance, but I wanted to make a bold statement to the industry – that I could do this and we should be respected. It remains a proud moment, with all of us staying at the recently opened Sandton Sun Hotel, at a rate of R19 per night.

Making that first movie from beginning to end was a steep learning curve for me, but I got it done and the lessons I learned then still apply. I came to realise that the best way to truly understand something is to do it yourself. We had to work hard and we had to take risks. It helped that I was in a business I loved and was becoming increasingly obsessed with, so I didn't mind either the hours the project demanded or the risks involved in such a bold venture. It also gave me the confidence to take on other projects and replicate the recipe. I was taken advantage of, yes, and I was naive, but it was worth the experience and it saved me millions later in production.

I always felt the need to tell our stories on film, especially those that demonstrated the epic tragedy of apartheid. The success we enjoyed with these early exploitation-type films made it possible for me to consider projects close to my heart, those that would contribute not only to a far greater social awareness but also showcase narratives that had, until then, never had a voice. Critics may have been scathing in their opinions of many of these films, but in reality they were a critical stepping stone towards doing the really important projects. In the process, I also proved that I could make films in South Africa for a quarter of the budget required to make them overseas. And with the financial success we enjoyed on movies such as *Deadly Passion* came the interest we had been seeking in the first place. The same people and vendors I had initially approached to invest in the film were now lining up to do business with me – now it was my turn to say no.

The modest success of *Deadly Passion* and some of our earlier projects took an interesting turn for us when, slowly, the big guns began to sit up and take notice. Who are these folk 'down in Africa' making waves, carving inroads? Why haven't we heard of them before? What are they doing, where are they going – and what are they going to do next? With that newfound recognition came clout, acknowledgement of the work we were doing and, more importantly, the work we were capable of doing.

Being reasonably well connected in Hollywood by now, I approached South African actor Marius Weyers. Marius had starred in *The Gods Must be Crazy*, which had grossed more than $10 million in the US alone. I felt that Marius was on the cusp of something great but, like so many local artists, despite worldwide acclaim for his work, he was struggling to crack the international market. It was time, I thought, for South Africans to make their mark on the world's stage and screen. So it was that Marius and I agreed that I would approach some of my contacts abroad, talk to agents and put out feelers for representation. It wasn't always easy to secure meetings, open doors and set the wheels in motion, but finally, following protracted negotiations, we managed to sign up an exclusive worldwide management deal for Marius with The Agency, which already represented the likes of Ron Howard (maker of *Splash*), Robert Wagner (of the TV series *Hart to Hart*) and Leonard Katzman (director of *Dallas*). Jerry Zeitsman of The Agency agreed that Marius had enormous potential for the US market, especially considering the success enjoyed by *Gods*.

It has always been something of an issue for local talent that the South African film and television industry, closed to the world for so many years, limited exposure to markets beyond the country and its audiences. We have seen it over and over again. Truly phenomenal performers and other industry folk reaching a ceiling locally, with few to no options beyond that. I felt then, as I do now, that there were numerous individuals with tremendous talent who needed international representation, not only to boost their own careers but also to prevent them from being taken advantage of. In many ways, this is what happened to Marius – with whom we later went on to do *Paljas* and *Red Dust* – and so many others in the entertainment industry. He had been in hundreds of plays and, at the time, more than 30 feature films, including his wildly successful *Gods*, as well as *Gandhi*.

Ladysmith Black Mambazo was another example. This extraordinarily talented male choral group had an international profile, particularly after their collaboration with Paul Simon on his *Graceland* album and their global hits 'Diamonds on the Soles of her Shoes' in 1986 and then 'Homeless' the following year. I got to know Ladysmith's Joseph Shabalala when we used his music in some of our movies, most notably his 'Amazing Grace' in *Cry, the Beloved Country* in 1995. It had then been nearly a decade since the group's worldwide success with Simon and *Graceland*, and they were still struggling. Joseph and I had become friends and, on one of his trips to Durban, I ventured to ask whether he was happy with his music deal and how the group was being handled. It appeared he wasn't. They'd enjoyed considerable success, both locally and internationally, but they feared they were being taken advantage of. Joseph was not satisfied that what they were seeing in terms of money and recognition was the best they could do. I suggested we show the numbers to my attorney in Los Angeles. If what they were pocketing was fair, then that would be that. If not, then we needed to put another plan of action into place. At the very least, I felt, they needed international representation more in line with their success and existing track-record. We met with Joe's lawyer, Edmund Radebe, and suggested he approach the group's representative at Gallo with a figure: R10 million. Of course, it was a wild, ball-park figure, but it gave Joe and his bandmates a starting point, some leverage for further negotiations. In the end, the number they settled on was considerably less, but also a lot more than their existing agreement had seen them getting, and certainly more than the paltry amounts so many South African artists had to settle for. The new agreement also saw them in far greater control of their own destinies. Black South African music artists were often abused by and taken advantage of by the music companies, who capitalised on their naivety in business. This saddened me, but I didn't really know the music business.

Opportunities such as these allow me to give back to the entertainment industry, drawing on my own experience of tough and turbulent times. My own hardships, particularly in my early years in film when I had to make my way through and over so many obstacles strewn across the path, put me in the privileged position of being able to smooth that path for others.

10

Place of Weeping

Navigating the 1980s in South Africa wasn't easy. Apartheid was still in full swing but the protests and rioting against oppression were spreading like wildfire. The state was under intense pressure from the outside world to bring an end to apartheid, with an increasing number of countries implementing trade sanctions and boycotts. PW Botha and his National Party government countered the groundswell by stepping up even more restrictive and oppressive measures. Following a fresh upsurge of violent and non-violent resistance to the continued racially exclusive system the government was enforcing, a first state of emergency was declared in 1985 and then extended, in an effort to regain and maintain control. In effect, this meant that thousands of Black, 'coloured' and

Indian people were detained, and movement was extremely limited – as was freedom of association. It was traumatic, it was violent and it was dangerous.

By 1986 I had fully embraced filmmaking but also continued with distribution, coinciding with possibly one of the worst years in South African history. The political chaos also wreaked havoc on the economy and that, of course, included the film industry. There was a dramatic collapse in the video industry, which saw more than 10 large national video distributors either liquidated or closed down. In cinemas, only the very big motion pictures were successful. Nelson Mandela was still in jail and the ANC was in exile. Matters were dire – for everyone. Globally, the creative community also joined our plea, many of whom participated in the cultural boycott of South Africa, which included music and film, and spoke out against apartheid.

A call from the ANC and from Madiba in prison encouraged supporters to speak out against apartheid and the regime in whatever way they could. I had already chosen to remain in the country and decided to contribute using whatever resources were available to me. And then – as the dust was swirling around me, as youngsters were being bundled into police vans never to be seen again, as activists and ordinary citizens succumbed to injuries inflicted behind closed doors in police cells – it came to me: I should make a film that took a stand against apartheid, a very public stand. That film would become the first anti-apartheid movie shot in South Africa, a defining moment for the country, its people and the world at large. A film could do that, but where and how?

The right project came from an unknown 24-year-old white filmmaker, Darrell Roodt, who approached me for help to finance his directorial debut, a film titled *Place of Weeping*.

Crossing paths with Darrell was to be our respective good fortunes.

He was and remains one of the most talented local directors I've ever worked with. Darrell had written the *Place of Weeping* screenplay himself; being in South Africa, he stated, one couldn't help making movies with political content, given there were very real political concerns. Because we shared the same beliefs, I worked well with Darrell, but *Place of Weeping* far from endeared him to his fellow whites. Yet, bolstered by the courage of his convictions, he forged ahead. Those people accepted that a Black producer like me could make a film like *Place of Weeping* but for a white South African to do so made him some sort of traitor. I financed *Place of Weeping* from my own pocket. It was a different, much smaller project than *Deadly Passion*, with a prospective budget of no more than R500 000 (the budget would eventually climb to five times that amount as the project went into production).

Place of Weeping tells the story of a brutal white farmer in a town called Weenen (Place of Weeping) who beats a Black farmworker to death for stealing a chicken. The worker's family and co-workers live in such fear that they are afraid to report the matter to the police. The narrative follows the efforts of a white Johannesburg-based journalist to expose the killer. It is also the story of Gracie (played by Gcina Mhlophe), a brave young woman who places her life in danger by taking on the voice of her suppressed nation, while trying to fight the unfair conditions so prevalent in the system. It reminded me of the auteur filmmakers such as Costa-Gavras, Norman Jewison, Stanley Kubrick, Michelangelo Antonioni, Wim Wenders, François Truffaut and Jean-Luc Godard, whose work influenced political thinking around the world, as well as other filmmakers such as Akira Kurosawa and Satyajit Ray, who were dealing with the art of cinema with provocation and sensitivity.

What appealed to me when I read the script was not only its political relevance but also its simplicity. Set in contemporary South Africa, it was the first locally made feature film that tackled the brutal injustices of the apartheid system. And so, despite the opposition it would inevitably meet from the state, we felt it important that we do it. In fact, we were so determined not to be talked out of what would be one of the most worthwhile projects we had ever embarked on that we chose not to consult with either the community or any of the liberation structures at the time, such as the United Democratic Front or the ANC-in-exile. Once we had made the decision to do it, it was a matter of following instincts that this was the right thing to do. My objective was to get the film made and not get involved in the politics as I wanted to make a statement with the film.

However, around that time I was introduced to Fatima and Ismail Meer by Len Konar, and shared the script of *Place of Weeping* with them. I knew a little bit about Fatima's background and her history and I had always been impressed by her and Ismail's activism. I also knew her daughter, Shehnaz, who was a contemporary of mine – we had participated in inter-school debates. Shehnaz is now a high court judge of the Western Cape and in 2021 was a candidate for a Constitutional Court post. Just spending a few hours with Fatima and learning more about her made me really value her opinion on *Place of Weeping*. What an incredible family of exceptional people, all of whom were hugely inspiring to me.

Making *Place of Weeping* did not come without risk, however. As it rolled into production in 1986, the country was deep in the grip of the state of emergency. Filming was considered subversive and the police were determined to shut us down. We were compelled to shoot the entire movie within 14 days and we – cast and crew – were forced to do it on the run. Every day the police would show up at the location where we'd been shooting the day before. Finally, as production shut down on day 15, I flew to London with the negative in my suitcase. When I returned, the police arrived at my Durban office, demanding to see the negative and all associated material. I told them that I sold the film to the UK. I had the film developed at Technicolor Studios in London and the film was completed in England. Meanwhile we were editing in Rockey Street, Yeoville, with David Heitner and Darrell.

Just as in the early days of my business when I rented out restricted films to Black audiences, I felt that I was taking a stand against the apartheid regime, but this time telling a story of the brutal repression experienced by Black people in South Africa and showing the world what was really happening in the country.

I arranged the film's commercial opening for New York City with distribution partner New World Pictures. I was firm that we had to launch the film overseas because if we had premiered at home first, it would almost certainly be banned. I gambled that the Pretoria censors wouldn't risk international humiliation by banning a political film for which major American critics had already been singing praises abroad. If it had the gravitas of a 'prestigious' film, it might get by the censors more easily.

The result was that *Place of Weeping* had its first screening in New York City on 5 December 1986 – 27 years to the day before we would premiere *Mandela: Long Walk To Freedom* in London – with an exclusive viewing at the new Carnegie Cinema in Manhattan.

Big-name anti-apartheid activists attended the screening, among them the guest of honour Martin Luther King III, actress Loretta Devine, actor Dick Gregory and many others. Fortuitously, our lead star, Gcina Mhlophe, was a visiting director at Boston's Brandeis University at the time and I asked her to attend the screening. She flew to New York to join us and she subsequently reminisced about the event. 'It was so exciting to be part of the premiere of *Place of Weeping* in New York. I was totally taken by the big names that were there to see the film we made in South Africa. What excitement – Martin Luther King III, Whoopi Goldberg and so many others ... I was star struck.' The film also marked the start of the film careers of Gcina, Darrell, Patrick Shai and others.

The movie won huge international acclaim, largely for its socio-political content rather than its creative content. The critics didn't hold back, but they did seem to understand the deeper message and the importance behind it. In her article in *The Wall Street Journal* in December 1986, Julie Salamon outlined the premise: '[The] film has a starkly melodramatic feel of a network docudrama. It is the story of a crude and cruel Afrikaner farmer who keeps his black workers on inhumanly short rations ... The characters are drawn starkly, with the aim of illustrating the issues ... And yet, despite its blatant bias, or perhaps because of it, the picture carries a kind of raw urgency.'

New York Times film critic Janet Maslin stated in her review that the film had 'a plain, clumsy style that does nothing to diminish its power'. Some critics nevertheless went on to suggest that the film was technically weak and over-hyped. What they neglected to mention, though, was our tiny budget and tight filming schedule. There was no way that, given our constraints, we would have been able to create a masterpiece, nor did we claim to have done so.

It was a protest film against racial oppression.

We had a point to make. And we made it.

In February 1987, *Place of Weeping* opened simultaneously in Los Angeles, where it played in the Beverly Center Cineplex, and back home in South Africa. In fact, Los Angeles mayor Tom Bradley even went as far as declaring 23 February 1987 Place of Weeping Day in his city!

Another strategy that helped ensure the success of the venture back home was that I secured a nationwide release, a ploy I had learned from handling other, less artful films. I also timed the release as close as possible to the city-by-city referendum on the desegregation of South African cinemas. At the time, cinemas in South Africa were still very much segregated, so this meant that Darrell Roodt – my white director – and I were unable to view our film together in our own country. On opening night in Johannesburg, I watched at the Eyethu Cinema in Soweto and Darrell attended the screening at Rosebank Mall. Afterwards we went for dinner at Le Français and compared notes. The full house in Soweto had risen to their feet and cheered as the credits rolled; the 10 or so individuals in Rosebank were less than moved. Our conclusion: white people seem not to be interested in the truth of what was going on.

The response in South Africa was interesting, a telling reflection on the reality of the fractured society echoed in the movie itself. The film broke opening-day ticket sales records in Soweto, Durban and Cape Town, as well as in the Black homelands, but nobody in Pretoria went to see it.

I was proud and felt it fitting that this narrative was produced by a Black South African, and to have made the first anti-apartheid film in my country and survive. *Place of Weeping* was finally made at a modest price and was very profitable and was pre-sold for $150 000 at Cannes, where we had shown a rough cut months before the first screening. A little controversy always boosts public awareness, but in this case the flap was about something other than just a stunt. We didn't have to hype the film one bit. When I got back to South Africa, I was – unsurprisingly – again harassed by the Security Police who had heard about the film and its content. But again they were too late, and in the end the censors did not ban the movie, although they did give it an X-rating (it had been PG-rated by the Motion Picture Association of America).

Place of Weeping became the first in a string of movies that demonstrated resistance against the system. For me it was a film of authenticity, portraying South Africa as it really was. The characters represented the full spectrum of views in the country at the time: the left, the right, the violent, the non-violent and the silent. For one thing, we'd hoped the film would help viewers to better understand the complexities and madness of the apartheid system and help kick-start a faster, more peaceful process towards real political change. A mainstream film, I felt, was the perfect way to open up the broader population to the possibility of change. It also had the potential to act as a catalyst for South African filmmakers to express their true feelings on apartheid. This was something most had for decades largely avoided. Darrell and I were on the same page, as were the cast, who had such strong convictions about the picture that they were willing to forego payment upfront, agreeing to earn their fees once the film's sale had been concluded. This in no small way contributed to the film's success.

By 1987 Videovision had come a long way, and we were already seeing the rewards. Considering our rapid growth, we could no longer afford to limit operations to Durban. Johannesburg was where it was happening for the industry and we needed to make our presence felt there, at the same time as increasing our exposure nationally and internationally. In 1987 we set up a Johannesburg office with Shan Moodley in Grant Street, Melville. In 1988 with the expansion of the business and the need for a bigger team in Durban, we purchased new premises in the whites-only suburb of Musgrave, establishing our corporate headquarters at 134 Essenwood Road. Again with the Group Areas Act still in force, we needed a white person as a nominee owner, which was really frustrating for me, especially as I had achieved a fair degree of success but was still being treated as a second-class citizen. But I knew this was soon going to change. We also established Distant Horizon, a wholly owned subsidiary of Videovision. Committed to independent filmmaking, the company was involved in all aspects of the film industry from development, financing, production through to distribution. It would produce films not only in South Africa, but in time in the United States, Canada, the United Kingdom and Hong Kong. Simultaneously, strategic relationships with film industry heavyweights, among them the major studios and leading distribution companies, would be formed and strengthened.

In 1989 we took over SCY Productions. There were two facets to this move: firstly, meeting the appetite for video by securing our shift to movie production and, secondly, turning the production infrastructure SCY already had into the production hub we required.

We were further able to consolidate the presence of Videovision and Distant Horizon abroad by establishing offices in London, New York and Los Angeles, which allowed us to produce 19 movies in the decade that followed. Things were happening for the little Movie Place, as a well-respected player in film.

Fortuitously, Paul Janssen, whom I had got to know when he was the entertainment manager at Sun City, was planning to move to the UK and was looking at prospects there at the same time as we were looking to set up our London office. He agreed to run our office in London for us. The New York and later the Los Angeles offices were headed by Brian Cox, whom I first met in New York in 1988 when I funded a small film, *Deadly Obsession*. Brian, who sadly passed on in 2019, ultimately became the creative head of our film business and contributed immensely to the films we made over the three decades he was with us. His creative acumen and literary knowledge was hugely beneficial, as was his brutal honesty.

Over the years, our relationship with CIC (now UIP) for the distribution of our films in South African theatres continued to grow. After Tim Ord headed back to New Zealand, in 1986 Peter Dignan was deployed to

South Africa from Japan as managing director for UIP in South Africa. Peter recalls how, after only a few days in the country, he had a sinking feeling that he had landed in the twilight zone, awash with white people in the comfort of their privilege. 'It was like they were not fully understanding what was really going on in their own country under the repressive apartheid regime against non-white people,' was how he put it.

The first time I met Peter was in his office in the UBS building in Main Street, Johannesburg, a few blocks down from the Carlton Hotel. It was a sunny winter afternoon and we spent it talking about films. By the end of the meeting, we knew we were kindred spirits in our passion for cinema. Peter credits me with giving him his first insight into the irrationality of the apartheid laws, but in truth all I did was simply point out to him countless scenarios that played out every day in the lives of Black people across the country. In the Johannesburg of 1986, I told Peter, I – as an Indian – was allowed to stay at the multiracial Carlton Hotel and enjoy a meal in the multiracial Mike's Kitchen restaurant across the road. But if I walked just around the corner to the Metro Cinema Market Street to watch a movie, I would be refused entry because it was a whites-only cinema. Peter was aghast.

We had many such conversations, Peter and I, where I briefed him and his company on the situation in South Africa. As a result, in 1986, UIP decided to take a firm stand against the injustices and inequalities faced by the majority of South Africans. The first thing they did was get multiracial status for all their cinemas in the country. Then they demanded that all independent distributors of their movies follow suit. Within a year, UIP went from 90 per cent whites only to 90 per cent multiracial nationally. The remaining 10 per cent had opted to remain for whites only, so UIP promptly refused to supply them with any further product.

After the release of and acclaim for *Place of Weeping*, before we'd

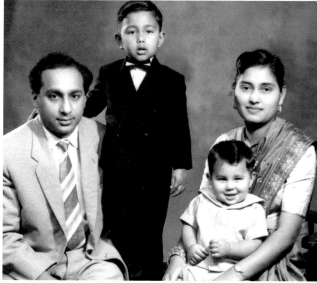

ABOVE LEFT: Anant with his grandmother, Parvati Singh (Ajee), 1958.

ABOVE: A family portrait with Dr Hareebrun Singh (father), Anant, Sanjeev and Bhindoo (mother), 1960.

LEFT: In Stanton Street, Reservoir Hills: Reshma Sathiparsad, Sanjeev, Nalin Sathiparsad, Anant and Sanil Singh, 1965/66.

BELOW: The pewter artwork Anant made when he was 11 years old, 1967.

Gcina Mhlophe at the *Place of Weeping* premiere in New York City, with Dick Gregory and Martin Luther King III, 5 December 1986.

Handing over a donation to the Aryan Benevolent Home: Kirit Trivedi, Shishupal Rambharos and Anant, 5 January 1991.

The Johannesburg premiere of *Sarafina!* with Nelson Mandela, Fatima Meer, Miriam Makeba, Leleti Khumalo, Mbongeni Ngema and Anant, 22 September 1992.

Anant with Danny Schechter, Pallo Jordan and Indres Naidoo, 1996.

Nelson Mandela, James Earl Jones, Jeremy Ractliffe, former CEO of the Nelson Mandela Children's Fund, and Anant at a press conference at the New York premiere of *Cry, the Beloved Country*, 23 October 1995.

The Videovision team with James Earl Jones, 1995. FRONT ROW: Celia Gritten, Mandy Mordaunt, Sudhir Pragjee SECOND ROW: Sanjeev Singh, Anant, James Earl Jones, Sharon Ramiah, Ken Kaplan THIRD ROW: Brian Ndwandwe, Aaron Ndwandwe, Elphas Dlamini, Robert Naidoo, Ronnie Govender BACK ROW: Amal Soni, Teddy Ravjee.

Anant and Vanashree with the Yamagata Mercedes-Benz in Cannes, 1996.

Dancing on the ceiling at La Chunga in Cannes, 1996.

The Dalai Lama and Anant in Johannesburg, *circa* 1996.

LEFT: Vanashree and Anant at their wedding reception at the Royal Hotel in Durban, 13 December 1997.

BELOW: Lisette Derouaux with Ahmed Kathrada (Kathy), Anant, Quincy Jones, Laloo Chiba and Vanashree on Robben Island, following a trip on the Blue Train with Madiba and Graça Machel, 1997.

Anant and Vanashree with Nelson Mandela at their wedding, 12 December 1997.

signed any sale agreement in Cannes, Videovision released a public statement urging that further international pressure be put on South Africa
to enable all cinemas across the country to allow multiracial audiences.
Videovision stated that we had decided to no longer supply any cinemas
that were segregated. In this we had the full support of UIP and Peter
Dignan, which made the impact even more significant. The line in the
sand had been drawn.

With acclaim for *Place of Weeping* still fresh and feeling buoyed by the
flush of the success it was enjoying, I decided to reach out to the most
famous Black actor of all, Sidney Poitier. He had done *Cry, the Beloved
Country* in the year I was born, 1956, and had always been a huge inspiration to me. Contacting him felt like something I just had to do. Rather than
writing, I took a real flyer and cold-called him one day, all the way from
Durban. In those days it was still possible. I simply went to a phone direc-
tory and, after placing a few calls, managed to reach him in Los Angeles.

'I'm Anant Singh,' I said. 'I've made South Africa's first anti-apartheid
movie in South Africa.'

Sidney was incredibly polite, supportive even, never mind that a complete stranger had had the audacity to call him up out of the blue. I went
on to explain that I travelled to Los Angeles once a year and said I would
like personally to hand him a copy of the film.

'Sure,' he said, 'come for lunch.'

I was weak at the knees, a little flushed, by the time I replaced the
receiver. I had essentially invited myself to the home of the most respected
Black actor of our time and secured a meeting with him. Sidney Poitier,
the *great* Sidney Poitier, would get to see my movie. Closer to the time, I
called him again to tell him I would be in Los Angeles in a week. 'Come

on over,' he said, and so I did.

I drove to Sidney's home in Beverly Hills and then it was just the two of us, enjoying a quiet lunch together in his private dining room. Sidney talked of his experience in apartheid South Africa. Racism had been alive and well during his visit in 1956, he said, and yet he was able to meet and befriend people from all walks of life. One of them, the man appointed as his driver, invited him to his home to stay as no hotel in South Africa would allow him as a guest. Out of this gesture a deep and long-lasting friendship had emerged.

Sidney made a huge impression on me and not simply because he was a much-lauded movie star – I had been in awe of his consummate skill ever since I'd watched his movies back in my days at the film rental shop – but also because of his deep-seated humility, the simplicity with which he lived his life and his down-to-earth nature. These were qualities that made me want to know more about him. I subsequently bought a copy of his autobiography, *The Measure of a Man*, which told me much more about his own hard upbringing and youth in the Bahamas, far more challenging and difficult than my own. I remember thinking then that if this man could achieve so much through such adversity, then there was hope for all who face daily challenges in their own lives.

Sidney and I never did get to work together, but we shared many ideas and good times. That's the magic of people, of connection. Today you could never reach out to a movie star like that. Despite social media and all the communication tools at our disposal, it is infinitely harder to make the sort of contacts I was able to back in the day when artists were just that: artists, no more. Today they are cogs in a well-oiled machine with a regimented, ever-vigilant army of handlers to guard them with the sole purpose of saying no.

In 2013, I visited Sidney at his home in Bel Air. Aged 86, he insisted on driving us to lunch at the Bel Air Hotel. He is a remarkable human being, gentle and sincere, genuine in every sense of that word. Meeting him was an extraordinary experience, cementing an admiration beyond compare. He has inspired me and has given all people of colour the strength to follow their dreams. This group includes Denzel Washington, Ossie Davis, Forest Whitaker and so many others.

11

Censored

By 1987 I had notched up quite a few deals in the movie business that had paid off. That kind of success comes only with hard work, perseverance and, in many cases, sacrifice. When I was in South Africa, I often worked well into the early hours of the morning, largely because of the time difference with the United States. Days were long, and for many of the small Videovision team that meant getting by on only a few hours of sleep, relying on adrenalin and our own drive.

If we were to continue to meet the challenges thrown our way by the movie business, I knew I had to grow the staff complement at Videovision, and delegate tasks and responsibilities to individuals I could trust. The notion made me anxious, but it was something I needed to do. Whereas before I had relied mostly on myself to do the hard slog, taking the long hours and late nights in my stride, I couldn't expect others to make the same kind of sacrifice. But the time had now come to consider the bigger picture, plan ahead and prepare for the growth that seemed inevitable. I knew it, and our team knew it.

By day Sudhir Pragjee was a partner at his auditing practice and by night – not every night! – he and I would work together (with Len Konar) at my house, devising strategy on structuring films and our future. Videovision had produced four or five movies within just a few years and moving to the company full time was a risk for Sudhir but he also saw it as an exciting opportunity. The film business in South Africa was fairly small, but successful and made up for what it lacked in security and certainty with excitement and creativity. Sudhir found that mix infectious. He had long since been bitten by the movie bug, but visiting the Cannes Film Festival with me in 1986 was the catalyst for him and he finally made the leap and came on board. As he put it himself: 'I left my three-piece pinstriped suit and secure audit partnership career to join what was then a small film business. I moved my vintage oak desk into an office at Videovision on Florida Road.'

Robert Naidoo, who was the auditor responsible for our company work, followed Sudhir to Videovision in 1990. Initially joining as an accountant, Robert became an invaluable member of the team as our financial manager. He recalls our association: 'When I was doing the audit for Videovision, I used to engage with Anant more on the financial side. Seeing that he is a man with no accounting background at all, I was pleasantly surprised that I could converse with him about the numbers and the manner that he dealt with this was amazing. You don't often get that when people have no accounting background but understand the financial aspects like balance sheets and budgets … I personally have a good relationship with Anant because there's mutual respect – he can call me and tell to do this or that, but I can also be honest with him and tell him this doesn't work, or don't waste my time. That's the type of relationship we have.'

The struggle was still in full swing in 1987, with the apartheid regime continuing to hold most of the cards. One lingering problem was the state-owned broadcaster, the SABC. It was a monopoly, effectively ensuring that certain programmes and particular individuals were never to be granted airtime, an easy way to censor anyone daring to speak out. Perhaps, given what was happening on the movie circuit and the successes we were enjoying there, they thought I was worth the risk, because in January 1987 I was invited to appear as a guest on the TV magazine show *Sundowner*, anchored by Penny Smythe, to talk about my work, which by then included *Place of Weeping*. But when the SABC backed out and at the last minute refused to show footage from the film, I walked out of the studio. I refused to compromise. There was no doubt in my mind that they did this for political reasons, kowtowing to the big guns who did not want to air any controversy relating to race or socio-political issues.

The incident was reported in the *Sunday Tribune* of 25 January 1987, under the headline 'Singh's film "too hot" for *Sundowner* programme':

> Film producer Anant Singh pulled out of the SABC's *Sundowner* programme on Friday night because he believed political reasons were behind the SABC's refusal to screen footage from his anti-apartheid film, *Place of Weeping*, which was released nationally on Friday.
>
> He has accused the corporation of backtracking on an earlier

agreement to screen footage of the film, which has had good reviews from foreign critics and began a successful run in the United States in December.

The significance of this narrative and its relevance to South African society in the here and now had been precisely what had inspired me to make the movie in the first place. What unfolded on that screen was not the story of a single individual, of one family visited by one of the greatest catastrophes of recent history, but that of hundreds of thousands of South Africans. This grinding tragedy, the pain and horror of it all, was not just the creation of a fantastic storyboard by a hive of creatives – among them a white director in Darrell Roodt and an Indian producer – and writers and storytellers gathered around a boardroom table; it was the lived experience of men and women across the country terrorised by this scourge. That the SABC – and those who controlled it – had refused to give voice to that narrative showed a complete indifference to that suffering. Again, I was having none of it.

This kind of blanket censorship was not uncommon, though. We saw it all the time, particularly in the draconian 1980s, when it must have felt that the wheels were coming off for the National Party and its apartheid government. Following increased pressure from 1986, particularly from the American film distributors, the state had declared that all movie theatres had to become desegregated. No matter this progress, the political atmosphere was still toxic, and 'controversial' films continued to be banned.

There was one surprising exception, however. On 28 November 1987, the South African Publications Board, the official state censors, unexpectedly approved the release of Sir Richard Attenborough's movie on Black Consciousness leader Steve Biko. The film was *Cry Freedom*

– which followed on Attenborough's extraordinary success with *Gandhi*, which had garnered a string of Oscars – and the board allowed the release without any cuts or restrictions. The decision-making panel, led in this instance by the enlightened Afrikaner Kobus van Rooyen, had viewed the film and decided, for some reason or another, that it wouldn't pose too much of a threat to state security. The decision on *Cry Freedom* was a surprise, especially because the writings of the two main characters, Steve Biko and Donald Woods, were still banned in the country. Biko had died under highly suspicious circumstances in police custody in 1977 and Woods was the white South African newspaper editor who had campaigned to establish the truth behind Biko's death – that he had been beaten to death by his captors. Due to the political climate in South Africa, the film had been shot primarily in Zimbabwe and Kenya. It starred Kevin Kline as Donald Woods and a young Denzel Washington in the role of Biko.

Opposition from the state towards the film was to be expected – it raised all sorts of issues that the apartheid government would have preferred to keep under wraps, especially at this turbulent time – but bizarrely the movie also caused some division among Black South Africans still fighting the regime. Black Consciousness groups such as the Azanian People's Organisation and the exiled Pan Africanist Congress were sharply critical of it, arguing that the story of the Black Consciousness hero as told through white eyes was not true to what Biko had stood for. At the other end of the spectrum, the African National Congress – which had been outlawed in 1960 – praised the film, suggesting that it would increase international awareness of the injustice and evil of the apartheid system.

The distributors of the film were my friends at UIP. When Peter Dignan approached me, we offered advice on the distribution of the film in South Africa, but it ultimately proved to be fruitless. First, the state appealed the decision by the Publications Board and lost. Naturally, there was an appeal – the state was not going to take this lying down – but a ruling was finally made by the Publication Appeals Board whereby, for a second time, it was declared that the film could indeed be shown. The board agreed that the movie was biased against the police but did not endanger race relations or state security.

But the matter did not rest there. Just hours after the Appeals Board judgment against them, the authorities banned the movie outright. This resulted in the police swooping down on theatres across the country, seizing film reels from at least 30 cinemas. There was an immediate uproar. Patrons at a big Johannesburg cinema broke into shouts of 'Amandla! Amandla!' when the manager announced that the screening had been cancelled by government order. In Pietermaritzburg, two policemen arrived in the middle of an afternoon show and agreed to the theatre manager's request that they wait until the screening ended to remove the film.

The police claimed that the film threatened public safety. According to reports in the media later, cinemas in Port Elizabeth, Pretoria, Durban and Soweto had reported bomb threats, probably orchestrated by the state. Finally Stoffel van der Merwe, then Minister of Information, had to step in. Van der Merwe stated that the government had seized the film because it was a piece of 'crude propaganda' that portrayed security forces 'in such a negative light that their public image would be seriously undermined' and 'could even lead to violence'. He added that the government had overruled its own censors' decision because the censor board had acted 'as if times were normal and times are unfortunately not normal in South Africa'. The police, he said, were in a better position to gauge 'what the implications of the film would be on the streets'.

The *New York Times* quoted Attenborough: 'I never believed they would show it. The overall reason for making the film was to tell people the truth about apartheid, and about how it struck both black and white South Africans,' he said.

The film nevertheless went on to receive critical acclaim. For his portrayal of Biko, Denzel Washington was nominated for an Academy Award. *Cry Freedom* was eventually re-released in South African cinemas on 27 April 1990, two-and-a-half years after its originally scheduled premiere and just months after Nelson Mandela was released from prison – and, coincidentally, four years to the day before the country's first democratic election.

12

The Stick

By the end of the 1980s, anti-war filmmaking had become something of a trend globally. Most likely, this renewed interest had been kick-started at the end of 1979 by Francis Ford Coppola's Vietnam epic *Apocalypse Now*. Within a matter of years, Oliver Stone's *Platoon* became a global blockbuster, taking $150 million at the box office. Then Stanley Kubrick did *Full Metal Jacket* – another massive hit, making $120 million.

I had turned 30 and my business was going well, but still I was a Black entrepreneur in apartheid South Africa, which came with many unknowns. I had grown Videovision by distributing movies to a market that had long been restricted and constrained by oppressive censorship laws in a society already ravaged by inequality and dire poverty.

The exploitation films made it possible for us to make anti-apartheid films that we knew were much riskier ventures, projects such as *Place of Weeping* and the next project I was set to tackle with Darrell Roodt, *The Stick*.

The Stick was an anti-war and anti-apartheid film that took a stand against the state. This time the focus was on South Africa's involvement in an increasingly controversial war in Angola that had claimed thousands of lives. In a sense, it could be seen as a parallel to the US stories about the Vietnam war – well, almost.

The opening shot focuses on a young man in a school blazer sitting at a fountain. He narrates: 'I remember my father once saying that the army will make a man out of you. He was wrong.'

With *The Stick*, however, we didn't purposefully set out to produce an anti-apartheid piece – the simple matter of it was that it was the honest reality at the time. The South African bush war (South Africa's Vietnam) was still in full force so, naturally, the film's narrative was firmly anti-war and anti-apartheid. The state was doing itself no favours by trying to dictate to the creative industry what we should and shouldn't be doing, just as the organisations actively fighting apartheid had no need to instruct creatives to oppose the system. What the state didn't realise was that, at the end of the day, political interference in art is little more than an extension of propaganda. You cannot tell the creative community what to do. When that happens, creativity is stifled, the entire process is tipped out of balance, and you find yourself in quicksand very quickly.

Again, I knew that *The Stick* would have to be handled very carefully, especially with all the controversy around *Cry Freedom* at the time. Darrell, inspired by some of his own experiences as a young white man, had written this script too. South Africa was one of the few countries that still practised conscription, forcing young men to fight an unpopular war beyond its borders, and Darrell had visualised *The Stick* as a way to highlight the breakdown in morality that it represented. It is a war film with two types of horror: horror not only within the characters themselves, but also a horror beyond that of an individual. The film speaks of war and what it does to people.

Another line was, 'This isn't a war any more – this is sick.'

And it was sick, a sick system. At once terrifying and nauseating, harrowing even, but a mirror of our times. Our film reflected the total madness of a war that was on our doorstep, and Darrell made it quite clear that real filmmakers can't really help making movies with political content. As he put it, 'Movies are the mirror of society.'

In South Africa, as in any country, there were truths that had to be exposed and we simply dealt with reality, just as we had done when we made *Place of Weeping*. I suppose Darrell and I were two of only a handful of filmmakers in the country at the time tackling the issues that needed to be tackled. *The Stick* highlighted the reality of kids who were barely 17 years old and wanted to be – deserved to be – just that: kids. Instead, they were leaving school only to be sent out to kill and be killed. That was the reality and so that's what we tried to depict: the sheer madness of it and the cause of scarred lives.

Of course this was not a story the state wanted told in a country that needed soldiers to defend the regime, so we were painting a target on our backs. It was not an easy road for us. Looking at those other war films, Oliver Stone made *Platoon* for $6 million, Francis Ford Coppola's *Apocalypse Now* was made for $31 million and Kubrick did *Full Metal Jacket* for $30 million; we made *The Stick* on a budget of R3 million.

It was originally meant to be filmed in the unsurpassed beauty of Botswana's Okavango swamps. Darrell and I, along with our director of photography Paul Witte, took a private plane, touching down in that remarkable landscape, which must be one of the most special places on earth. Sadly, the location proved too much of a logistical nightmare. In view of the heavy artillery, arms and choppers of the South African military machine that would have had to pass over those borders at the time, that plan turned out to be too costly and entirely unworkable, so we settled for the mountains of the Magaliesberg. One of the principal settings was an army base camp. This we constructed over a period of two months in an area covering 30 000 square metres, using a construction team of more than 200 people. First we went in with a front-end loader and cleared away the bush. Then followed the gruelling ordeal of building platforms and roads from the barren land. Construction costs alone totalled R1 million.

One of our saving graces was the cast. Here we had young actors who would go on to do great things in the industry, among them Sean Taylor, Gys de Villiers, Frank Opperman and the legendary Winston Ntshona.

Still, it was hard, often back-breaking work. But that is what making movies comes down to. It doesn't necessarily require any great genius. It's really about knowing all there is to know about the industry and applying those principles properly. Experience – all those years since I was a young boy working in a film shop rewinding films – had taught me to know the market. I had spent years preparing and getting to know the industry inside and out, understanding the varied aspects of it. That helped. And then it is about working really hard – I was still pulling 18-hour days.

That's what it was like back then. Working hard was the only secret. The magic recipe. I imagine that would be the same in every industry. It also helped that I understood what people wanted and how to generate awareness about the products I wanted to make.

The Stick had its start at the Cannes Film Festival. The world market premiere was at the Olympia Theatre in Cannes on 14 May 1988. Distributors rely heavily on the advertising of their product; in the film industry the thinking is that if the advertising is big the film must surely be big – which is dumb, I know, but that's how it is. So at the festivals it is especially important to attain high visibility for your film. At Cannes this is even more significant and infinitely more difficult, because there are just so many films vying for attention. In 1988 there were at least 500 others on sale, from all over the world, so marketing was as important as the picture itself.

So, how do you play this game and win without wasting your money? The problem, particularly for the little guy in the business, is that marketing at Cannes during the film festival can be very expensive. Everything comes at a price and that price is high. Place a poster on a wall at a hotel and that's $5 000 right there. Back then, my budget was extremely limited but I understood all too well the need for solid marketing, so I came up with an ambush campaign. The idea was to print large posters and slap them on the windshields of parked cars. That wasn't done back then. But I had these metre-wide posters made up – very simple: it just read, *The Stick* – we took Teddy with us and we paid five locals to go out with him at the crack of dawn every morning and slap them on windscreens, under the wipers of all the cars parked along the two-kilometre Boulevard de la Croisette. The ingenuity behind the idea was that no matter who you were, the head of a big film studio or an actor or a big producer, to attend the festivities you had to walk or drive the Croisette, and of course all the cameras and news media followed you every step of the way. And there was no way anyone could miss those giant posters in the background of every television interview and shot. Cars all along the promenade were emblazoned with the name of my movie – and it was everywhere.

We also hit Cannes with daily airplane banner advertising – the banner made in South Africa and brought over in our luggage – which hovered over the crowds of filmmakers and stars at the Côte d'Azur. Ambush marketing at its best! Every distributor in Cannes that year knew all about *The Stick* and went to see it. So it was that the psychology of 'If you advertise big, then it must pay off big' was born for me. It was the most cost-effective marketing we had ever done. In fact, it worked so well that we employed the same strategy for at least 10 years after that. We owned Cannes with our banners printed in South Africa.

As a result of our fierce marketing campaign, *The Stick* was licensed to major distributors from all around the globe and became a major hit at the festival, playing to standing ovations. It was sold by my friends Christian Solomon, who I had met at New World Pictures, and Marco Colombo from Vestron who formed FilmTrust together.

Two weeks after its premiere at Cannes, *The Stick* was banned by the South African Publications Board. The censors put forward a three-page list of reasons, stating, 'There is no doubt that the film has very high artistic merit. The script, photography, acting and directing are all of a very high standard and the tension very convincing.' It went on to compare the movie to the likes of *Apocalypse Now* and *Full Metal Jacket*, but then declared it 'undesirable' because 'the South African Defence Force are presented as ruthless and indiscriminate killers of innocent Black people'. And, it went on to say, 'White and Black are shown in basic and insoluble conflict. The film is highly detrimental to the safety of the state, as well as to the peace and good order in the countries involved.'

The board instructed us to make 48 cuts to the film before they could consider unbanning it. We refused. The result was simple and predictable: we were forbidden from screening the film in South Africa. Nationwide the controversy was still swirling around the state's actions against *Cry*

Freedom, so we threw a Hail Mary pass. We appealed. This led to an anxious wait for the Appeal Board's decision. Would the film be screened in the country in which it had been made? A decision would take months.

In the interim, we watched developments from the sidelines, revelling in the ripples that the board's decision had cast on the waters of South African cinema. The banning of the film saw global interest skyrocket and the industry embraced the movie even more. On 24 August 1988, in its official world premiere, *The Stick* opened the prestigious World Film Festival in Montreal, at the time one of the top four such festivals in the world, attracting around 270 000 festivalgoers. The irony did not escape Darrell that South Africans had to travel thousands of miles to see a film we should have been able to see at a local cinema.

In July the following year *The Stick* was screened behind the Iron Curtain at the 1989 Moscow Film Festival, the first time that a South African film had been screened in the Soviet Union. We attended the event and took great pleasure in the massive success the film enjoyed there. It was screened four times, each time in front of audiences as large as 5 000 people. *The Stick* was eventually only unbanned in South Africa in June 1990, four months after the release of Nelson Mandela.

In those early years and being somewhat naive, I did not realise the significance of the film festivals and the potential impact they could have on the commercial success of a film, especially securing distribution. While we premiered *Place of Weeping* in New York, it also went on to premiere at the Toronto Film Festival and several others festivals around the world. Like *The Stick*, we also had *Quest for Love*, which premiered in Montreal, as well as at the London Film Festival. It was quite ironic that we had all of these films playing globally while *The Stick* was banned in South Africa and we had immense challenges getting *Place of Weeping* released. It was a fascinating time as cinemas were segregated and if we think back, that was just over 30 years ago!

At this point, I was spending a lot of my time travelling: Los Angeles, New York, Tokyo, London, Paris, Toronto and Cannes. I attended the London premiere of *The Last Emperor* and came within $25 000 of securing the rights to distribute the film in South Africa. I had read the script three years earlier and knew immediately that it would be a winner, so I made a bid for distribution rights in South Africa, but Columbia wanted it too and had much deeper pockets. I had to admit defeat and give it a pass, a decision I would of course regret. Another lesson learned. You win some, you lose some, and you've just got to live with it – but you also have to make sure you win more than you lose.

In 1982 in South Africa, Sylvester Stallone was very popular with his *Rocky* films and *First Blood*. Videovision bought the video distribution rights for *Rambo: First Blood Part II* for a record $100 000, and we released it on video cassette in January 1986. Within a matter of days, over 2 000 copies were sold, a huge number for 1986. But *Rambo: First Blood Part II* also became one of the first films to be pirated on a large scale in the country, the unprecedented demand far outstripping supply. This led to some video stores making unauthorised copies of the film and we had to rapidly establish a special security network to investigate the piracy. We had limited success in this.

Sadly, little has changed since. Piracy of copyrighted material in recent years has become huge as internet access and speeds have improved. At one stage we were ranked 14th in the world for illegal downloads; in fact, South Africa was the country where *Game of Thrones* episodes were the ninth most downloaded globally. Unfortunately, as internet speeds and access continue to improve, this is probably only going to increase, especially as police enforcement struggles to keep up with the blistering change in the online world and the sheer speed of developments in the industry.

Fortunately, Videovision's successes have never been due to just one thing; it was always more of a progression and a combination of elements. Still, the acquisition of *Rambo: First Blood Part II* gave us our first real presence in the market. Prior to this, we had been largely limited to Black and Indian cinemas and rental stores, but the real money was to be made in the white market, which had opened up to us to a much larger extent thanks to CIC/UIP. As it transpired, our early success with Rambo was worth a lot more than the money I had spent. We were still oppressed, but forging ahead with our own business in an industry in which I had steadily been making some strong alliances.

Videovision Enterprises was by now the exclusive distributor of all titles from global film distributors such as New World Pictures, Kings Road Group Films and Alliance Entertainment.

Unexpected successes and severe disappointments are both part of the game. The dance that is distribution takes place in an industry that thrives on lightning-fast moves, bold decisions and huge amounts of cash – and one setback wasn't going to stop me. So, as taxing as the constant travelling had become, it also exhilarated me, gave me purpose and reason, and drove me onwards. These trips made it possible, for instance, for me to sign my biggest deal yet – with a newly formed South African distributor by the name of T-Vision, a division of Teljoy, in 1988. I sold them a package of video distribution rights worth more than R5.5 million. This gave them the rights to distribute blockbusters I had already acquired, among them *Rambo III* (with Sylvester Stallone), *Angel Heart* (starring Robert

De Niro and music by Trevor Jones, with whom I would later work), *Running Man* (starring Arnold Schwarzenegger and Rob Cohen, with whom I collaborated later in my career) and *Ironweed* (Meryl Streep and Jack Nicholson). Although the figure may seem paltry in current terms, this was one of the biggest deals of the time and it enabled me to fund a number of the productions that followed.

None of this had come easily. I was living with one hand on the phone and the other grasping my hand luggage. I was told that I was one of the most frequent travellers out of Louis Botha Airport – the name by which the airport in Durban was known back then – both domestically and internationally. It was brutal and certainly less glamorous than it might sound.

When I was in Johannesburg I was based in Rockey Street, Yeoville, which was considered something of a creative hub at the time. We'd been rather busy making a number of films, including *Quest for Love* in 1987, written and directed by Helena Nogueira. The movie starred Afrikaans actresses Jana Cilliers and Sandra Prinsloo in a sizzling lesbian love story, with the drama unfolding over the course of a passionate weekend affair between the two women. This was to be not only one of the first cinematic productions in the world entirely dominated by women in both cast and crew, but it also triggered in me a determination to tell women's stories, particularly to focus on themes that celebrated women. A possible result was that, in 1997, I was presented with the International Women in Film & Television Award, and then in 2015 the International Women's Forum Legacy Award, the first to be awarded to a male. In 2016, I helped finance the production of the Canadian film *Below Her Mouth*, which set a precedent as a film made entirely by women in all aspects of the production.

Because of the low-cost action and horror fare I had been serving up, I was being increasingly described as a schlock filmmaker. Some may have considered the label insulting – and it was indeed derogatory – but I have always held firm that, as much as some of these movies were exploitative, film was film, and they all had the same intention: storytelling in different ways. That they were targeting different audiences was not in question, but the intention was always to entertain, inform, educate and offer some kind of escape, irrespective of the genre. George Lucas made *Star Wars* and Federico Fellini *La Dolce Vita* for the same reasons I ventured into genres others considered schlock.

One such genre was kickboxing, which was for the most part targeted at a video market that had an avaricious appetite. In 1991 I made a movie with American martial artists John Barrett and Keith Vitali. Ritchie Mohamed, a big film distributor based in Johannesburg, suggested I title the movie *American Kickboxer*. We shot large parts in Eldorado Park, a 'coloured' suburb in Johannesburg. It became a stand-in for parts of LA and no one was any the wiser. In the movie the characters get into a brawl at a party, with the protagonist accidently killing a bystander who tries to break the fight up. The actor who portrayed that bystander was a young Gavin Hood, who went on to become a famous and highly regarded Hollywood director, particularly of *X-Men* and the Oscar-winning *Tsotsi*.

Ritchie Mohamed and I had been doing business together since the late 1970s. He was one of the original distributors to Black townships and independent cinemas in South Africa and had landed big contracts supplying movies to the country's mines, where entertainment was needed for the hostels. Locally, he was known as the King of Martial Arts, the guy bringing into the country every martial arts movie being made. His Spaghetti Westerns and Kung Fu movies were hugely popular on the independent circuit. He had incredible contacts in places such as Hong Kong and had been visiting international film festivals since the 1960s. Ritchie knew all about working the system, but remained legit because he was doing big business with the mines. He, too, would complain about having to comply with orders to cut films. He was once ordered to cut the word 'God' from every 'Goddamn' uttered in one particular movie, which meant more than 40 cuts, thus completely butchering a brand-new print.

Often local productions suffered from poor content and were thus unexportable. Because of the newly introduced generous tax benefits, up to 40 movies were being made in South Africa every year, but no more than two or three were being released internationally and, even then, with limited success.

In the 1980s, making films in South Africa to sell abroad was becoming increasingly difficult. Following louder and louder calls for the tightening of sanctions against the apartheid government, there were growing whispers about big movie distribution companies pulling out of the country. The international press, particularly in the US, were stepping up their campaign, criticising producers who appeared to be placing profits above morals, the accusation being that the industry was full of individuals who were prepared to circumvent the rules simply to make a quick buck.

But there were also grey areas – and I was caught in the crossfire. Some of the big studios simply wouldn't deal with any South African, Black or white. In America I would need to point out that I was a Black filmmaker, a strange concept to those familiar with a more transparent, more obvious definition of 'Black', as opposed to the vagaries of 'non-white' or 'Asian' as determined by the apartheid government and terms I refused to acknowledge or give any credence to. Describing myself or allowing myself to be described as 'non-white' or 'Asian' would obliterate all I had accomplished and nullify any steps I had already made in the opposite direction, away from National Party delineations and classifications – they were white and we were Black. The term 'non-white' indicated that white South Africans were superior. And that made a difference. As did my support of the Sullivan Code.

Described as 'guidelines for American businesses operating in South Africa', the Sullivan Code – or Sullivan Principles – was developed in 1977 with the express goal of applying economic pressure on the country in protest at apartheid. The principles consisted of seven requirements a corporation was to demand for its employees as a condition of doing business in South Africa. Amongst others, they demanded the equal treatment of employees regardless of their race, both within and outside of the workplace – a demand that flew directly in the face of the official South African policy of racial segregation and unequal rights. The Sullivan Principles were the brainchild of Reverend Leon Sullivan, pastor of the Zion Baptist Church in Philadelphia. His opposition to apartheid had its roots in a tour of African countries back in 1975, when he was approached by anti-apartheid activists to take on the issue of South African apartheid.

Whenever I was in America, I would take the two-hour trip on the Amtrak train from New York City to Philadelphia, just to spend an hour with the Reverend in the Zion Baptist Church at 3600 Broad Street. Here we would talk things over, thrash out ideas, and unpack theories and resolutions. I learned a lot from the Reverend. He became a mentor during a difficult time in our history. The principles he stood for and, in fact, demanded, gained much traction and were widely adopted by US-based corporations but, unsurprisingly, by very few South African businesses. At the time, the Reverend was the first African American to have been appointed to the board of directors of General Motors, which was a big thing. On reflection, Sullivan was very intuitive, and I'm sure he must have felt that he had nothing to lose by throwing his hat in with this young man. It could certainly do no harm, so he let me loose on some of these entities that would have otherwise not given me the time of day, allowing me to lobby South African entities to sign the code. Videovision was the first South African-owned company to become a signatory and so, with his consent, I then wrote to all the listed entities on the stock exchange. By far the majority didn't bother to respond, and those who did made it quite clear that they felt they were doing enough and didn't need me to tell them what to do. Only a fraction even entertained the idea of a discussion, and even fewer, including retail giant Raymond Ackerman of Pick n Pay, actually invited me to meet them.

In 1985 I issued a public statement, endorsed by Reverend Sullivan, that outlined our commitment to the Sullivan Code. In it, I stated that by adopting the code the intention was to have private companies as well as public companies follow suit. 'Its success,' I said, would be 'dependent upon the response it receives amongst the South African business community, which I hope will be mostly positive.' In a press statement made at the launch of the drive, I quoted the Reverend: 'The Principles are not an academic response designed to advance the views of those who are proponents of either investment or disinvestment. To the contrary, the Principles are a pragmatic policy based on the most judicious engagement of the available resources and are intended to improve the quality of life ... and to help build a peaceful and free South Africa for everyone. I would like to see South African-owned companies adhere to these Principles, report on the compliance, including the strongest amplification of those Principles, which calls on all companies to oppose all apartheid laws.'

I know I was 'small fry' but there was nothing to lose, and I couldn't subscribe to a situation of 'money talks, equality walks'. Videovision had always been proud to endorse Sullivan's stand, as was I personally. For years the international entertainment industry had been stepping up its opposition to apartheid; Woody Allen, for instance, had included clauses in his film contracts that stipulated that his movies would not be released in South Africa. The Directors Against Apartheid Movement, and actors such as Jane Fonda, spearheaded a campaign protesting against having their films screened in the country.

Still, apartheid largely got off easy. The reason, I think, was simple: the industry outside South Africa had limited knowledge about what was really going on inside the country and so failed to grasp the full extent of apartheid. The extreme censorship imposed by the state meant that that message was simply not getting out, certainly not clearly enough. I hope that what helped open the eyes of the entertainment world to apartheid and the everyday reality of it for so many South Africans were my films, *Place of Weeping* and *The Stick*. That those films had been popular and had garnered so much attention made artists and producers – the industry as a whole – sit up, take notice and understand what apartheid was about. And so they started mobilising and getting more involved.

In 1989, a very influential group known as Artists for a Free South Africa (AFSA) was founded by Alfre Woodard, Danny Glover, Blair Underwood, CCH Pounder, Mary Steenburgen, Robert and Donna Brown Guillaume, Roderick Spencer, Samuel L Jackson and his wife LaTanya Richardson Jackson. By launching such an initiative, the founders, as well as other members of the creative community, many of whom – including Sharon Gelman, head of AFSA at the time – had long been involved in efforts against apartheid in some form or another, recognised the role artists and the arts could play in galvanising public attention at a time when media coverage of South Africa was scarce. This was largely as a result of not only stringent South African censorship and the expulsion of foreign journalists, but also lagging US interest in what was unfolding down at the bottom of Africa. AFSA's intention was to mobilise the entertainment industry in support of the cultural boycott, economic sanctions, and other international campaigns to help end apartheid. By involving celebrities in their efforts, AFSA increased media coverage and generated significant public awareness about apartheid. I became heavily involved with AFSA and many of the individuals behind its campaigns.

All these powerful and like-minded people soon became, and still are, friends. One of the people I introduced them to was Ahmed Kathrada and they continue to tell me to this day what a blessing this was in their lives that they got to know him and Barbara Hogan and were inspired by him and his journey.

Chippendales®

13

Who bans the Chippendales?

To the Editor:
[The New York Times]

For partition to succeed in a country as a means of avoiding conflict, certain basic prerequisites should prevail: Partition should be a last resort, after all attempts at reconciling differing aspirations have failed; it should bear the freely given approval of those affected by it; it should be fair to all groups, and it should insure the viability of the hived-off territories, free of economic bondage.

The homelands policy of the National Government in South Africa meets none of these criteria. Partition in South Africa is certainly no last resort. Blacks have historically been excluded from the decision-making process and even today are not part of the constitutional debate.

Furthermore, the Balkanization of South Africa does not carry the approval, freely given or otherwise, of the majority of South Africans. The concept's only endorsees are the Nationalists and the presidents of the new 'states'.

The black majority has had little say in the matter. Homeland or no homeland, to the blacks, who are increasingly urban-based and industrially active, these territories are no more than remote, depressed areas, meaning nothing to their everyday lives, which continue to be governed by the Pass laws, the Group Areas Act, race discrimination and apartheid. The homelands concept is seen merely as a method of depriving them of their South African citizenship and of a stake in the greater whole ...

The homelands have one major export in common: human labor. More than 50 percent of the homelands' work force can find employment only outside the borders of their 'states.' Except for the Transkei, all the homelands are fragmented and comprise unconsolidated parcels of land, hardly resembling a picture of free and independent states. None of the states concerned are self-sufficient in food production, and probably never will be. They are all tied to Pretoria's pursestring largesse. Most are landlocked, without untrammeled access to harbors, airports and markets.

The homelands policy is no more than a mechanism to exclude the majority from the mainstream of South African politics. It can only fail. No policy in South Africa can succeed unless it includes the right of all citizens to a say in the making of the laws which govern people, where they live and work, nor can a philosophy founded in race discrimination survive in the long run.

These were the words of Progressive Federal Party MP David Dalling to *The New York Times* on 31 December 1980, following the launch of the apartheid government's brazen new Homeland Policy, designed entirely around its own needs and to further augment its existing segregationist programme.

From 1979 the apartheid state created 10 tiny areas within South Africa designated as 'homelands' for Black people. These included the Transkei, Ciskei and Bophuthatswana. This essentially meant the permanent removal and resettlement of Black people from a white South Africa where its Black South Africans (including Indians and 'coloureds') had no citizenship and no vote in a place with virtually no viable economy. The plan was to grant citizenship only to the people of these new, 'independent' bantustans or homelands, but their 'rights' would of course be applicable only there, far removed from the everyday lives of white South Africans. *Out of sight, out of mind.*

Apart from the outrageous socio-political implications, however, there was a carefully manufactured spin-off that suited the South African government very nicely, satisfying the needs and – dare I say it – desires of its white citizens without having to save face or admit any moral failure on their part: a Vegas right on their doorstep.

Since the 'homelands' had been declared independent by the apartheid government (although never recognised as such by any other nation), they were free to flout the rigid, Calvinistic laws that prevailed within South Africa itself, and so provide such hedonistic entertainment as gambling and topless revues, trading 7 days a week, 24/7 for South Africans. However, although this proved rather handy for the National Party government – it could quite comfortably and without reservation wash its hands of what was happening in the Sodom and Gomorrah across the border – it also played right into the hands of the entertainment industry.

Since the state's censorship laws did not apply 'across the border', the homelands could, for instance, also release films that were banned and censored in South Africa.

In fact, the South African hotel magnate Sol Kerzner – the CEO of Southern Sun and Sun International who went on to open exclusive resorts around the world in places such as Dubai and the Bahamas – built a chain of resorts in the homelands, including his crown jewel, Sun City, which opened in Bophuthatswana in 1979. These high-end resorts, with their gambling, sensual extravaganzas and six-star leisure experience, were enormously popular. It was like travelling to another country within the country. The Wild Coast Sun, for example, was just two hours from Durban, but once you crossed the Port Edward bridge into the Transkei, there was a real sense of freedom. People from Natal flocked there for live shows, dance extravaganzas, movies and gambling. Over weekends it was impossible to find parking at the Wild Coast Sun, that's how busy it was. There were even arranged tours, with busloads from the Indian areas whisked off to the resort. A coupon for as little as R50 included the bus ticket, entrance to the casino, a meal and some cash for gambling. Heaven for entertainment-starved South Africans of every hue.

Outside of the 'homelands' South Africans also found freedom from the restrictions of apartheid in neighbouring countries like Lesotho and Swaziland and often made weekend trips. My group of friends, among whom were Larry Kulpath, Wally Mistri, Mohamed Cassimjee, Chris Naidoo, Pickey Dass and Dave Naidu, took full advantage of this. For us as young men, it was reasonably priced as we could drive into either country and minimise our accommodation costs by sharing rooms.

The censors' attempts to safeguard South African morals thus ensured massive profits for cheap films showing some skin on the homeland movie circuit. Movies such as *Emmanuelle, The Perils of Gwendoline, One Night Only* and *Cousins in Love* may not have had much going for them in terms of the normal standards of cinematic excellence – plots and character development were generally very feeble – but that didn't matter. What seemed to matter was that they were all deemed unacceptable for visual consumption in South Africa. *Emmanuelle IV*, starring the sultry French actress Mia Nygren and Sylvia Kristel, had the incredible plot of a frustrated middle-aged socialite who undergoes a rejuvenation operation at a South American clinic. Halved in age, she is let loose in Europe and her exploits soon earn her the distinction of becoming the most experienced virgin in the world. The film enjoyed so much popularity at Sun City that the original print wore out and had to be replaced. It was the highest grossing film in the homeland states and ran for more than 12 months, establishing a record in South Africa and earning more than R200 000 for one tiny cinema at Sun City. It went on to play at cinemas at the Wild Coast Sun, Mmabatho Sun and the Thaba Nchu Sun near Bloemfontein. I became friends with the Paris-based producer of the *Emmanuelle* series, Alain Siritsky, who was very smart and talented.

In South Africa all these films were banned and not allowed to be screened under any circumstances. They were being sold to Zimbabwe, Namibia and the homelands. One could argue that we should not have played these movies in the internationally unrecognised 'independent countries' the South African government wanted the world to believe the homelands were, that we should have been boycotting them, but I took a different view. Not all of the films we distributed there were 'risqué' and banned in South Africa because of their explicitness when it came to nudity or sexual content. *Eddie Murphy Raw*, for example, was an indictment on racism and stereotyping of Black people. It was only one of several other films I felt were important to show, making audiences aware of such issues. Also, the ability to sell some of these films internationally and to the homelands enabled me to then finance movies like *Place of Weeping* and *The Stick*.

Another film I bought was *Private Lessons*, starring *Emmanuelle*'s Sylvia Kristel, who had featured in the earlier *Emmanuelle* movies. The tale was of a kid exploring and learning about sex, but was really quite innocuous, although it still played to a 16 age restriction in the US. It came as no surprise that the apartheid state promptly banned it, but we swiftly took it to Sun City and the Wild Coast Sun where, just as promptly, it was a hit.

In a country where the populace was fed a diet of sanitised *Huisgenoot* magazine features and the SABC, the homelands became havens of forbidden pleasure where flexible morals could be exercised without embarrassment. Those who went did so to escape and do the things they couldn't do in South Africa, like gambling and watching risqué films that were explicit but not exactly intellectually challenging. The banning of a film would almost guarantee its success at the entertainment resorts of the homelands. In fact, when many of these films were later unbanned, they didn't fare well on the local circuit; it was as if cinemagoers suspected that all the good bits had been cut.

The successes in the homelands, however, led to even better things for us, allowing us to remake movies such as *Bedroom Eyes*, starring Kathy Shower, Playboy Playmate of the Year in 1988. Canadian Robert Lantos and I had been working together since his very early days in Montreal, distributing his films *In Praise of Older Women*, *My Ticket is No Longer Valid* and all the others he made. The original *Bedroom Eyes* did so well in the homelands that he sold me the remake rights to *Bedroom Eyes II*, which I went on to produce. He and I shared a similar vision, a united understanding of the audience. Neither of us took ourselves too seriously

– for us, it was always about the market. (Robert said he remembered me when we first started doing business as having 'a head full of hair and of smart ideas' and also that I'd paid for one of the movies I bought from him with a carpet!) Long story ...

There was an ever-growing market for this type of movie, an appetite that seemed insatiable, and South Africa proved no exception to the trend. Following the worldwide success of *Bedroom Eyes I*, the sequel was a sure-fire hit for us, as were many others along similar lines.

In his piece in the Arts & Leisure pages of *The New York Times*, Donald McNeil expressed his understanding of why I ventured into these types of films: '[Anant Singh] is no fool: American B-movies that go straight to video are staples of third-world cinemas. And video-rental fees his films earn in America mean serious money here.'

He was right of course. Catering for a mass market in one genre allowed me to tackle others that brought with them meaning and substance, messages that would otherwise remain unfinanced, unheard and unseen. They allowed me to make movies that referenced who I was at heart, which was why I was in the movie business in the first place. These films provided me with the cashflow I needed to finance films that were socially relevant and politically savvy.

The notion of me, a South African, taking films from America and Canada, aggressively marketing them and selling them internationally – even remaking them, in some cases – was beginning to bear fruit. I knew what the markets were like and how they worked, and that allowed me to take something, buy it from Robert Lantos and turn a profit, simply because I had better international contacts than many others in the business, including in Hollywood. We filmed *Bedroom Eyes II* in New York, with Wings Hauser in a starring role. He'd flown to the Big Apple immediately after *Reason to Die* had wrapped for us in South Africa. Our posters of big-breasted women in flimsy negligées and in mortal danger drew viewers like moths to a flame.

Although this was the era of cocaine, loose living in the very broadest sense of that term, sometimes the Calvinist restrictions played right into our hands, sometimes not. When it came to Eddie Murphy and the Chippendales, they certainly did.

In May 1989 the South African Publications Board banned our film *Eddie Murphy Raw*, the American comedian's record-breaking stand-up comedy film. Eddie's massive popularity came on the back of the huge success of his *Beverly Hills Cop* series of films. *Beverly Hills Cop II*, which came out in 1987, had been the highest grossing film at the US box office that year. The South African censors banned outright the local release of *Eddie Murphy Raw*, stating that 'in no way can this act be cleaned up'. So, naturally, we showed it to sold-out audiences at Sun City, Morula Sun and the Wild Coast Sun, three casino complexes in the then homelands.

Then, that same year, the Chippendales visited South Africa with their world tour show *Chippendales, Tall, Dark and Handsome* at the Sun City Superbowl, the resort's giant arena. The troupe's live shows were mammoth successes. South Africans rushed to the homelands to see the Chippendale hunks in action. The shows always sold out way in advance and a black market was created for tickets to the live shows, attended by fans of all shapes, colours, races and creeds. There was actually little about the show that was salacious, with nothing more offensive in their attire than would be found on any public beach, but this clearly wasn't putting people off. Women were going nuts.

The Chippendales had made a video of their show, and I had no doubt that it would do excellent business. The film had been shot in the United

States and was advertised as featuring a scene on a secluded beach where 'a lifeguard comes to your rescue' and another where 'you could take a ride with a biker that moves too fast'. I didn't hesitate.

There was a huge market for this type of entertainment in South Africa, so I secured the video distribution rights and immediately submitted the film to the censor board so that it could be approved and released as soon as possible. It should have come as no surprise that the Publications Board banned the video outright for all South African audiences. In a statement released by the board, it said that the video would clearly adversely affect the moral life of the South African community and would lead 'a substantial number of viewers to breaking the existing moral code'. Among other things, the film would be 'lust provoking', offensive and aggravating.

By this time, I had something of a history with the Publications Board. They had passed other films that were considered female erotica, such as *Stripper*, for example. Emboldened by this, I took the Chippendale decision on review. This time our appeal was successful and the release was delayed by only a few months. And it proved to be as successful as the live shows, demand far outstripping supply, with copies in video rental stores often booked out days and even weeks in advance. It was an enormous hit on home release, with South Africans buying thousands of the videos as Christmas gifts, continuing to generate huge sales until Easter 1990.

For every success story, there's another of dismal failure and disappointment. Things can change very quickly in the film industry, likewise in politics. In 1989 an amendment to the government's tax subsidy to filmmakers had a devastating impact on the industry. The state had been offering filmmakers highly advantageous tax concessions for many years, which in turn had led to a proliferation of so-called filmmakers chasing tax breaks. Many had made a lot of money by playing the system during the tax-break era. South Africa had become the third largest film-producing nation in the world after the US and India. At the same time, the country was only 80th on the World Bank's ranking of nations by income per capita, between Algeria and the former Yugoslavia. All that came to an end when the state cancelled the tax incentive programme.

Gene Louw, Minister of Home Affairs at the time, was inundated with furious industry folk who pulled up at his office in BMWs and Mercedes-Benzes, all crying that they couldn't possibly survive without the special concessions. Most of them were not actually filmmakers, but accountants, bankers and lawyers; many had never even seen a script or a production budget. They had been drawn by the smell of a handout from the public purse and had been making so-called films ever since. All the usual arguments about job losses and strategic assets were made but to no avail. Louw stood firm. The party was over.

Film production in South Africa crashed from 50 projects per year to fewer than 10. The accountants, bankers and lawyers all left in pursuit of new prey and the guys who had always been the real filmmakers were left stranded amid the ruins. The effect of this was that by 1990 Videovision, which had made only a handful of titles utilising the programme, was the only South African company still producing movies. Our good fortune was that we had always been very clear on where we stood: that Videovision was in the business of making films and telling stories, particularly South African stories, but we believed that, subsidy or no, our products still had to be able to succeed in the global marketplace. That was the philosophy I had employed from the beginning.

I didn't let any film out on the market if I didn't think it could succeed; nor did I rely on subsidies to bail us out. For years the subsidy system that had been in place had ensured that filmmakers made a profit irrespective of whether the film was a commercial success or not. In fact, many projects never even reached cinema screens. With the withdrawal of the scheme, work in the industry ground to a halt.

The men were being sorted from the boys.

14

Meeting Mandela

It's late afternoon on Friday, 12 June 1964. Home from his rooms uncharacteristically early for a weekday, my father walks into the kitchen of our house in Reservoir Hills. My mother is busying herself over the pots steaming on the stove top, Sanjeev and I within eyesight. I'm eight years old, drawing at the kitchen table, while five-year-old Sanjeev is putt-putt-putting his tractor along the lines of the tiles at my feet. On the radio perched on the windowsill The Dixie Cups are singing about the Chapel of Love, but Daddy has no patience for this. Pecking Mummy briefly on the cheek, he heads swiftly over to the radio, tuning to short-wave and turning the knob as he hunts for the BBC News frequency.

'You hear about the nonsense going on in Pretoria?' He's irritated by the loud hiss from the radio, but determined to find the news.

Mummy, ever the picture of grace and dignity, looks up from the curry bubbling on the stove and shakes her head.

My father has found the station he's been searching for. 'Just listen here. Shhh, boys ...' Irritated, he puts his finger to his lips when Sanjeev accelerates his tractor up the table leg. 'Listen.'

> Following Judge Quartus de Wet's guilty verdict yesterday at the Palace of Justice in Pretoria, Mr Nelson Mandela and his co-accused were today sentenced to life imprisonment for sabotage, Judge De Wet likening their action to 'one of high treason'. The convicted have been transported to Robben Island where they will serve out their life sent—

'Dammit!'

Dead silence. My mother stops mid-stir, her hand hovering above the pot. Sanjeev and I are shocked, our eyes wide, mouths hanging open. We have never seen our father this angry. Not even when Sanjeev tried to flush his shoes down the loo that one time. Mummy resumes her stirring, but I can see how rattled she is.

'It could have been the death penalty,' she says. 'They could have hanged them all.'

'But, my love ...' Daddy appears to have been calmed somewhat by Mummy's levelheadedness, 'the man's already serving a sentence. For leaving the country without a passport. How did it get to this?'

There is a brief silence. No one moves, not even Sanjeev.

'There was a young man in my rooms this morning. He says his cousin was there at the court in April when the defence launched its case. Nelson gave a long speech – very long. But Nelson wanted to make it very clear how he felt, how everything he's done is for his people. The people want to see the end of domination of one over another. A "democratic and free society", he said.' Daddy lowers his head into his hands. I think he wants to cry. 'This is the ideal for which he said he was prepared to die. That's what he said.'

Mummy lifts the pot from the stove top and places it on the table 'We hope it won't come to that,' she says.

On 11 February 1990, Nelson Mandela walked out of jail a free man.

On leaving Victor Verster Prison just outside Cape Town, Mandela held his wife Winnie's hand as he faced the huge crowd pressing for a look at the man who had last been seen in public 27 years previously. Broadcast live across the world, the moment was iconic. Pure film magic. Cinematic gold.

At the time of Madiba's historic release I was in a remote place on the KwaZulu-Natal north coast with a few friends. The TV signal there was poor so we left early in order to watch this watershed occasion live on television at home. What a memorable day for us all.

Mandela was driven to Cape Town. His driver got lost on their way to Dullah Omar's house, where his first meeting was to take place before he spoke to the nation and the world. That evening Mandela appeared on a balcony at the City Hall before a huge rally of more than 60 000 citizens gathered below on the Grand Parade. Beside him stood his lifelong friend and fellow activist Walter Sisulu and Cyril Ramaphosa, who went on to become president of South Africa. The crowd was euphoric, the excitement and jubilation palpable, audible. Apartheid was not yet behind us, however, and tensions were continuing to build, with many on the far right vitriolic in their condemnation of FW de Klerk's government for releasing Mandela from prison and unbanning the ANC and other anti-apartheid organisations. Mandela appeared to rise above it all, however, giving a rousing speech, his first delivered in public in three decades, declaring his commitment to peace and reconciliation. He was insistent about his focus: to bring peace to the Black majority and to secure for them the right to vote in their own country.

That evening the Mandelas stayed at the home of Archbishop Desmond Tutu in the Cape Town suburb of Bishopscourt. What an evening of fun and joy that must have been.

A few months later, my life and the path it would take would be changed forever.

Something of that conversation between my parents on the day Nelson Mandela was sentenced in 1964 lodged in my child's mind, but my own political consciousness and awareness of the struggle was shaped in high school. Some of my schoolmates at Sastri College in Durban had been student activists and it was through them that I became increasingly aware of the inequality of the society in which we found ourselves, of the untenable political situation and the dire consequences it visited on ordinary South Africans. Mandela, Walter Sisulu, Ahmed Kathrada, Oliver Tambo and their comrades became our heroes, as did many activists like Steve Biko, Ahmed Timol, Pravin Gordhan, Andrew Zondo, Archie Gumede, Ruth First, Dulcie September, Solomon Mahlangu, Rick Turner, David Webster, Griffiths and Victoria Mxenge, and so many others. They were the ones who helped guide us to a freedom already hard fought.

In the 1970s, South African politics was a hotbed of activism, and Nelson Mandela was the symbol of the struggle. It was a time, too, when pictures of Mandela were still banned – no one even knew what the man looked like anymore. To me he was not only one of our liberators but the epitome of a towering Hollywood leading man: romantic freedom fighter, champion of the rights of the people. The perfect poster shot.

A few years later, on one of my trips overseas, I bought a wristwatch bearing the face of Nelson Mandela and smuggled it into the country. I looked at it often and his face reminded me of the struggle, of the violence that the quest for freedom had wrought on the people, inspiring me and motivating me to use film as a tool – as my tool – to oppose apartheid.

In the early 1980s, when Mandela and the ANC called for people to do what they could to speak out or fight against the oppressive regime, the people responded. Some decided against buying South African oranges, a simple act that gained traction as the movement grew and resistance spread. In 1986, I took the decision to make *Place of Weeping*, the first anti-apartheid film to be shot in South Africa. Making this film and then, thereafter, continuing to tell the anti-apartheid stories that I did, saw me reach out to anti-apartheid activists with whom I was set to establish strong ties that lasted a lifetime.

One of these deep and lasting friendships was with renowned anti-apartheid activist and ANC stalwart Fatima Meer. She became a close mentor. I spent a lot of time with her in the late 1980s and learned an enormous amount from her. She and her husband Ismail had sheltered Mandela in their home in Durban in the 1960s, when he was still underground and known as the 'Black Pimpernel'. Fatima, having known the Mandelas for decades, was also a close friend of Winnie Mandela, with whom she had been detained in 1976. The two were like sisters. They spoke whenever possible and as often as they could, and I enjoyed the benefit of hearing about some of those discussions, further influencing my own political thinking and strengthening my admiration for both Fatima and Madiba.

Fatima was exceptional, a champion of the less advantaged and a woman of extreme integrity, dignity and strength. In 1988, at the request of Mandela himself, she wrote *Higher than Hope*, an authorised biography of Nelson Mandela, while he was still in prison. She gave me the manuscript to read and, further fascinated by Mandela's extraordinary story, I immediately realised what an incredible motion picture it would make. Fatima and I had many discussions about the prospect and the potential it held for strengthening a global awareness of our struggle for freedom.

One day she called me. 'I'm going to visit Nelson,' she said, 'and will discuss your idea of a film with him.' A few weeks later she received a handwritten letter from Mandela in which he referred to me by name and, in his humble manner, questioned the need for a film. *A film about my life? But why? Why would anyone want to see a film about me?* I ended up writing to him, putting forward the idea and eventually – he took a lot of persuading – he became amenable. Fatima suggested Mandela be played by Sidney Poitier, to which he promptly acceded, adding, however, that he was not sure that the actor would accept the offer, considering that Poitier was such 'a super star'.

On the release of the book, there was a lot of interest in the film rights to *Higher than Hope* and it wasn't long before an international bidding war raged, one that drew entities with an eye on doing a miniseries on Mandela. These included Lorimar Television, the studio responsible for *Dallas* and *Falcon Crest*, both massively popular television series at the time.

Fortunately for me, I had enjoyed a long relationship with Fatima, helping her with the many needs of the not-for-profit Institute for Black

Research, which she headed, assisting her with fundraising, media and publishing.

I was also still the only Black filmmaker in South Africa.

This all helped make it possible for me to step up and step forward, and acquire the rights to Fatima's biography of Mandela in 1990. But events soon overtook this plan.

My personal relationship with Madiba began a few months after he was released from Victor Verster Prison. Amid the flurry of excitement, the interminable meet-and-greets the man was expected to conduct, the one-on-one, face-to-face visits to comrades and supporters to thank them personally for their support over the years, he was travelling across the country and had come to Durban, where he visited and stayed with Ismail and Fatima Meer.

At around 5 am one morning in August, in 1990, my phone rang. I had probably gone to bed at about 2 am and, jolted from my sleep, I could hear the ringing somewhere in the house. I had purposely turned off the ringer of the phone in my room. I ignored it at first but, after five calls of long and persistent ringing, I finally picked up. It was Fatima.

'I want you to come to my house. Now.' I turned to the digital clock next to the bed.

'But, Fatima, it is 05:40!'

'Yes, I know that,' she said, 'but this is something you want to do. There is someone very important I want you to meet.' Perhaps we could do it later, I urged, unaware of course of who she meant.

'No,' she insisted, 'you have to come now. This is urgent.'

I still lived with my mother in Reservoir Hills and Fatima and Ismail lived in Burnwood Road in Clare Estate, 10 minutes away.

And so I got up, washed my face and, without even showering, rushed over. Immediately, she walked me into the garden – and there was Madiba, an empty chair next to him. And that was where and how it happened.

I spent an hour with Madiba that day, discussing issues that touched both him and me, including the media, family, films, globalisation and his life in prison. He showed great interest in my films. I was surprised that he knew of the films I had made and that he knew about my battles with Ster-Kinekor, SABC TV and the censors with *Place of Weeping*. I later learned that when he was at Victor Verster Prison, he had access to a television and newspapers. I told him of the movies I had made to which he would not have had access. I told him that I was preparing to make a film about *Sarafina!* the stage play, which he was aware of as he was the inspiration for the character Sarafina and had read about its success in the US. He was very pleased as it also celebrated the youth of 1976. He asked of my views on many things, politics, our leaders, my family and friends. He asked how I came to be in the film business. He told me about the movies they watched on 16mm in prison on a rare 'movie night'. We talked about Kathy – Ahmed Kathrada – whom I had already met, as well as the simple things in life. He made me feel important, and I know that he genuinely cared as his sincerity came through. I remember feeling it then – and knowing it now – that that was the most incredible and fascinating hour I have ever spent with anyone in my entire life. As he was to prove in the years that followed, and as reported in countless articles, reviews and interviews, Madiba was every bit the charming, modest, down-to-earth man he was made out to be. He was always intent on making me feel important, keen to know everything about diverse topics. He had a special charismatic quality and calming aura about him. We could have chatted for days but, alas, he had to be shared. Our interaction nevertheless reinforced my passion to make a movie about his journey. He told me about his biography, *Long Walk to Freedom*, which he wrote in prison and was smuggled out. It was going to be published soon, he said, and suggested we wait for this rather than do *Higher than Hope*. I agreed. His modesty and humility were ever-present. It was then that I committed myself to assisting him in any way possible, in full support of his initiatives.

Later that year actors Alfre Woodard, CCH Pounder and LaTanya Richardson Jackson (Samuel L Jackson's wife) of AFSA travelled to South Africa. I told Madiba of their visit, and within minutes of touching down in Johannesburg I called to tell them that they were invited to lunch with Nelson Mandela. It had been a long flight and they were desperate to shower first or at least get a clean change of clothes, but I had to spell it out to them. They were taking a chance, I explained. Did they want to do it or not? And, of course, no one ever turned down an invitation from Madiba.

Shortly after our meeting, Madiba visited the United States where he embarked on a nationwide tour. AFSA arranged a massive fundraising dinner in Los Angeles that collected $1.2 million for the Nelson Mandela Freedom Fund. I had the great honour of being elected to the board as the only South African representative. (After South Africa's first democratic election in 1994 the organisation changed its name to Artists for a New South Africa, known as ANSA.)

The road to freedom was a hard one. It was achieved through blood, sweat and tears. Over and above the liberation fighters taking on the might of the apartheid regime with thousands losing their lives, Natal and the Witwatersrand was plagued by ethnic violence, which was only resolved when Madiba intervened and brokered a peaceful solution.

The year 1994 was a momentous one – for the nation, of course, but also for me personally – and one that changed everything. It was the culmination of centuries of struggle by freedom-seeking South Africans, a hard-won victory that had taken its toll on a nation suppressed and oppressed for so long. But, on 27 April that year, the people of South Africa put that behind them for a while, and turned out in droves to make their cross on the ballot and claim their place in history.

The dawn of voting broke bright and fresh, in every sense. That afternoon we made our way to the church hall in St Thomas Road. It was significant for us as the area was the bastion of white old Durban families and it was unthinkable for us to venture into this part of town in the apartheid years. It was as though we were seeing the world in an entirely different light, seeing it all for the first time. As though, suddenly, all around us was a saturation of colour, of light dancing, the opening scene of a movie playing out right in front of us. The queues were long, the would-be voters patient, an excitement so real and so tangible that you could feel it in the air. Voices were animated, the buzz punctuated here and there with laughter. At other voting stations across the country, the lines snaked across city streets, through open veld, down dusty roads. There was dancing and singing, ululating and laughter, an especially poignant and moving moment for those – like myself – who were casting their ballot for the very first time. The entire election process, from being screened, to having our thumbs marked, to making our X, was almost overwhelming, and the most amazing thing was that everyone was patient and in the queues there were people of all race groups and ethnicities – a true Rainbow Nation.

The movie industry was clearly in the doldrums, but there were some early green shoots, one of them the unbanning of a number of films and books following Mandela's release.

In 1994 came a once-in-a-lifetime opportunity that cemented a long-standing relationship with New York-based activist and documentary film director Danny Schechter. In his book *When South Africa Called, We Answered*, Danny outlines the hard road he faced documenting behind the scenes on some of the projects we worked on together or that he tackled on his own:

> I was involved in making six documentaries about Nelson Mandela in the 1990s ... Many of these documentaries were co-produced with Anant Singh's South African company, Videovision, requiring thousands of hours of effort. I did not and could not have done it alone.
>
> *Free at Last*, about Mandela's release, 'went out' in 1990, and then I played a role in his first hour-long American TV interview from Lusaka where he was visiting the ANC HQ in exile. Later, I travelled to Sweden when he reunited with his ailing law partner and then ANC president, Oliver Tambo, after three decades.
>
> Months later, I was with him on his triumphant eight-city tour of the United States where he packed stadiums and inspired millions. I filmed it all for the documentary, *Mandela in America*.

Following Danny's documenting of the US tour, Madiba invited him to South Africa to document his run for the presidency in 1994. The result was *Countdown to Freedom: Ten Days That Changed South Africa*.

Selling the idea to interested buyers, however, proved really tough, with Danny encountering one obstacle after another, one disappointment running into the next.

'I contacted Anant Singh,' Danny says in his book. 'Responsible for [a number of] before-their-time anti-apartheid films, he was known for being gutsy. He was my last hope. I wasn't sure if a documentary project would be appealing because he is primarily in the feature movie business. I asked to meet him ... It took Singh about a nanosecond to recognise the importance of documenting the unprecedented events underway in his own country.'

Danny was forthright in his approach, outlining the history of the project and the attitude of TV networks that had vacillated between enthusiasm and utter disregard. He became rather emotional about it all but, in all honesty, I didn't need any persuading. It was already a notion endorsed by Madiba himself – what else was there to consider?

'Anant's response was: "Fine, let's do it." We shook hands. That was it. No contracts, no deal memos. No long months of high-priced lawyers negotiating miles of boilerplate. Singh said he'd pay for a crew and ten days of shooting. And then we'd see what we had – and where to go next.

'We would be partners, the first international co-production of its kind in the "new" South Africa. I wasn't sure if we could do it, but there it was – a green light, and a not yet fully committed "low budget", which is always better than no budget. I now had a dare: "Show me what you can do."

'I was lucky to find a South African with faith in me, faith in his country's history, and the bucks to get the film going. Race never entered into it. Our project was now back on track – a narrower track to be sure, but at least, at this late hour, we would finally be able to do something.'

Countdown to Freedom was a fascinating experience. Here we were capturing the run-up to the first free elections with unfettered access to Madiba and the ANC war room as they strategised their campaign. For me, the most significant part of this was being at Madiba's inauguration

– it was mesmerising to be in the midst of all the dignitaries, heads of state and celebrities, and I was lucky to meet Yasser Arafat, Colin Powell, Maya Angelou, Randall Robinson and a host of others, including Quincy Jones. With the exclusive access that we had, we were flies on the wall, following the ANC leadership around to shoot everywhere they went. On one occasion we were in the Union Buildings, waiting to film the moment when Madiba and Fidel Castro were about to meet privately. It was such a special moment when Fidel Castro arrived and Madiba and he walked towards each other, with Madiba saying, 'Hello, Fidel' and Fidel, speaking through his interpreter, reciprocating the greeting. They embraced each other warmly. It was moving to see the love, camaraderie and friendship between these two world leaders, who had barely met each other before. Madiba, being his gracious self, kindly introduced me to Fidel, telling him that I was to make a movie about his life. In turn I said that a film should be made about Fidel's amazing life and legacy.

Danny and I would collaborate on a number of other productions over the years, among them *Prisoners of Hope*, *A Hero for All* and *Viva Mandela*. I also brought Danny back to South Africa to produce and direct the documentary *Beyond Long Walk to Freedom*, a five-part series on the making of the film. Sadly, this was to be his last film project. He passed away on 19 March 2015. His departure was a blow, his contribution to society having been immeasurable. It was from Danny that I learned that if one is driven by a cause, nothing is impossible.

Despite the slump in the fortunes of the film industry at the time that Danny and I first collaborated, 1994 was a pivotal year. There was a real sense of excitement in the air, a sense of freedom and real change.

I was happy that Danny and I got to have a front-row seat to the show. Even today when I am in New York, I think of Danny and the great discussions and robust debates we had.

In time, following our first meeting in 1990, my relationship with Madiba grew and I regularly joined him on his international trips. I had the privilege of experiencing first-hand his gentle nature and ability to disarm individuals, to make them feel perfectly at ease. He had this knack of making everyone feel important – whether it was a chef, bellman or a king or queen. We spent many precious moments together. Madiba was not a man of protocol and it was amusing to me that he defied royal protocol which required that Queen Elizabeth II be addressed as 'Your Majesty'. Madiba called her Elizabeth and she in turn called him Nelson.

It was in light of this relationship that Madiba asked me to help set up a gathering at the Presidential Guest House in Pretoria in the run-up to the launch of the Nelson Mandela Children's Fund in 1995. A handful of guests, among them captains of industry, high net-worth individuals and corporates, were invited to commit R750 000 towards the fund, matching Madiba's own commitment to donate one-third of his salary for his five-year term as president, and so become a founding member. Naturally, a number of these individuals, largely CEOs of companies, signed up. Jeremy Ractliffe, head of the fund, asked that they pose for a picture with Madiba. As they lined up, it was striking to me – and a little embarrassing – that all of those individuals were white. Startled, I leaned over to Jeremy, who was standing beside me, and whispered, 'But that's not right.'

'Maybe I should step in there,' I ventured, 'but I just can't afford it.' Mulling it over very quickly, I added: 'Perhaps I can pay it off over five or six years, if that works?'

A broad smile spread over Jeremy's face. 'Yes, please do,' he said. 'Go ahead.'

And that was how I became actively involved as a founding member of the Nelson Mandela Children's Fund, and one of the first President's Club members.

15

Exit, followed by an elephant

It was Sudhir Pragjee who came up with the idea.

The year was 1990. Madiba had just been released from prison and South Africa was experiencing the euphoria of the impossible becoming possible. Sudhir was driving his parents in downtown Durban when he tuned the radio to Lotus FM, the local Indian radio station. Kirit Trivedi, the manager of Amitabh Bachchan, the wildly popular Indian film star, was in the country and being interviewed. After Sudhir heard him say that he hoped to bring Amitabh to South Africa some time, he rushed straight to my office. The chance of a lifetime, he said. We had to get to Amitabh and bring him over. No question about it.

I wasn't convinced, but Sudhir was adamant. In the end I said: 'Sure.

See what you can do.' Sudhir immediately kicked into overdrive. He called the radio station and, pulling a few strings, managed to track down Kirit and set up a meeting. As it happened we were not the only suitor. Kirit admitted right off the bat that Amitabh would require £1 million to do two shows in South Africa. That, of course, was completely beyond our budget – there was no way we could do it. We told him this upfront, but still we spent two days with him, showing him who we were and what we were about. When it was time for Kirit to leave, we drove him to the airport to see him off. As he was leaving he turned to Sudhir. 'Look,' he said, 'if Amitabh does come to South Africa, he will only come here to do it with you guys.'

Needless to say, Sudhir's eyes lit up. There was just one snag – we didn't have the money. Amitabh was a huge star, his film persona described by Brenda Kali in *The Star Tonight* as the 'Lone Ranger-type champion of the downtrodden, a crusader against villainy and a campaigner for justice'. His following was enormous, so much so that in 1999 he was voted the Greatest Star of Stage or Screen of the Millennium in an online BBC poll.

Sudhir was determined to come up with a way to get Amitabh to South Africa. He remembered some government tax scheme that had been used in the past to bring superstars to southern Africa where corporates could sponsor the arts and receive a massive tax break in return. This 'loophole' had been used to get Frank Sinatra to Sun City. When he investigated further he discovered that the programme, which had been designed to bring sports stars and popular performers to South Africa in defiance of the sporting and cultural boycott, still existed. The programme allowed for a sponsor to claim 180 per cent of the sponsorship amount in tax credits ... so off we went – farming our idea around until finally we found a sponsor who saw an excellent opportunity. First

National Bank seemed keen to get behind a ground-breaking production of this magnitude, which, at the same time, could allow them to tap into what they must have seen as the booming middle-class Indian market. They stepped in with an offer. Now we had a show, but that was only the beginning.

We had no idea what we had signed up for. Live entertainment was something we had never done before. Our fears, however, were premature. Amitabh's show, the first international concert in South Africa following Mandela's release, would become the biggest, most incredible extravaganza South Africans had ever seen.

Despite countless challenges, including political interference, when Amitabh touched down at the airport in Durban there were 7 000 fans waiting. Authorities had to shut the parking lot to vehicles to allow fans to see him drive past. There was an unprecedented outpouring of love for their number one superstar.

The first show, on 5 January 1991, was to be at Kings Park Stadium, Durban's premier rugby venue (ironically, one to which we as Indians would not have been granted access during the apartheid years), the second show just 24 hours later at Soccer City in Johannesburg, some 600 kilometres away. In order to keep to the scheduling commitments of the Bollywood star in India and elsewhere, this was quite a logistical challenge. We had to dismantle the set and then transport, overnight, all the equipment, the entire stage and the crew – mostly by road – to get everything set up in time for the next night in Johannesburg.

But we did it. The shows were sold out and, in fact, massively oversubscribed.

The production was not without its drama though. Another promoter who was keen to bring Amitabh to South Africa turned to the courts, claiming he had had a verbal agreement – and the photo of a handshake to prove it – which resulted in an interdict being served. It was the end of December 1990 and everyone in South Africa was on their summer holiday – it seemed as if there was not a single lawyer in town, and the show was just around the corner. Fortunately, we were able to rope in some legal help, with lawyers drafting court papers at our offices at the very last minute to ensure that the show went on.

In Durban there was such an incredible vibe, an excitement that was almost tangible, that I asked Amitabh whether he might be prepared to visit the Chatsworth Centre, the popular mall in the biggest Indian township in Durban, to allow more people to see him in the flesh. He readily agreed, understanding the demand and also that not everyone would have been able to get tickets to the show. As keen as Amitabh was, however, the logistics here also proved extremely challenging. The traffic jams were so horrific, vehicles backed up for kilometres, that I had to arrange a helicopter to pick Amitabh up from the road and fly him to the centre, where at a rough count at least 40 000 ecstatic fans had gathered. The place was charged with excitement, a sense of grand theatre and dramatic tension. This was Amitabh mania on a scale never seen before in South Africa. When he stepped out of the helicopter onto the roof, the throng erupted.

We had a local singer there, Mervyn Pillay, who is an Amitabh impersonator; he looks a little like him and performs shows like Amitabh's. In fact, Mervyn performing Amitabh's songs received so much applause that Amitabh joked that the South African Amitabh was better at playing him than he was himself.

The show at Kings Park that evening was South Africa's first major international event and our first live stadium extravaganza, and we had never seen so much cash. Because not everyone had access to Computicket, the country's computerised ticketing system, we had to physically collect ticket money from local vendors dotted around the city. While these mom-and-pop operations (an established network traditionally utilised for the purposes of ticket sales) were not accustomed to dealing with the numbers we were expecting, it was essential that we support those who had not only always stood behind us but also provided a direct link to folk on the ground. And, proving how significant a role word of mouth plays, it was a spectacular success – ticket sales boomed and the money came in, almost all of it in cash. It was extraordinary, unimaginable.

Following our collaborations with Amitabh, we set about establishing an effective way to support a worthy charitable cause. We donated R65 000 from the proceeds to community and welfare organisations, and R250 000 to the Aryan Benevolent Home, which cared for the aged, orphans and other vulnerable people in our society. With the funds, they built a training facility, the Amitabh Bachchan Centre.

The show boasted a 40-piece orchestra and 35 dancers, but the *pièce de résistance* was to be Amitabh's grand entrance – on the back of an elephant. So off we went to fetch an elephant from Brian's Circus. Unfortunately, we hadn't factored in the possibility of stage fright. On the night the elephant refused to budge, and when it became clear that nothing was going to tempt it to change its mind, we were forced to abandon the spectacle at the last minute.

Those days there weren't the big high-resolution screens we have at concerts today. All we had were some Jumbotrons, old-style video display units with terrible resolution by today's standards, but a real hit back then. The shows were hugely successful and ground-breaking for South Africa.

Building relationships that last has always been important to me. I have only ever distributed Bollywood films because Amitabh asked me to, the first the highly acclaimed *Bombay*. Following the 1991 shows, he came out again in 2002 to do a promotional tour for *Aankhen* and once more – this time at the Pavilion centre – there were thousands of fans lined up to see him. Again, we had to close off all the parking lots. South Africans just love the man. And he loves South Africans right back.

While the shows were modestly profitable, we gave the artists and our South African fans the time of their lives, and an event that is still talked about today.

16

Whoopi, Leroy and Harvey Weinstein

In the 1980s the Market Theatre in Johannesburg was a real melting
pot of culture and art. It had been founded in 1976 by Mannie Manim
and Barney Simon and was built on the site of Johannesburg's Indian
Fruit Market, which itself had been built in 1913. During the dark days
of apartheid, with freedom of expression restricted and bans and cen-
sorships the order of the day, the Market Theatre, armed with little more
than the conviction that culture can change society, always challenged
the apartheid regime. Based in the downtown bohemian suburb of
Newtown, it operated as an independent theatre, one of the few places

where Blacks and whites could mix on equal terms. There were other similar theatres, including The Space Theatre in Cape Town, but the Market Theatre was probably the biggest, internationally renowned as South Africa's 'Theatre of the Struggle'. *The New York Times* referred to productions there as dissidents 'urgently telling and retelling the atrocities of apartheid'. It spoke glowingly about the defiance of the regime by the theatre in Newtown.

It was during the turbulent 1970s, on 21 June 1976 – less than a week after the Soweto uprising when police opened fire on students who were protesting against Afrikaans as the medium of instruction in schools – that the Market Theatre opened its doors, with Simon as its artistic director. Many productions that were staged there were subsequently made into films by me, among them *Township Fever* and *Road to Mecca*.

It was here, in 1987, that KwaZulu-Natal-born songwriter and playwright Mbongeni Ngema – born only three days after me in Verulam, just a short distance from my home – debuted his ground-breaking musical *Sarafina!*, which was directed for the stage by John Kani, with additional music by Hugh Masekela. The story was based on the revolt by students from Morris Isaacson Junior High, the site of student protests during the Soweto uprisings of 1976, and recounts the students' efforts to create a play out of their tragic history. It follows the lives of the teenaged Sarafina and her classmates on two fronts: surviving the madness and pain of their daily lives, and revelling in the rhythms and energy of the school musical they were creating.

It was a spellbinding story of freedom. But what many forget is that the inspiration went all the way back to Nelson Mandela. The story of *Sarafina!* is a celebration of the day Mandela was released – a somewhat outlandish notion for 1987, when the man himself was in prison for life and with images of and articles about him still banned. At the time

Sarafina! debuted, it seemed that there was no chance of Mandela ever walking free – no one had even seen a photo of him for years – yet the kids in *Sarafina!* all had his picture pasted up on the walls of their homes.

Mbongeni had crafted the musical with immense care and ingenious creativity. The obvious influences were both Nelson and Winnie Mandela, and indeed part of the message was about the strength of Winnie and young women in general, which became a central theme of *Sarafina!* It was no coincidence that the lead character, played by unknown 16-year-old Leleti Khumalo, was a woman aspiring to be the next Nelson Mandela. Leleti and the bulk of the cast – two dozen of them, most of them in their late teens – were all youngsters, regular township teenagers with no formal training. Mbongeni had scoured the country for his cast and found them in his many countrywide auditions, before he set about establishing a rigorous training programme that schooled them in song and dance. They were courageous and highly talented.

Once I saw the show I was immediately enamoured. I knew instinctively that this was a project that had to be done as a film. With this in mind I approached Mbongeni and we had a series of meetings to explore the possibility of working together. Initially, he appeared to be very interested, but what I didn't know was that he was also negotiating with the Brooklyn Academy of Music to take the show to New York. And, of course, when that deal was finally cemented and he set off for New York, our discussions ground to a halt. As it turned out, the show became a huge hit for Mbongeni and, as it toured the US, ending with a long run at Broadway's Cort Theatre, I was facing stiff competition. Everyone was clamouring to be part of what was fast becoming a global phenomenon. Unfortunately for me, Mbongeni had already signed a deal so nothing further came of our negotiations.

In the meantime, though, the stage show was proving an immense hit and it wasn't long before an invitation was extended to take it abroad. Leleti and her 23 co-stars travelled to New York in 1988 where the play debuted on 28 January at the Brooklyn Academy of Music. The run was meant to be only two months but, in the end, the show played for more than a year and then went on to Broadway. Leleti did not have an understudy so she had to stay and perform while her co-stars took turns to go home and come back. She was terribly homesick, which confused a lot of people. In New York, they would say, 'But why would you want to go back to South Africa?' Her answer was always the same: *Because it's home.*

The stage musical was nominated for five prestigious Tony Awards in 1988, including Best Musical and, for Leleti, Best Performance by a Featured Actress in a Musical. The award went to Judy Kaye for her performance in *The Phantom of the Opera*, a decision that set a cat among the pigeons: the judging panel was too white, said the critics; Broadway itself was too white. Leleti had been robbed.

And yet, despite the enormous success of the stage show and all the accolades bestowed on it, Mbongeni and his team just couldn't get it to the big screen. Mbongeni had explored the possibility of working with a number of individuals on the project, but couldn't find someone who shared the same vision.

Eventually, the show returned to the Market Theatre in South Africa, by which time the film rights were held in conjunction with the BBC. David Thompson, head of BBC Films, approached me to help make *Sarafina!* the film a reality. They required a South African partner and a large part of the funding because the BBC was primarily interested in the UK broadcast rights.

And so I did some homework, a call here, a suggestion there; my Little Black Book did overtime, its pages worn thin as I scoured my contacts, determined to set this project in motion and make a movie. Eventually, it all started to come together. During the development process, I held several meetings in London with writer Bill Nicholson and producer David Thompson, as well as Hugh Masekela and Mbongeni. As with most film projects, it didn't happen overnight; in reality, it took some four-and-a-half years before we made the movie, on a budget of $3 million in a Videovision collaboration with the BBC and the French company Les Films Ariane.

One of the early reasons for the long delay was finalising a script. It was one thing to have a smash stage musical, but quite another transforming that to film. Musicals are a very unforgiving genre, and one misstep can prove disastrous. We had a story of youth being killed, and it was a musical. The odds seemed stacked against us. Fortune was, however, on our side: by the time we finally got around to filming, it was 1991 and Mandela had been released. It became easy to go straight into production, shooting on location in Soweto with the support of Madiba and the local population and, for a change, with no apartheid secret police interference or bullying.

David Thompson remembers that his three-year-old daughter Sophie slept through the entire shoot of the riot scene in Soweto in the back of his car; and that his son Joshua played football in his Manchester United kit on the set with the schoolkids. What I remember – which seemed to have slipped David's memory – was how he came close to blowing up an almost-new BMW when he ran the vehicle's aircon for the whole day while it was stationary.

At the time, many exiles who had left the country during the dire oppressive years of apartheid were returning home. One of these was the legendary songstress Miriam Makeba and her collaborator and ex-husband, the musician Hugh Masekela. We became firm friends, so much so that when Hugh was a guest lecturer at the University of KwaZulu-Natal in the 1990s, he stayed at our apartment on the Berea in Durban, which was close to the university. Both Miriam and Hugh became involved in the film. *Sarafina!* was, after all, a story everyone knew and loved, and the involvement of Miriam and Hugh, both globally recognised as extraordinary talents, added considerable gravitas to the project. We decided early on that no one but Leleti should play Sarafina and that Darrell Roodt would be brought in to direct.

Darrell and I had made names for ourselves with several international award-winning films, including our collaborations *Place of Weeping* and *The Stick*. But if we thought it was all slotting neatly into place, we were wrong. This was to be no smooth ride. For one, to retain the authenticity of the story, I firmly believed it was essential that it have a South African director, but it proved difficult to get our overseas partners to agree to my vision. I had to convince them to let Darrell do it, particularly as stage and film are two very different mediums. Signing Darrell was swiftly followed by other significant breakthroughs. First I managed to secure Michael Peters, the choreographer behind Michael Jackson's *Thriller* video, to do the film's choreography.

And then ... the big one. Our star: Whoopi Goldberg.

Since its New York premiere, Whoopi had been an ardent supporter of *Place of Weeping* and, given its context and that she was a member of Artists for a Free South Africa, she had publicly endorsed the movie. Later, when we met up at the 1991 Cannes Film Festival where she was on the jury, we started chatting. Having been raised in segregated South Africa, in a society where people of colour were required to know their place, to speak only when spoken to, to watch their words, I had already learned that that was going to get me nowhere. Although I was a little intimidated by Whoopi's star status, I was determined to have my say. During our conversation, I mentioned *Sarafina!* and asked her advice on elements of the project. My boldness paid off. She told me how much she had loved the play and, she suggested, she wouldn't be averse to a role in the movie edition. 'You need to be in it,' I dared and, later that evening, dropped a copy of the script in her mailbox at the Majestic Hotel, where we were both staying. In my note, I explained how important it was for us that she consider a role in the film. To be honest, though, I didn't hold out much hope. These types of interactions happen every day in Hollywood and all too often nothing comes of them: a promising project with a great script – and polite enthusiasm from an award-winning actor who gets to read some of the finest work the industry has to offer.

When I enquired a few days later whether she had had the opportunity to read any of the script, she admitted that she hadn't. So, more than a little disappointed, I let the matter go. The last thing you want to do in this business is harass an A-list star. But I was so sure that this would be right for both her and us. A few days later I received a short note from her in my message box at the hotel: 'I love it. Any chance I can be in it?'

As it was, she had indeed read the script and had loved it. She was excited that the project was about to get off the ground and, she said, the role of the teacher was 'something I could do'.

Dared I get excited? Whoopi had just won an Oscar for *Ghost* and was thus in incredibly high demand, able to ask between $1 million to $3 million per project. We, of course, didn't have that kind of capital – that was one-third of our budget for 12 days – so we had to make a plan. It was time to get creative. I suggested we bring Whoopi on as a partner. Under this arrangement she would take a lower fee than her usual one but share in the income when the film started to earn revenue. Whoopi agreed – and she became my partner. Her initial fee of no more than $100 000 for her role in *Sarafina!* would multiply tenfold with her earnings as an investor. Hooray for Hollywood!

Securing Whoopi was a significant coup, an indescribable boost for the production, but there was one small hiccup: we were set to film in South Africa and Whoopi Goldberg was reluctant to fly. Anywhere. Years earlier, she had developed a serious phobia of flying after witnessing the mid-air collision of two aircraft in San Diego. She had insisted on driving everywhere ever since – even today, she still drives around the US in a huge touring van. But there would be no keeping her from this, the opportunity to share in this story. And so, despite her personal fears, for this movie, this *Sarafina!*, Whoopi climbed on a plane and flew halfway around the world.

Whoopi remembers it like this: 'I said, "Do they know I hate to fly?" and they said, "Yeah, they kinda know, but they figured you might be interested in this." So I talked to Anant. And I thought, well, boy, I really want to do this. And I wanted to go to South Africa because Madiba had just been released. I wanted to be part of that because I was part of a concert for the freeing of Nelson Mandela. And never in a million years did I think that somehow I would get to meet and spend time with him and be friends.'

But we were to face one more challenge before filming started. Unaware that we had the personal endorsement of Madiba, the Film and Allied Workers Organisation threatened to derail the entire project. Essentially, Whoopi's involvement in the project transgressed a blanket ban on international artists performing in South Africa. The trade union movement was very powerful in the anti-apartheid struggle and its membership was steadfast in adhering to their principles. Politically and socially, matters were still very fragile. We had reached an impasse on the issue. To try to restore a little sanity to an otherwise bizarre and

potentially explosive situation, Whoopi agreed to go along to a meeting with the labour representatives. The conversation with me was not
progressing well. I had said to them that I had been trying my best to do
whatever I could to speak out without consultation. Of course, Whoopi
being Whoopi, she charmed them, later describing the encounter in her
inimitable way: 'After having a conversation with them, where I kinda
said, "Hey, ya know, we're all fighting for the same thing, man. We're all
trying to fight for the same thing, because we are one human race. So you
can't be nasty to me, because I came to shine light." And so they were
like, "Ya, we know ... we noticed. You're all right. You're fine."'

And she certainly was. Whoopi was a real trooper. She bit the bullet
on the challenges, faced her flying fears and came to South Africa. Her
presence was reassuring to many of the actors – most of whom were
young and very nervous, virtually none of them having acted in a movie
before. Whoopi would call the youngsters over, calm them down and
help them through their scenes. It was really inspiring to watch.

But Whoopi was not the only star, of course. Back home we had our
own constellation we were determined to make good use of, showcasing
a star-studded cast and crew in what was set to be one of the most ambitious productions the country had ever seen. Among the extraordinary
talents we were able to assemble were Miriam Makeba, John Kani (as the
school principal) and Mbongeni Ngema himself.

In a strange twist of fate, the result of me coming up with the idea to
cast Makeba in the movie as Sarafina's mother, she had in 1988 met the
theatre cast of *Sarafina!* in New York when the show was on Broadway.
Makeba was still in exile at the time and it was a highly emotional meeting. She apparently declared that she would die happy knowing the
young cast would continue what she had started years before, spreading the message to the world through their music. 'We are a proud and

struggling people and we will win our independence and we will be free,'
she told them. Within five years, Makeba was back home.

Hugh Masekela shared a similar journey of exile from his land of
birth. In 1960, at the age of 21, he left South Africa to begin what would
be 30 years abroad, returning only in 1990, following the unbanning of
the ANC and the release of Nelson Mandela. Miriam and Hugh had
been married but since their parting had remained on good terms.

I ran my suggestion past Darrell and Mbongeni. 'Hey,' I said, 'let's
develop the role of Leleti's mother and ask Miriam to play her, as a
cameo? And maybe we do a song with her?'

Everyone bought into the concept right away and I was delighted.
I went to Miriam with the idea and she liked it too. We made a deal.
Then I got Mbongeni to write a new song with Hugh, and that was how
'Thank You, Mama' came about. A salute to The Mother and the Black
women of South Africa who bore the brunt of the harshness of apartheid, the song featured in the original movie. Later, when Disney bought
the film for the US, they substituted the song, claiming that it was 'too
South African'. I bristled at this but relented, although I insisted that it
be retained for South Africa and the rest of the world.

The pre-production period on *Sarafina!* was incredibly challenging,
for the movie's leads as well as the kids who put everything they had into
their performances. We actually sent them on a training camp for months
so that they were able to learn the moves and the music. Pre-production
was thus an intense six months but, interestingly, here too Sarafina's
journey and Madiba's journey became intertwined. In February 1990,
Madiba was released from prison and we began shooting the following
year.

In October 1991 an American delegation of TransAfrica members were in Johannesburg to see Madiba, probably 30 of them in all, a mix of political bigwigs and a host of anti-apartheid celebrities and activists. I came up with the idea of putting on a show for them with some of the *Sarafina!* cast – as a thank you, but also to showcase our spirit and energy. When Madiba said, 'Good idea,' we leapt into action.

The event was held in a hall in Hillbrow and in the audience were the legendary muso Quincy Jones, congressman John Lewis, Randall Robinson and tennis player Arthur Ashe. The kids pulled out all the stops, performing their hearts out in a line-up of song and dance numbers that blew the visitors away. That night I had a memorable dinner with Quincy and John Lewis at the Carlton Club, which began at about 1 am and finished at 4 am.

I had met Quincy some years before and we had become good friends. 'We were all fighting the battle,' Quincy said of our first encounter, 'to free South Africa, and then I heard about Anant's work. Here was a South African filmmaker making movies about life during apartheid in the 80s and early 90s. I admired his courage to make these movies and wanted to meet him. It was through one of his movies which screened in the States that I first met him … What has developed between us is a valued friendship, a kind of brotherly bond that I truly treasure. I came to South Africa shortly after Madiba was released from prison and met Anant again. He was about to make *Sarafina!* and had a launch, which I had the privilege of attending. I knew the kids that were in the stage musical when they played on Broadway, and it was so good to see them all grown up, but that event was even more special because Madiba was there to give Anant his support for the movie.'

I remember in particular one incident involving Quincy in London in July 1996 when we were getting ready to make our way to the Royal

Albert Hall for a concert in which the Queen was set to honour Madiba on his state visit. I was in the lounge of Quincy's hotel suite at the Dorchester reading a magazine, and he was freshening up in the bathroom, when the phone rang.

'Could you get that?' Quincy called.

'Sure.' I put the magazine down, and picked up the phone. 'Hello?'

A husky male voice on the other end said, 'Leroy?'

'Leroy? No, there's no Leroy here.'

'Who is it?' Quincy shouted from the bathroom.

'Someone looking for Leroy,' I replied, about to replace the receiver.

'Tell him to come up. Give him the room number.'

I gave the caller the room number, told him to come up and went back to the couch to read. A little later the doorbell rang. Quincy was still in the bathroom so I got up, walked over and opened the door. My jaw dropped. For a minute I was completely speechless. What does one say when the Godfather himself is standing right in front of you, after all?

'Mr Brando ...' I stuttered.

'Where's Leroy?' Brando asked, brushing past me into the room.

I was still struggling to explain that there was no Leroy here when Quincy bounded into the room.

'Leroy!' he shouted.

The two men hugged, calling each other Leroy over and over as though it was the most natural thing in the world, the best joke ever. I'd get it only later: the night they met, they went to a jazz club in Harlem and Brando got into a spot of trouble with a pimp after he'd smoked a joint and taken one of the pimp's girls dancing.

'He was convinced the pimp was out to get him,' explained Quincy, 'so he went back to the pimp and said, "I was a gentleman, man. I came and asked first, man." But the pimp would hear none of it. "I ain't no man, man," he said. "The name's Leroy. L-E-R-O-Y. Leeeee-roy."'

And Quincy and Marlon had called each other Leroy ever since.

My meeting Brando was one of those defining moments, one that lingers in the memory. When Quincy introduced us, there was already a thread that connected us. Naturally, Brando being Brando, I had followed his career with keen interest, but the project that meant the most to me personally was his involvement in *A Dry White Season*, the screen adaptation of André Brink's bestselling novel. I wasted no time in telling him. Brando was an outspoken human rights activist and Brink's novel was one of those anti-apartheid stories just begging to be retold on screen. That Brando chose to be a part of that earned him immeasurable respect in my eyes, and his involvement opened the floodgates to a heart-to-heart conversation that has stayed with me all these years. We unpacked his long career, his human rights projects and the roles that meant the most to him, including Bernardo Bertolucci's controversial *Last Tango in Paris*, in which he had starred and which had been banned by the apartheid authorities.

When Quincy visited South Africa, I introduced him to Nando's chicken, which he just loved! On one occasion, I arranged for a platter of chicken to be sent to him at the Dorchester Hotel in London. The snobbish hotel staff refused to accept it and Nando's head Robbie Brozin called me to let me know. I immediately called Quincy and, of course, it was promptly delivered to his suite. He enjoyed it tremendously!

For years before the scandal that broke around his head, I had a love-hate relationship with Harvey Weinstein. He was a master of marketing and distribution of kind of high-quality films. We had many run-ins over the years. He was always a passionate film lover and bought several of my films, among them the rights for *Sarafina!*

We had started shooting *Sarafina!* in 1991, then broke for our summer and Christmas holidays, to resume as soon as Whoopi was available in January. This meant we had finished the initial part of the shoot without Whoopi and, once we were done, I put together a 15-minute show reel with the idea to go out and try to market the film. So, reel tucked under my arm, I set off to Los Angeles and called on some of the contacts I had been making in the industry there. One of these was Quincy, who immediately set about arranging meetings with Warner Brothers, while I secured screenings with a few other companies. One of those screenings was for Harvey Weinstein. In those days, the 15-minute reel was on 35mm film – not for us the luxury of today's technology where all you need is a memory card. Back then you had to cart the film, sound, everything around. Everyone loved it, but as soon as Harvey saw the footage, he was most aggressive. When he had to have something, he would pursue it doggedly.

'I want to buy it right now,' he insisted.

I, however, wasn't quite ready to sell.

Harvey was adamant.

'Then make me an offer,' I prompted.

'I'll make an offer,' he said, 'but then you close it right away. Deal?'

'No. Let me think about it first.' He was making me anxious, and I wasn't going to buckle under the pressure, or succumb to his intimidation but it was good to know that I could make a deal.

Now, just as a precursor, I had obviously been keeping agents and managers in the loop regarding the progress we were making. That night I was sitting in a restaurant with Alan Grodin, my friend and lawyer who had represented me in the US since my very first film, having dinner. Harvey was seated at a table behind us.

Strange coincidence, I thought. Then he sidled over. 'You ready to make a deal?' he said. He stood there chain-smoking – smoking was still allowed in restaurants then – waiting for my answer.

'Okay,' I said. 'I am. Tomorrow morning, 10 o'clock. We'll meet in Alan's office.'

It was only much later that I found out that the reason Harvey was in the restaurant at all was because two of Whoopi's representatives I'd been keeping updated on developments had leaked the information. They had told him that we were going to be there, and while I was navigating through the quagmire of negotiations, considering our options, juggling offers –Warner Brothers, Sony and many more – they were trying to close their own deals.

The next day, as arranged, Harvey showed up – *still* smoking. Alan said, 'Hey, get out of my office! There'll be no smoking in here.' I was concerned that the meeting was already off to a bad start.

'So, what's your offer?' I ventured.

Harvey threw out a sum – $6 million, or whatever it was – and I said no. 'Sorry, I'm not interested – don't even bother,' I told him.

'How much d'you want then?' he threw back at me.

'What I want is irrelevant,' I said. 'I need to know what you want to do, how you're going to release it, how much you're going to spend on it and only then how much you're going to offer. I have a lot invested here, and Whoopi's a partner.'

'Sure,' he said. 'No problem. We'll make sure you have approvals.'

I suppose I was still somewhat naive in the way the world of sales works, especially at this level, because when he then said, 'I'll give you $9 million,' I heard my voice stutter.

'Okay,' I said. 'Maybe there's room to talk.'

Finally, we ended up on $10 million. The money upfront or guaranteed.

We also agreed on certain conditions, one of these being that he was not to sell the movie to any third party without our permission – a clause

I actually had to write in by hand – and that I would have total veto on everything. Why, I don't know.

He agreed. The paperwork was completed, and the deal essentially closed.

At some point later I reminded Harvey that it was time to pay up. *Show me the money.* Suddenly there was uhm-ing and aah-ing, stalling, protracted delays about this and that, before Harvey eventually agreed to pay upfront in a letter of credit. Only later did I find out that Harvey and his team were, not to put too fine a point on it, on the bones of their asses. His company, Miramax, had burned through all its money, but he managed to get Technicolor, a film laboratory which provided rebates, to underwrite the letter of credit in order to activate the deal. The problem, though, was that there was very little money left in the business to honour the guarantees concerning marketing and related issues, but by that stage it was already too late to do anything about it, and I did not know this.

I soon realised that while I thought I was doing well in the negotiations with Harvey and Miramax, he was in reality using my movie, *Sarafina!*, as leverage to sell hundreds of other films to Disney and, soon thereafter, to sell his company to them. Simply put, Harvey was using *Sarafina!* to get in with Disney. As it transpired, Disney wanted *Sarafina!* as they had just had a mega-hit with *Sister Act* starring Whoopi, but the success had been followed by a falling-out between the star and the studio, with Whoopi swearing she would never work with Disney again. Disney believed that if they managed to nab *Sarafina!*, which also starred Whoopi, they would be able to win her back, which would inevitably lead to a sequel to *Sister Act*. All of this was going on behind the scenes of course. We remained blissfully unaware of the machinations taking place backstage – although Harvey knew full well the motives behind

Disney's desire to secure *Sarafina!*

Harvey went on to sell *Sarafina!* to Disney for $20 million without my permission. When I found out, I held him to our contract. Tempers flared, accusations and counter-accusations were flung about, and Harvey threatened to bury the movie. He swore he'd make sure nobody ever saw it – until we reminded him that we already had the $10 million upfront payment and pointed out that he'd be burying his own money.

Eventually we settled and he finally paid over another $4 million, but it dawned on me then that you never really know the full and true context of the plays being made in Hollywood. The result was that for many years I had a tumultuous relationship with Harvey Weinstein. He could be vicious, nasty and extremely abusive; he really was the epitome of a big Hollywood bully. We had many aggressive run-ins over the years, either via email or one on one, often punctuated by threats. But little did I know how dark and deep his web of deceit really went. That would be revealed in time.

17

Sarafina!

Sarafina! premiered at the Cannes Film Festival on 11 May 1992, screening in its Official Selection Out of Competition – a huge honour for the film and all its participants. *Sarafina!* became the first South African film to make the Official Selection of the Festival, receiving a 20-minute standing ovation from a capacity audience of 2 200 at the Grand Théâtre Lumière at the world's most prestigious film festival. It was such a special event, especially to celebrate with so many of the creative team in attendance.

For me it had always been an easy decision to make *Sarafina!* Under apartheid, when you were a Black South African without a vote and one of an oppressed majority, you had to be politically active. Cinema has always been a powerful medium and through my films I would continue to try to communicate the point of view and political perspective of the oppressed. That was what I told the world in Cannes after the exhilarating screening of *Sarafina!* Warner president Wayne Duband confided that he hadn't seen Cannes react to a film like that since *E.T.*, while French cinema magazine *Le Film Français* described the Cannes viewing as 'powerful' and 'soul stirring'. It was fresh and new.

Of course, it was all that and more, with even our peers, colleagues, critics and associates singing its praises. When *Sarafina!* was presented at Cannes, *Reservoir Dogs* was showing too, and Darrell Roodt and Quentin Tarantino subsequently went out for lunch, where Quentin raved about *Sarafina!*

We were on top of the world, the talk of the town. That evening following the world premiere, we – the stars and principals – celebrated with a party on David Bowie's yacht, where Hollywood was introduced to the talent, our very own stars. In attendance was an array of international celebrities, among them Robert De Niro, supermodel Naomi Campbell and Sharon Stone. Later that week we hosted our own party on the Majestic Hotel beach with 250 guests. Among them were Hollywood legends Jerry Lee Lewis, Peter Weller, John Turturro, Robert Altman and Spike Lee. And our own Leleti Khumalo, Darrell Roodt, Mbongeni Ngema, Miriam Makeba, Bill Nicholson, David Thompson and Whoopi Goldberg. We were walking on air.

Following the success in Cannes, Harvey Weinstein leveraged *Sarafina!* in his deal with Disney, resulting in Disney taking over the distribution of the film. Jeffrey Katzenberg, head of Walt Disney Studios, was passionate about musicals and decided that the best launch for the film was to host the premiere at New York's prestigious Radio City Music Hall on 14 September 1992, which was quite mind-blowing to us, especially having created this little film in South Africa. Jeffrey subsequently decided that the Los Angeles premiere would take place 24 hours later. Leleti, Whoopi, Darrell and several other members were in New York for the historic premiere, which was followed by a very exclusive after-party at New York's prestigious 21 Club. We left the 21 Club early, before the party ended, and flew with Jeffrey on the Disney corporate jet to Los Angeles. This was my first, and most remarkable experience, of flying on a private Gulfstream. The Los Angeles premiere was equally glamorous. It was held at the newly opened El Capitan Theatre in Hollywood, followed by a party at the Los Angeles County Museum of Art, another exceptional event!

But with jubilation there is often disappointment and ours was tempered by developments in the US that threatened to derail the success we had enjoyed so far. For one, due to their money issues, Harvey Weinstein's promises turned out to be less than sincere and, for another, by the time *Sarafina!* was released in the key market of Los Angeles, the timing for a movie about violent unrest, riots and protests could not have been worse.

In a troubling echo of the themes of *Sarafina!*, LA was rocked by violent riots in April and May 1992. Unrest had begun on 29 April, after a jury acquitted four officers from the Los Angeles Police Department of the use of excessive force in arresting a Black man, Rodney King. The event had been videotaped and widely viewed on television broadcasts. The acquittal rocked Los Angeles, with violent protests spilling out onto the streets. By the time peace was eventually restored, 63 people had been killed, 2 383 injured, and some 12 000 arrested. The *Sarafina!* riot scenes therefore came at an extremely tricky time. Still, the movie made more than $20 million at the US box office.

After securing the US distribution for *Sarafina!* prior to Cannes, I approached Patrick Wachsberger to distribute the film to international territories. He was able secure deals with high-profile companies like Warner Brothers and Gaga Communications in Japan. We also acquired films from his various companies, including Odyssey Distributors, from which we bought films like Tom Stoppard's *Rosencrantz and Guildenstern Are Dead* and the film version of *The Handmaid's Tale*. I liked the way Patrick conducted business and his skill in selling films and offered to him to sell *Sarafina!* As I had structured a co-production with France, he readily agreed. This was the beginning of a long friendship and distribution relationship, which continues today. He also sold several films for us, among them *Yankee Zulu*, *The Mangler*, *Face*, *The Theory of Flight*, *The Legend of Zu* and *Paljas*.

Back home, on 24 September 1992, *Sarafina!* premiered at the magnificent Carlton Centre before an audience that included Nelson Mandela, Oliver Tambo, Joe Slovo, Walter Sisulu, Ahmed Kathrada and Fatima Meer – a who's who of the anti-apartheid political struggle movement – together with activist poets Barbara Masekela and Mongane Wally Serote, as well as other celebrities of music, dance and literature. For us, the producers, and guests, as well as for the country as a whole, it was quite a moment. A moment when you really felt anything was possible.

Madiba paid an emotional tribute to the movie. 'The verdict of June 16 is clear – apartheid has failed,' he said. 'The story is still being told and impacting on new generations in faraway lands. Here is the spirit of freedom. The youth are still demanding freedom. *Sarafina!* speaks of today and yesterday ... It is up to us to see that it speaks for tomorrow. This film tells of hope and courage and the triumph of the human spirit.'

After the screening, he recalled how he and his comrades in prison had learned of the 1976 student protests. 'The prison walls could not keep this information from us,' he said. News of the sacrifices made by black youth had heartened the imprisoned anti-apartheid leaders and forever 'changed the course of our history'.

The future belongs to our youth. So, yes, *Sarafina!* was topical – the Soweto uprising, which occurred 13 years after Mandela was imprisoned, signalled the beginning of a chaotic decade in South Africa, culminating in a four-year state of emergency that ended only after Mandela's release in 1990 – and even a little painful, given the truths it espoused and how it echoed the angst of so many South Africans. But relevance and truth are no guarantee of success.

It's impossible to tell in advance of its release whether a film is going to be a hit. The industry measures you according to the level on which you have worked, by the people with whom you have rubbed shoulders, and the responses from critics. And in this regard, *Sarafina!* was a quantum leap forward. Its credit list included international stars such as Whoopi Goldberg, choreographer Michael Peters and, through Quincy's introduction, Grammy winner James Ingram, who did the song 'One More Time' for the end credits. These were names that opened doors in the industry and benefited the film enormously.

Sarafina! was a prestige project that attracted plenty of interest from major Hollywood studios. As a stage production, it had drawn more than a million people during its run on Broadway. The subsequent movie catapulted us to international stardom, especially after Disney acquired the rights from Miramax. Following the success of *Sarafina!*, Disney wanted both Darrell and me to drive new projects for them.

I said no thanks. I wasn't interested.

They threw money and promises at us. They were relentless. Eventually, finally, I gave in. 'Okay,' I said. 'Let's go for six months.'

It would not turn out well at all.

Our first project was to be a film with Patrick Swayze and Halle Berry titled *Father Hood* – somewhat ironic given that we had just done *Sarafina!* with Whoopi and then moved straight on to a project with Swayze, who was fresh from his collaboration with Whoopi in the Oscar-winning blockbuster *Ghost*. The Hollywood machine swallowed us whole, crushing every ounce of creativity and innovation left in us. The movie became a nightmare. The version we were initially promised included Richard Gere and was an entirely different script and story. But, as we discovered in Hollywood, things change and we no longer had any control. Darrell set out to do a good film, a serious film, but then Disney wanted to turn it into a family movie. First Gere pulled out, then the scripts changed, and it all got progressively worse until it didn't work at all. Patrick Swayze was great, but really desperate to break out of the mould of *Dirty Dancing* and he was not committed to making a family comedy either. It was difficult to get all the moving parts going and working in the same direction. On the one hand, the keys to the Magic Kingdom had been held out to us; on the other, the bosses refused to let us in. Darrell had no say in the final product. He believed Disney had used him. As Darrell once commented, 'When you are there, you must play the Hollywood game and dance with the devil.'

As for me, I ended up with a mess that had my name all over it. But, one moves on and I learned from the experience. It was the last time I made a film for a studio.

The only positive for me personally was that *Sarafina!* led to me becoming the first South African to become a member of the Academy of Motion Picture Arts and Sciences, which hosts the Oscars every year. After *Sarafina!* a producer friend, Alex Ho, asked, 'Hey, why don't you become a member of the Academy?'

'Well, what does that mean?' I asked. 'How does that work?'

What it boiled down to was that you had to make a movie that was released by a major studio in America – and, of course, *Sarafina!* had been released through Disney. Step one: *tick.* Alex nominated me for the Producers' Branch of the Academy.

For me, the Oscars have always been a special occasion. My first experience attending the awards had been a full decade earlier, in 1982, a significant year for film and one in which a host of truly exceptional films were honoured: *Chariots of Fire*, *Reds* and *Mephisto*.

The night remains etched in my memory, as much for the fact that this was the culmination of a dream for me as for the movies being celebrated. South Africa was still in the throes of apartheid and I had essentially snuck in through the back door, but that took nothing from the experience. As I had done so often, I had simply cold-called from South Africa and told anyone who cared to listen that I was a film producer. It was a bold move but it paid off: I was offered two tickets. Purchased for about $50, my seats were obviously in the cheap section, but I was elated. I was going to the Oscars! It was 29 March 1982, no prestigious before- or after-party, no limo with tinted windows, no chauffeur, but I was going nevertheless. I had no date, so I took a friend; I didn't own a tuxedo, so I wore a dark suit and bought a bow tie – and the next thing I knew I was at the Dorothy Chandler Pavilion in Los Angeles.

For that starry-eyed Indian boy who had screened movies against a sheet in a tiny house in Springfield, I could scarcely believe that here I was making my way up that famous red carpet. It was all I imagined it would be: the much-hyped glitz and glamour that only Hollywood, in all its finery, can pull off. A sea of faces otherwise seen only on the big screen, talent I admired not only for their creativity but for their staying power in an industry that can be both demanding and fickle.

Much has changed over the years, of course, and my experience of the Oscars is today very different, but I have always felt it a tremendous honour not only to attend but, in recent times, to be a member of the Academy – and, as a producer, to put forth nominations in the category Best Film. Once the votes are in and the list is finally announced, members then get to vote in all the categories.

Despite what Oscar night may appear to be, however, the Academy is not without its problems. For years the Academy has been struggling with issues of inclusivity, diversity and gender and race representation. It is run by a 54-member board of governors, which oversees the Academy's strategic mission, financial health and the Oscars. Board members represent the 17 branches of the Academy (Producers, Directors, Music, Actors and Writers among them) and may serve up to three consecutive three-year terms.

I have had my run-ins with the organisation about all sorts of matters over the years, especially when it came to the issue of them opening up to international members. The thing is, it had always been open to international members, but they had just never appointed anyone. Suddenly, they were protecting their own interests; cinema was becoming more global and yet the Academy remains so very American, still so very white and still so very male. It has taken an extraordinarily long time for international films to make inroads not only into the world market, but also, particularly, at the Academy Awards. It was therefore remarkable that in 2020, the South Korean film *Parasite* was able to garner no fewer than four mainstream awards rather than be restricted to the Best International Feature Film (previously Foreign Language) category. In the modern era it is becoming increasingly impossible to shy away from harsh realities and structures; as such, the Academy will need some deep introspection regarding its future and has recently taken bold steps to ensure racial parity among cast and crew.

As for me, I remain a member, honoured to be part of the group, but I will never be silent. There is too much at stake.

18

Towards the new millennium

The two decades that preceded the new millennium were quite a roller-coaster ride for me. I was doing enormous amounts of travel and acquiring films for distribution in South Africa and elsewhere around the world. My journey of finding films for distribution took me to Asia – Japan and Hong Kong – as I was a fan of Asian cinema; to Europe, including France, Italy, Germany and the UK; and to the United States and Canada, where most of the content came from.

Those partnerships and acquisitions I made were pivotal. They allowed us to benefit greatly from the pervasive new medium that was video when this emerged and took hold. The appetite for home entertainment was voracious and we were eager suppliers. More important for me were the relationships I established along that journey, many of which still stand solidly right till today.

In the days when there was less security around international flying, before 9/11 changed everything, one could arrive at the airport 15 or 20 minute before for an international flight and make it. On one occasion, Sudhir and I arrived at the PanAm boarding gate of New York's JF Kennedy Airport and saw that the aircraft door was closed. To our relief (and surprise), they allowed us to get on. They opened the door and let us in. There were people already in our seats, which – unfortunately for them – they had to vacate.

One major benefit travelling from South Africa was that the fares were a lot cheaper than if you bought a ticket anywhere else in the world. The fares we paid in South Africa were rand denominated and the rand at the time was strong against most currencies, including the US dollar. During that period, British Airways had an exceptional special offer: if you flew business class to the US, you would get a free one-way upgrade to fly Concorde. I have a keen interest in aircraft and I immediately grasped the opportunity and subsequently flew many times on this incredible aircraft that took you from London to New York or Miami in half the time, at twice the speed of sound at almost 2 000 kilometres an hour. It is unfortunate that all Concorde flights ceased in 2003 soon after one of the Air France aircraft crashed, killing everyone on board.

The wonder of flying Concorde was amazing – on one occasion, on 13 July 1985, I had work in London, and attended the Live Aid Concert at Wembley. While the concert was still in progress, I flew out on the Concorde to New York and watched the second segment of the concert, which was in Philadelphia, from my hotel room in New York. It was mind-boggling and surreal that I could travel between two continents and catch the same concert within a matter of hours.

In the latter part of the 80s there were various film markets around the world, the most obvious one being Cannes. Another, called MIFED, was in Milan and was held in November every year. We would attend screenings there and buy films for distribution, travelling to Milan by train from Zürich. Some of these memorable journeys I made with Jimmy Pereira. Talking on the train over leisurely lunches, I learned much from Jimmy and eagerly imbibed his knowledge. On weekends I would try to explore and experience some of the places in and around Milan, like the Piazza del Duomo, the villages, the lake region and the shops that sold leather goods. I still wear the jacket I bought 40 years ago from the Pollini store when the Italian currency was still the lira.

I became a creature of habit. We would go to the same bars and restaurants every year in Milan. Many of the staff could not speak English and I couldn't speak Italian, but when I walked in, they knew what I was going to eat or drink. That was really quite special. During the MIFED market, it was the season of porcini mushrooms and that was our staple diet. Something I learned early on was that as you go back to the same places, you build relationships and trust. This paid off on one occasion when I had forgotten my wallet and went to one of the restaurants that I frequented annually. They said no problem, pay us next year! I went back the very next day and paid them. Brian Cox, who was very well read and astute, joined me on various trips as we explored and acquired films, learned from the people we acquired the films from, and got to understand their cultures. He was even more adventurous than me.

On one of my early trips to Cannes, I stayed at the Hôtel Martinez, which was right next door to a live music bar and club, La Chunga, where the musicians would rotate every 30 minutes. We would go there for dinner at about 9 pm and when we left at 5 am, the place was still pumping, with people dancing on the tables. By 8.30 am we were back on the road, watching movies and making deals. We played hard and worked hard.

Another time in Cannes, I was on the street walking to my next meeting when I bumped into the legendary *Chicago Sun-Times* critic, Roger Ebert. I greeted him and introduced myself. He told me of his time in Cape Town as a lecturer and how much he enjoyed it. He was wandering about trying to find a European adapter to charge his computer. No problem, I said to him, don't worry, I will find one for you and get it to you – and I did. I had an adapter delivered to him and probably made his day as he could get his reviews out to the US on time. And out of that simple gesture began a friendship that endured until he passed on 4 April 2013. He and his wife, Chaz, visited us in South Africa and, when my wife Vanashree hosted a Children's Fund auction event, they bought a Christmas tree, which Chaz still uses to this day.

Through Fatima Meer and Kathy, and soon after Madiba's release from prison, I was fortunate to meet many liberation leaders and activists and get to know them on a more personal level. Two people in particular were Dullah Omar, who was appointed Minister of Justice in Madiba's cabinet, and Advocate Ismail Mahomed, who later became South Africa's first Chief Justice of the Constitutional Court. Advocate Mahomed also represented us in the mid-1990s in our case against Ster-Kinekor for their anti-competitive actions in the film exhibition and distribution business. These astute legal minds made profound impressions on me.

South Africa was the flavour of the decade – business, the economy and international investment soared. Stockmarket listings were flying and many brokers approached us to list on the JSE. I called my friend and mentor Michael Katz and set up a meeting, which Sudhir, Robert and I attended. We discussed the idea and Michael said to me, 'Anant, I know you and the way you work, and the creative process of your decisions. A listing and answering to a board is not for you or Videovision.' Sound advice, which I follow to this day.

In mid-1994 I attended the Soccer World Cup in Los Angeles with newly appointed ministers Jeff Radebe and Bantu Holomisa. Sudhir and Chris Naidoo were there as well. On our way to the stadium, already running late, the limo became stuck in very heavy traffic en route. I noticed a motorcade that was making its way past us and instructed our driver to slip in behind them, which he did. We didn't get very far before the police pulled us over. A little anxiously, I asked Jeff for his card and asked the driver to show the officer that it was Jeff Radebe, Minister of Public Works. For a brief moment there was an awkward silence before the unsuspecting cop barked into his mouthpiece, 'I've got the Minister of Africa in the car,' and, following what must have been a clear directive from his superior, he waved us back into the motorcade. We followed the string of cars right into the stadium grounds. As it turned out, the entourage was that of US Vice President Al Gore …

At dinner in January 2020, when he was in Davos for the World Economic Forum, I relayed the story to him. Gore threw back his head and laughed. 'Happy to have been of service,' he said.

On 16 July 1994, the eve of the World Cup Final – Brazil vs Italy – the Three Tenors, Luciano Pavarotti, Plácido Domingo and José Carreras, performed in a reunion concert at Los Angeles' Dodger Stadium. It was a concert that everyone wanted to attend but tickets had sold out shortly after bookings opened. I saw this concert as an opportunity to build goodwill among people I worked with in Los Angeles and, as I knew the promoter, I had secured VIP tickets early. I hosted a group of 20 people in a private suite at the concert, among whom were former Investec CEO Steve Koseff, who was in Los Angeles for the final. The funny story is that when I offered tickets to Steve, he asked why he would want to go to a classical concert. A short while later he called me back and said that he had spoken to his wife, Sheryl, and she said he was mad to pass on the opportunity and they definitely wanted to attend. You can take the boy out of Benoni, but you can't take Benoni out of the boy ... The Three Tenors gave a phenomenal performance and our guests were bowled over.

A few years later, on 18 April 1999, the Three Tenors came to South Africa and performed at the Union Buildings. Having the privilege of seeing the Three Tenors for the second time, it was even better, especially as it was at home in South Africa. Barbara Hogan and Ahmed Kathrada were our guests, and needless to say, Kathy enjoyed it immensely.

Just months later, on 21 August, together with Barbara as my co-conspirator, we decided to surprise Kathy with a party to celebrate his 70th birthday. I hosted the party in the large formal dining room at Investec in Sandton. I concocted a story about going to a private dinner there and Kathy reluctantly agreed to join us. When Vanashree and I ushered Kathy and Barbara in, the look on Kathy's face when he saw all his friends and family there was worth all the pain and aggravation of organising the surprise. It was so special for him to celebrate his mile-stone birthday with an amazing group of guests, all of whom were big fans and close friends of his. Cyril Ramaphosa was there, as were Laloo Chiba, Mac Maharaj, Tokyo Sexwale, former Reserve Bank Governor Gill Marcus, Chris Hani's wife Limpho Hani, Shan Balton (now executive director of the Ahmed Kathrada Foundation) and a host of others.

I was also privileged to host Walter Sisulu and Kathy at my beach house for a weekend in 1996. They were to attend the funeral of Ma Luthuli in Groutville, and I suggested to Kathy that he spend the night before the funeral with me. What a fascinating experience it was, listening to their stories of the liberation struggle and their prison days. I hung on every word like a child enchanted by a bedtime story. They jovially argued about details like exact dates and times of events decades before, but with great modesty, humility and mutual respect.

From 2001 Vanashree and I were very fortunate to attend several of the World Economic Forum Annual Meetings in Davos, where I was honoured with their Crystal Award. It is a fascinating experience, especially for me not being in the big business world, and it generated many friendships and enriching experiences for me. The visionary work of its founders, Klaus and Hilde Schwab, encompassing big business, academics, scientists, professionals and cultural leaders, makes it quite special. It was there that my friendships grew and flourished, with fellow and Crystal Award recipients like Bono, Peter Gabriel, Angélique Kidjo, Paulo Coelho, Quincy Jones, Youssou N'Dour, and Platon and Romero Britto.

Many coincidental meetings with people led to long-lasting friendships, something that I realised years later. Meeting people who inspired me, getting to know them and becoming friends with them has been a blessing. For me, it has always been so important just to be considerate and warm to others, and the relationships forged with many people has enriched my life immensely.

One of these relationships was with Deepak Chopra, the world-renowned medical doctor and 'mind, body, spirit' guru. He and I met by coincidence in LA in the 90s, and the meeting led to a friendship that has endured over 30 years. We met frequently when I visited New York. On one of these meetings he mentioned his fiction writings, which piqued my curiosity. I sought out the books and two works in particular stood out for me – *The Return of Merlin* and *Soulmate*. When Deepak came to South Africa in March 2002, we discussed adapting these books into films and in June of that year, I optioned the film rights.

A year earlier, Deepak had come to South Africa for a lecture series in Johannesburg and Durban. In Johannesburg, he stayed at the Michelangelo Hotel and on his way to his lecture at the Sandton Convention Centre he suddenly found himself stuck in the lift. He called me in a panic (I was in Durban). He said he was on his way to the lecture and there were about 5 000 people waiting for him ... My immediate response was, don't worry I will see what I can do. Don't fret, I added, Madiba spent 27 years in a prison cell, which was a bit larger than the lift Deepak was in, and he survived. He thought this was quite revealing and, to my surprise, I heard from many people who attended the lecture that he mentioned the story when he got there, perhaps 10 minutes late. I reminded him of this when we met in August 2021 and we had a good laugh.

In the 90s and beyond, my relationship with Fatima Meer became stronger. We would speak almost every day and I tried to help her with all the incredible work that she was doing at the Institute for Black Research, which she had founded in 1972. It became the leading Black-run research institution, publishing house, as well as an educational and welfare NGO in South Africa. One of the things I assisted her with was the design of a series of book covers, including the cover for *Higher than Hope*, her Mandela biography.

One of the greatest lessons I learned from Fatima is the immense power of the written word. She inspired me to expand on my early reading experiences, which were somewhat modest, and to appreciate literature fully. I enjoyed reading at school and growing up my favourite books were *A Tale of Two Cities*, *Othello*, *Cry, the Beloved Country*, *The Story of an African Farm, Siddhartha* (after viewing the film) and the Hardy Boys series; and of course American comics. But film was where I found my voice and my literature.

Fatima had also written the book *The Trial of Andrew Zondo* about the Umkhonto weSizwe operative's trial for the bombing of a shopping centre in Durban. I tried to develop a screenplay around this book as I was moved by the fascinating story of this brave young man, but, unfortunately, I could not get support to make the film or get it released in South Africa as it was too controversial due to the fact that Zondo was hanged on 9 September 1986 when he was 20 years old.

It was through Fatima that I got to meet Winnie Mandela. I was very inspired by her, especially her immeasurable courage living in the apartheid system, being jailed, banished and subjected to many days of solitary confinement, one for a stretch 491 days. She experienced the full wrath of the apartheid government, including being subjected to torture by the most notorious Lieutenant Swanepoel. I had the privilege of sitting with her at Ismail Meer's funeral in May 2000 and we shared this very emotional moment. Ismail's passing was a deeply personal loss for her, given her relationship with him and his unstinting support through all of her challenges.

Fatima was a wonderful sounding board for me. In my discussions with her, I explained my approach of using the medium of film independently, of not being governed by political forces or outside influences. She was fully supportive of my view and of how I elected to speak out against apartheid using my chosen medium as I deemed appropriate. She was also a great resource, especially when it came to confirming the facts of the South African stories that we made into films. It was a huge personal loss and a very sad day for me when she passed on, on 12 March 2010. I was abroad at the time but had been to see her in hospital before

I left. She was my 'political mother'.

During the 80s and 90s, I loved listening to music. Some of my favourites were Van Morrison's *Moondance* album, Jimi Hendrix, Santana and classical jazz artists like Duke Ellington. What's really amazing is that today my son, Kiyan, enjoys the same music, which shows how timeless these artists are. I listened to them on audio cassette and vinyl, while today Kiyan listens to them on Apple Music and vinyl as well – we've come full circle.

As we approached the end of 1999, I decided to host a New Year Millennium bash to see in the new century. We rang in the new millennium at my favourite restaurant, La Dolce Vita at the elegant Durban Club, with the talented and legendary Durban dance band the Duke's Combo providing the entertainment. Among the guests who saw the New Year in with us were UK producer of *Who Wants to be a Millionaire?* Paul Smith and his family from London – we were in the middle of producing the show in South Africa – SA *Millionaire* host Jeremy Maggs and his wife Anne, and Douw Steyn and a group of his friends. What a wonderful 'party of the millennium' it was. It ended with breakfast at 5 am!

19

Cry, the Beloved Country

In December 1992, Richard Attenborough's next big biographical movie after the acclaimed *Gandhi* was *Chaplin*, which had its US premiere in New Orleans. It starred Robert Downey Jr, who would go on to be *Iron Man* in the Marvel cinematic universe. We were shooting the Disney film *Father Hood* in Louisiana, and because I knew Richard from *Cry Freedom* and remained a huge admirer of his work, I was invited to the *Chaplin* premiere. We arranged to meet at the cinema at 11 am one morning when he was doing a run-through test of the projection before the premiere. When he was done, we chatted about *Cry* and *Mandela: Long Walk to Freedom*.

Attenborough's *Chaplin* was a full-circle moment, whisking me back to where it all began …

Save for the flickering on the screen, the dance of light against the white sheet, the room is in darkness. The only sounds are the distant calls of the mynahs on the roof and the chewing of my brother and I as we munch our way through the sweet treats left for us by Ajee. On screen The Tramp is waddling in his peculiar manner, hitching his trousers up as he wanders down a busy street, cane twirling, bowler hat typically askew. I can feel the laughter and excitement already building in my throat; I see Sanjeev's shoulders begin to shake. We are captivated. Charlie is our favourite.

But then there's a subtle change on screen, a swing in the action that neither of us has anticipated. It takes us by surprise, this sudden shift; there's no sound but the moving image on screen has us enthralled. A cop is towering over The Tramp, a frown on his face; he is wagging his finger. The Tramp is in trouble, we can tell. We stop. Our eyes are wide, hearts beating a little faster. What will the policeman do? What will become of The Little Tramp? Does this mean jail for him? Does it?

But then, just as suddenly, Charlie steps up, puffs out his chest and staggers forward, cane in hand, and gives the cop a swift kick up the butt. No one is going to bully The Tramp and get away with it. Not even a cop. Not today, not ever. The Little Tramp will have none of that.

Sanjeev and I turn to each other, hands over our mouths. Then we double over, collapse onto the floor, hugging our tummies in laughter. The Little Tramp, vagabond champion of the downtrodden, the harassed, the hard-done-by, has saved the day. Gentle, kind, humble and forgiving he may be, but he is also not to be messed with.

The icon that was Charlie Chaplin changed cinema, changed the very notion of entertainment as we know it. I knew it. Attenborough knew it.

And, it seemed, Hollywood now knew it too. Susan King, writing about Chaplin in the *Los Angeles Times* on 24 January 2014, summed it up: 'Cinema was just emerging from its infancy when Charlie Chaplin created his comic character The Tramp a century ago. With his bowler hat, baggy pants, endearing little moustache, exaggerated shuffling walk and cane, The Little Tramp was an instant star.' She went on to quote documentarian/film preservationist Serge Bromberg: '"The cinema was not yet 20 years old when he made the first Tramp film ... What is so amazing is that 100 years later, he remains the absolute icon for cinema."' And, said Bromberg, '"the reason the character has remained a part of culture is straightforward ... We are all The Tramp. He has no nationality. When a kid watches Chaplin, it's simple. He doesn't speak, he just shows. He shares the most common values of generosity."'

'That's just a part of it,' noted Ohio University professor and Chaplin historian Lisa Stein Haven. 'He's not above kicking somebody in the pants and making the authority figure look bad.'

Making the authority figure look bad. That was the very crux of Alan Paton's acclaimed classic, *Cry, the Beloved Country* and Attenborough's take on Chaplin. I first read the Paton book in 1971 when I was at school. I was young, but I knew instinctively that it was a powerful work, an allegory of South African politics and our history, as much as it was a human story of two people of different races who find common ground to reconcile. I read it again in 1988 and by then its resonance was even more profound. To me, the real truth of it would only be apparent in a post-apartheid South Africa, but it was so powerful, so captivating, that I decided I would turn it into a film.

The first movie version of *Cry, the Beloved Country* was shot in 1951. When it was finally released, it was well received but was never really considered controversial, despite what must have been a challenging notion

Barbara Hogan and Ahmed Kathrada with Anant and Vanashree, 1996.

Anant with Sidney Poitier at the Directors Guild of America Awards, 2000.

Mickey Nivelli with Gyana (daughter), Anant and Kiyan (son) in Durban, 2003.

Anant and Winnie Madikizela-Mandela at the Johannesburg premiere of *Mandela: Long Walk To Freedom*, 3 November 2013.

Anant with Alan and Ann Grodin, 1999.

Anant and Vanashree with Sam and Helga Ramsamy and George Bizos in Athens, 2004.

Anant, Leleti Khumalo and Denzel Washington at the Venice Film Festival for the film *Yesterday*, 2004.

Anant and friends, 2005. STANDING: Rajesh Rajkumar, Pickey Dass, Dino Pather, Wally Mistri, Robert Naidoo, Nilesh Singh, Ronnie Govender, Rajan Pather. SEATED: Anant, Chris Naidoo, Sanjeev Singh, Teddy Ravjee, Larry Kulpath (front).

Anant at his 59th birthday with his mother, Bhindoo, and Kiyan, 2015.

LEFT: Sanjeev and Anant, *circa* 2011.

BELOW: Brian Cox and Anant on location in the Drakensberg for *Mandela: Long Walk to Freedom*, 2012.

Vanashree, Michael Jackson and Anant in Cape Town, 1997.

Anant and Vanashree at the *Mandela: Long Walk to Freedom* premiere at the Toronto International Film Festival, 2013.

Anant and Vanashree with President Barack Obama at the White House screening of *Mandela: Long Walk to Freedom*, November 2013.

Anant with Naomie Harris, Vanashree and Idris Elba at the White House screening of *Mandela: Long Walk to Freedom*, November 2013.

Anant and family at his
60th birthday in Durban,
29 May 2016.

Anant and family with the Heung family from Hong Kong in Cannes, 2016.

LEFT: Anant's 60th birthday gift personally painted by U2's Bono.

BELOW: Anant and Sanjeev with their families: Tasha, Nikita, Gyana, Vanashree, Anant, Bhindoo (mother), Kiyan, Sanjeev and Chandra, 2019.

Anant, Vanashree and Robert Lantos in Cannes, 2017.

Anant and Gyana in Cannes, 2017.

ABOVE: Sudhir Pragjee,
Chris Tucker, Fani
Titi, Anant and
Nilesh Singh in
Durban, 8 November
2018.

RIGHT: Anant and
Kiyan in New York,
July 2021.

in those early days of apartheid. Penned by Paton in distant Norway, the novel carried with it a deep nostalgia for home, particularly the landscapes of his childhood.

In 1950 two black American actors, Sidney Poitier and Canada Lee, visited South Africa to film the movie for director Zoltan Korda, who had snapped up the rights in 1947, offering Paton £1 000. On his entry into the country in the 1950s, Korda fooled the authorities into thinking Poitier and Lee were his servants rather than professional actors. Due to the restrictive race laws, as actors they would not have been allowed to work. Already, Sidney and Canada were not permitted to stay in the same hotel as their white co-stars and filmmakers. Sidney had stayed with an Indian family, which had allowed him to see first-hand how the system worked, allowed him to live it. In his memoir *This Life*, he tells of some of his own experiences at the time, including the fact that the studio had segregated bathrooms. Sidney used the whites-only toilet, which led to an altercation with a young white man whom Sidney came close to punching in the face. Later, when filming was over and Sidney was leaving for the airport, he was chased by a car full of gun-wielding white men, one of them the young man from the studio.

The movie was released a year later. It was the first time that the world would see some of the devastating effects of apartheid's terrible segregationist laws on film. Sidney was not allowed back into South Africa to attend the premiere in Johannesburg. Paton himself was seated next to DF Malan, prime minister of South Africa at the time, and Malan's wife Maria. At intermission Mrs Malan is reported to have said, 'Surely, Mr Paton, things are not like this?'

'Oh, they are much worse, madam,' was his reply.

To succeed in anything, my firm belief is that you have to be passionate about it. The life of a movie producer may seem glamorous and fun, but in reality it is a lot of hard work. And, as I explained to journalist Steve Wright when he interviewed me for a piece on the state of the local film industry, 'It's as difficult to make a bad film as it is to make a good one, so unfortunately it doesn't always turn out the way we intended.' It is demanding work and requires all of your attention all of the time. A producer must put together the entire package, secure the story rights, sign the right director, set up the financing and so on.

Although Nelson Mandela had been freed, the country itself was not free yet and I realised that the time wasn't right for a remake. *Cry, the Beloved Country* should not come out of a nation still feeling the burden of legalised racism. It would hold more meaning once we had accomplished our freedom in totality. After all, Paton wrote of reconciliation and introspection. That day had not yet come.

I started planning, doing my homework, setting it all up and trying to find a writer – the hardest task – to make it relevant in today's world. Along the way, Paton's wife Anne put several of his original manuscripts, including the 1 000-page handwritten *Cry, the Beloved Country*, up for auction with Sotheby's in New York. She had done so – apparently – against the wishes of Paton's son by his first wife, who believed the manuscripts should remain in South Africa. It was speculated at the time that all the extraordinary works would raise at least R1 million, with *Cry, the Beloved Country* expected to be the top performer with R500 000. I was very interested and, because I owned the film rights by then, I desperately wanted the manuscript; mostly, I wanted to ensure that the manuscript stayed in South Africa. I believed it should remain where it was conceived, a legacy to the nation itself. On the day of the auction, I couldn't be there in person, so I participated in the bidding via a car-phone, one of the first mobile phones in South Africa – remember it was 1992. Everything was progressing in my favour – I was bidding excitedly on the lots – when, at the worst possible moment, just before the most important item came under the hammer, the phone connection dropped. Paton's *Cry, the Beloved Country* was on the block and I was in the dark. The auctioneers managed to reach me only after the hammer had fallen. It was too late. Fate, I suppose. It sold for a bargain R300 000 ($120 000) to mining magnate and former Anglo American and De Beers chairman Harry Oppenheimer. At least I was able to buy some of the others on auction that day, including the original manuscripts for *Ah, but Your Land is Beautiful* and *Towards the Mountain*, for R94 000 and R39 000 respectively. It is consolation to me, however, that the Oppenheimers had the same intention: to keep the manuscript in the country, where it belongs, and where it remains to this day at the Brenthurst Library in Johannesburg.

Following on from our previous collaborations, the movie was to be directed by Darrell Roodt. Ronald Harwood, the Sea Point-born, Oscar-winning writer of *The Pianist,* who also wrote the Oscar-nominated *The Dresser* and many other films, penned the screenplay.

When we finally got around to filming in a post-democratic South Africa, we also set our remake in 1946, two years before the first apartheid laws were passed, but at a time when the terror of segregation was already visible.

We stuck as close to the book's plot as possible: a humble Christian Zulu priest from the hills of Natal journeys to Johannesburg to find his son, who had gone there a year before to look for work and then vanished. A prosperous English farmer makes the same journey to bury his son, a white liberal writer killed in a burglary gone wrong at his home. Inevitably, it is revealed that the priest's son was the panicky burglar who had pulled the trigger, and the two fathers meet.

At its core, *Cry, the Beloved Country* is a film about two fathers, one white and one Black, who find common ground amidst the terrible times of segregation in South Africa. It is a story about two men, a white bigot and a Zulu country minister, who are able to see past their different cultures and recognise one another's shared humanity in a celebration of the human spirit.

The film also served as a reminder of the reality that was apartheid, of what one people's hatred for another could do if unchecked. The remake was thus set to be much more than just another movie.

While it was certainly special for me personally, it was also the first film to come out of a democratic South Africa. Under apartheid, Black South Africans were prevented from watching movies such as this, so making and releasing it when we did was also a victory over oppression. While it promoted reconciliation, at the same time it was a reminder of a time that had passed and to which we should never, ever go back.

In the 1951 version Sidney Poitier had played the young priest and, initially, our idea was to get Sidney back to play the father in the remake. This didn't work out, however, so we went with iconic American actor James Earl Jones and Irishman Richard Harris as the two leads.

I had first discussed the project with James Earl Jones five years before when we spoke about the timing of the project given the state South Africa was still in. Fast-forward a few years and we had seen Nelson Mandela rise as the new president, extolling many of the same virtues as the Reverend Kumalo, the character portrayed by James. That patient gentleness, humility and forgiveness were virtues that would not have played out the same had we done the film any earlier. James played the role Canada Lee had portrayed in the original, a role Lee imbued with stoicism and toughness. In our remake James made the role his own, bringing in elements of humility, shyness and gentleness, which added depth to the character and layers to the narrative.

We also fleshed out the role of the white farmer, played by Richard Harris, who would in later years go on to be Albus Dumbledore in the Harry Potter movies. Just as we were about to begin production, I was warned about Richard's reputation for being a difficult actor to work with, and the more I heard the more anxious I got. We really couldn't afford to risk this project being scuppered by the reckless escapades of an individual, no matter who they were, so – probably about a month before we were set to begin shooting – I braved the possibility of a confrontation and called Harris from South Africa.

'I think we need to talk,' I said. 'I have something I need to discuss with you.'

'Awright then ...'

'I'll happily come to New York. When are you free?'

'Right. I'll see you next Wednesday. Dinner?'

So I flew to the Big Apple, and met Richard for dinner at Jezebel, a Southern soul food restaurant on 45th Street that was one of my favourites.

Cautiously, I began to set out the purpose of my visit.

'Richard,' I explained, 'I'm financing this movie myself, out of my own pocket. I really can't afford any setbacks. But I've been told there were problems on the set of your last film: you not showing up, or worse, showing up drunk.'

He didn't say a word.

'Personally,' I tried to assure him, 'I'm always reluctant to listen to gossip. There's way too much of that in our business. But, Richard, this project is important. To me, and to so many others. I can't take any risks. There's too much at stake.'

Still silence.

'I do not wish to speculate on any of the stories, so the only way I felt it appropriate to deal with this,' I continued, 'was for me to speak to you face to face. Because if there is a potential for problems, I'd rather deal with it now.'

Richard was very open about it all. He looked me in the eye and extended his hand to shake mine. 'You have no reason to be concerned. I'll give you my word right now to be on time every day – and no more than one pint of Guinness a day.' That characteristic smile of his played at the corners of his mouth.

And that was that. He assured me of his co-operation and his commitment to the film. And indeed, he delivered on both. In the week or so he was required on set, he was at the shoot promptly every day. There were no problems, and he delivered what I consider one of the most outstanding performances of his career.

Cry's soulful music was composed by five-time Oscar winner John Barry, the composer and musical director for *Out of Africa*, who also created memorable scores for many of the Bond films. Signing John Barry was not difficult. Having shown the film to John and his wife Laurie in New York in my hotel room on a poor quality video, his immediate response was, 'Yes, I'd be delighted to do this.'

On one of the days when we were recording the soundtrack at the famous Abbey Road Studios, Harvey Weinstein's minions showed up to watch some of the takes of John's resounding music conjured up in all its magnificence by the 50-piece English Chamber Orchestra. They immediately indicated that Harvey would want in, so I suggested that they get him on the Concorde right away.

It might seem surprising, after our dealings on *Sarafina!*, that I should even entertain doing business with Harvey. But there is a very simple truth to this industry: he wanted something I had. Many factors go into the making and financing of a film. Regardless of its beauty and worth, you'll hear 'no' over and over again because of a distributor's corporate mandate, some executive's personal taste, or general industry trends. Every 'yes' needs to be taken seriously, especially when it comes fast and furious, regardless of who is in the driver's seat, and can disappear as fast.

Weinstein touched down the very next day, headed straight to the studio, and after observing some two hours of recording, said, 'Yes, we have to do this – let's go to dinner.' So it was at The Ivy restaurant that Harvey and I negotiated our deal, outside on the pavement in the freezing cold, so that he could have a smoke.

Cry, the Beloved Country had it all – period sets, costumes, cars and trains that American audiences love so much, along with helicopter shots and an original music score – and still it cost less than a quarter of what the average Hollywood production would have cost, delivering quality as good as theirs.

The American distributor was again Harvey Weinstein's Miramax, and this time around they seemed genuinely as excited about the film as I was and had high hopes for it in the US. In *Cry* we had a truly international movie. We even went as far as to shoot extra scenes for the American version, in part to satisfy Harvey. As usual, he was full of praise. 'When all else fails, Anant sends me so much South African wine that I agree with everything he says,' he stated in the press at the time. But he does not drink alcohol.

In South Africa, the hope was that this would be the country's breakout film, the one that would do for the local movie industry what *Breaker Morant* and *Crocodile Dundee* had done for Australia in the 1980s.

The world premiere of *Cry, the Beloved Country* was held as a fundraiser for the Nelson Mandela Children's Fund on Monday, 23 October 1995, at the Ziegfeld Theatre in New York, where *Lawrence of Arabia* and *Cabaret* had had their premieres. The event raised over $1.5 million and was the platform that secured several long-term donors for the fund. Our premiere – and the party that followed at Remi just across on 54th Street – was attended by Whoopi Goldberg, Donatella Versace, Glenn Close, Sharon Stone, Bob Iger (former head of Disney) and Pauletta and Denzel Washington. Madiba attended both the screening and the after-party to address the guests. He was also the guest of honour, along with former US First Lady, Hillary Rodham-Clinton, who spoke of reading the book in high school and being very moved by it.

The most expensive tables we sold, which included 10 tickets to the premiere, cost $25 000. The first buyer was a company called Forstmann Little, a company I had never heard of. I immediately enquired from the events manager who they were, and he said it was the company of investment banker and philanthropist Teddy Forstmann. I was happy to learn this, and at some point at the party, I had a walkie-talkie and I heard that some guy called Teddy Forstmann was trying to get in, saying he'd bought a table but didn't have a ticket as he hadn't gone to the premiere beforehand. I told them to let him in, and about an hour later, Jeremy Ractliffe, the CEO of the Children's Fund, came over to me and asked if I knew who Teddy Forstmann was; he needed to find him. I immediately said I knew who he was and asked why he needed to find him. Jeremy exclaimed that Teddy just given Madiba $1 million as a donation to the Children's Fund. I said, don't worry, I know where to find him. Unfortunately for Jeremy, I left immediately after the screening to come home to premiere the film in Johannesburg the next day with Darrell. In those days there were no cellphones so when I called from Paris in transit, my assistant said Jeremy had called 10 times!

Teddy was a remarkable human being. I called him when I returned home and asked what he thought of the film, only to find that he hadn't seen it. I said to him that I would be happy to host a private screening for him and his guests when I returned to New York for the opening a month later.

This was the beginning of a friendship that led to him coming to South Africa and meeting two young boys, Everest Matross and Siya Madikane, who were in a children's home. He funded their schooling and eventually adopted both of them. Teddy and the boys returned to South Africa for the 2010 World Cup. Today they are remarkable young men, with whom we have maintained a strong friendship.

I had exceptional experiences with Teddy, including the Paris Air Show when he owned the aircraft company, Gulf Stream Corporation, and launched the Gulf Stream 5 there. It was a beauty parade and show of state-of-the-art aviation, from military and commercial aircraft to private jets and I found it fascinating. Teddy hosted the annual Forstmann Little Conference in Aspen, Colorado, and one year he invited Madiba, along with other guests, among whom were Jeff Bezos, Eric Schmidt, philanthropist Eli Broad and the NBA's David Stern.

Over the years, Madiba had remained a supporter. He often attended the premieres of our films, where he was always guest of honour. So it was with *Cry, the Beloved Country* in New York where Madiba addressed the audience after the screening of the film. He did not see the film in New York as he had other engagements in between.

Much of *Cry, the Beloved Country*, said Madiba, evoked such strong emotions about the terrible past from which South Africa had just emerged. The film, he added, 'for my generation, will evoke the bitter-sweet memories of our youth'.

The promotional schedule for *Cry* was incredibly demanding and tough on everyone. After the benefit premiere at the Ziegfeld in New York, we were due to host the South African premiere at the Kine Centre in Johannesburg on 25 October – just 48 hours later. Logistically, this might have seemed like an insurmountable obstacle, but somehow insurmountable obstacles have never discouraged me.

Darrell Roodt put it this way: 'The reasons for Anant's massive success in the movie game can be attributed to many things: he's smart, he's got good taste, he knows how to crunch those numbers! But, above all, he's cool! How cool? Well, let's take the world premiere of *Cry, the Beloved Country* as an example. There we were, having a screening with Hillary Clinton and a roster of heavy hitters in New York City. The thing is, we were supposed to be in Johannesburg the following evening with Nelson Mandela. In Johannesburg! Half a world away! How was that possible? *Anant Singh* possible! Straight after the screening, we were whisked by a limo to the 55th Street helipad where we jumped into a chopper with James Earl Jones. We flew directly to JFK. Landed right next to the Concorde, which we promptly boarded. Everyone was glaring at us, but we were soon on our way! We landed in London, boarded a 747 Jumbo within a few minutes of our arrival and before we knew it, we were touching down in Nairobi – where a Lear jet was waiting for us! A few hours later we were in Johannesburg, standing alongside the one and only Mr Mandela, welcoming everyone to the screening! And Anant made Miramax, the American distributors, pick up the tab!'

Despite Harvey being Harvey, *Cry* was a success because Disney became involved. All along, my journey in film has meant instilling the belief that one person can make a difference and then striving to be one of those people. I never wanted to politicise any of my projects, or allow politics to be the sole motivation, the driving force behind them, but it is a simple fact that everything in South Africa is political. Every fragment of life here is interwoven with politics. This remains true today. What further interested me – and my responsibility as a filmmaker, in a sense – was making people aware, through film, of what they do. How individual actions can make a difference, positively or negatively. I saw that in my early politicisation when I first encountered the work of Sidney Poitier, James Earl Jones, Quincy Jones and Bob Marley; and I see it now in the influences that continue to creep into my own work.

While filmed entertainment is undeniably escapist by nature, all creative expression weaves a web that allows people to identify with others and, by implication, become galvanised to make a difference. This remains the motivation behind much of my work. It is an attempt to do what I can to contribute towards freedom and the liberation movement without expecting reward and, at the same time, not consulting with the ANC or any other party. At times, this was to my own detriment; there were occasions that organisations made a concerted effort to put an end to projects I had embarked on. These issues are certainly not unique to South Africa, and are true in other countries around the world, but while political issues may be omnipresent, there is also – in my opinion – less of an edge elsewhere, certainly less than what we experience here. For most, in those countries where politics may seem to dominate, life itself goes on relatively easily, often without any real connection to the issues at hand. In South Africa it's all a little different; it feels at times as though the entire country is living on a knife's edge. And yet, somehow, we always find a way to avoid stepping too close, never quite tumbling over the edge.

Before I started making *Cry, the Beloved Country*, I recall a long night at the Saxon Hotel debating the relevance of the film with Thabo Mbeki, a senior leader in the ANC at the time and the man who would become president after Nelson Mandela. Mbeki argued that I should not make it and I argued that I should. Over a four-hour debate, him having many whiskies and me cognacs, we agreed to disagree. He felt it was time to move on from all that *Cry* represented.

'Why are we still dwelling on this old historical context?'

But I was adamant. 'I hear you,' I said, 'but I am going to do it.'

Holding firm to my decision paid off. In January 1996, I received a letter from Miramax informing me that *Cry, the Beloved Country* had been honoured in the category of Best Picture in the 1996 Christopher Awards (as *Sarafina!* had been in 1993), following the likes of *Apollo 13* and *Dead Man Walking*. The awards recognise writers, producers and directors of film, television and books whose work 'affirms the highest values of the human spirit'.

Today I think the film and the story may be even more significant than they were then. I think it is the quintessential South African story, an important legacy of our history, and it remains timeless. I watched it again in 2020 and I am astonished how well it holds up. This story of humanity, I truly believe, is even more poignant than ever and I sincerely hope that it will be a poetic reminder to generations to come.

20

More than just business

When I started out in the movie business, Harry Alan Towers was already a famous producer, having put his hand to more than 250 productions. He started out as a child actor, then became a celebrated radio writer and television producer, and, finally, in the early 1960s, he delved into film. I got to meet him and, over the years, bought a number of films from him, screening them for local audiences at a time when that appeared a near-impossible feat. Most notable of those acquisitions were *The Picture of Dorian Gray*, *Fanny Hill* and Joan Collins' *The Stud* and *The Bitch*, all of which had previously been banned, thus ensuring a ready and enthusiastic viewership in South Africa. I liked and admired Harry. He had a certain style and was modestly successful, sometimes producing up to 10 films a year. Over time, our relationship grew and when I got into production, I could go to him and learn from him.

I learned many tricks of the trade from Harry, including how to secure rights and produce films. What I tried to do was absorb and interpret the good and disregard what I didn't think worked. He had so many contacts and such a long career that he knew everyone, among them Orson Welles and the players of the original *Cry, the Beloved Country*, so that when we were negotiating to buy the remake rights, he was instrumental in helping me secure them.

Traditionally, when I tackle a demanding, socially relevant project that resonates, I try to change tack completely with the next film. Between *Sarafina! and Cry*, I made *The Mangler*, a Stephen King short story about a giant laundry-folding machine with a blood lust, and another project facilitated by Harry, who had recently enjoyed huge success with *The Lawnmower Man*, a loose adaptation of another of Stephen King's stories.

I bought the rights to *The Mangler* in 1994. Tobe Hooper, who directed *Texas Chainsaw Massacre*, was the director and co-writer of the screenplay. The distributor, New Line Cinema, wanted to have Stephen King's name in prominence above the title, so Tobe and I were asked to visit Stephen to negotiate using his name on the poster. Often these projects are all about marketing, and I wanted the movie poster to read 'Stephen King and Anant Singh'. Stephen lives in Maine, north of New York City. It's a very pretty part of the world, despite what Stephen tends to write about so magnificently. He is a friendly, polite family man, and, of course, a writing genius. We had a fruitful meeting and I got his blessing to use his name on the posters. The next project was set.

The Mangler continued my tradition of doing some commercial movies – a market I knew well. In those days many of today's blockbuster comic adaptations would also have been called B-grade films. Although American B-movies may often go straight to video, they are the staple of international cinema and can mean serious money. This is also true in America. While critics slammed our efforts, we sold hundreds of thousands of videos. I remember my smirk when Brian Cox and I saw the poster and marquee for the movie when we drove by the prestigious then Mann's Chinese Theatre on Hollywood Boulevard with Stephen's name shouting boldly and just below it 'Anant Singh'. As an added bonus, Stephen later told me he had been very impressed by the film version of his story and, if he hadn't known better, he would never have guessed the film had been made in South Africa. I was proud to be pushing the message that our filmmaking was on par with the rest of the world.

It was in pursuit of films such as these that I cultivated contacts in Hong Kong and managed to not only get access to incredible martial arts films from the East but also start buying up Asian movies in this genre to distribute globally. The first Asian film I brought over was *The New Legend of Shaolin*, starring Jet Li, who at the time was not known outside the East. I also bought the worldwide rights to his *Black Mask* in 1996 and dubbed the movie to English in South Africa, after which I sold it internationally.

International sales were becoming increasingly important to us, and during the 1990s we took a number of bold steps in that direction, most significantly introducing Asian films to the US market. Asia was where all the action was. Our relationship with Charles and Tiffany Heung's Hong Kong-based China Star Entertainment saw us handling not only films such as *Black Mask* and *Black Mask 2*, but also China Star's megabudget fantasy action movie *League of Gods*.

Naturally, when you're talking Asian movies in the US market you cannot fail to mention the inimitable Jackie Chan and the influence he has had on American audiences. Introducing Jackie Chan and Jet Li to the US market, as well as films from Japan and South Korea, was an important milestone as it started a new trend of success for Asian cinema.

This set us on a new road and, in later years, we managed to pick up the remake rights for a number of other Asian films, among them *Pulse*, a remake of the Kiyoshi Kurosawa Japanese horror film *Kairo*, starring Kristen Bell, co-produced with Dimension Films. This was followed up with a remake of Japanese filmmaker Hideo Nakata's *Don't Look Up*, directed by award-winning Hong Kong filmmaker Fruit Chan and starring Henry Thomas, Carmen Chaplin, Kevin Corrigan and Lothaire Bluteau.

And yet, despite the successes, the accolades, the triumphs in business and on the world stage – a stage that was growing all the time for me, particularly during this period – it always came down to one simple truth: success means different things to different people. One of my favourite movies is the Orson Welles classic *Citizen Kane*, in which the title character becomes the richest man in the world and yet something is still lacking in his life. At the end of his life, he whispers a single word – Rosebud – but no one knows what that means. This is the catalyst for a plot that concludes when the secret is revealed, one that takes us back to his youth when he had nothing. In the end, it's about the value of simple things, value we don't recognise when we're young. By the time we realise what's important, it's often too late.

I identified in some small way with the character's sense of loss. For me it has to do with the beginning. As a youngster, my father would take out his small handheld 8mm camera and film us. We would spend hours watching those films together. Those home movies, my first tentative steps in this industry, were – and remain – precious to me, even more so since my father passed when I was young.

Sadly, at some point all those films, those reminders of bygone memories, were lost. I vaguely remember a whole bag of these old films, which by then had all come off their reels, just a giant jumbled mess. When we were packing to move out of the home in Reservoir Hills, we had all the 8mm home movies in a plastic bag and they were accidentally trashed. They're gone.

Initially, when I realised that they were gone, I didn't really care too much. But, now, years later, that loss is immense. I mourn them and carry with me a deep sense of grief for those moments that were captured and then lost, never to be recovered. I don't have a single frame of those films. And, apart from my parents' wedding day, no moving images of my father.

And so, while I vaguely remember the images, at the beach or wherever, and can see them in my mind's eye – my father's steady hands, his ready smile, the laughter in the eyes of my mother as a young woman – I know I won't get to see them ever again. No matter how many movies I get to make or be a part of. It's taught me a lesson about our value systems, what we prioritise. Understanding that it's the little things that matter later.

There is, though, one good-news story from all of this. As an 11-year-old, I remember a particular piece of art I had made at school, a pewter sculpture of sorts – although quite complex in form, 'sculpture' is perhaps too fancy a term for what it really is – on which I had worked really hard: head down, brow wrinkled in concentration, eyes bright, laughter bubbling from my chest as I screwed and hammered and banged and fastened. But that, too, vanished decades ago and, I believed, was lost forever. It was a simple object made of metal, but it carried many memories that were irreplaceable. Then one day, one of my uncles, VS Maharaj, was digging through his garage and called me. 'Hey,' he said, 'I think you should have this.'

And there it was, some 20 years later, in my hands, a tangible memory of my childhood I had long thought forever lost. It's in my home study today where I can look at it. And remember the amazing foundations of my creativity.

By the time I turned 39 I had produced nearly 40 films, many of them international productions. I had signed on accomplished directors and a range of talent, including South Africans in, for instance, the film versions of Athol Fugard's classic *Road to Mecca*, as well as Katinka Heyns's *Paljas*, which was our first Afrikaans project in the democratic 'new South Africa'. Making *Road to Mecca* was special for me as I am a huge admirer of Fugard's exceptional stories depicting South African life.

Now into my 40th year, I was still single, still putting in 18-hour days and working most weekends. I was still living with my mother whenever I was in the country – which at that point was not very often; I was spending at least 150-plus days of the year overseas. My mother spoiled me, I am the first to admit, making sure my laundry was done and cooking for me, caring for me as doting mothers tend to do. Her efforts made my work possible because she took care of the mundane daily chores for which I had neither the time nor the patience. As a result, I could devote all my energy to the business, work harder, push harder, focus. In an attempt to keep myself rounded and grounded, I did make a special effort to get out – to movies, shows, jazz, parties – and see my friends. However, apart from perhaps one or two that seemed to stay the distance, relationships were very low on my list of priorities. Working relationships, however, were a different story.

At work we were beginning to grow, expanding into other areas. One of those areas was broadcast radio. It was in 1995 that I received that call from Anton Harber informing me that the SABC had decided to sell off its six commercial regional radio stations. Anton asked whether I'd be interested in partnering with Kagiso Trust and going into the radio business. I said yes immediately.

We became part of the New Radio Consortium, which included Kagiso Trust Investment Company and acclaimed South African muso Johnny Clegg, with Fani Titi, who is now joint CEO of global private bank Investec, representing the trust. Together we acquired the two formerly state-owned radio stations East Coast Radio and Radio Oranje. Later, New Radio Consortium took over the JSE-listed company Publico in a reverse takeover that resulted in Videovision and Kagiso acquiring 15 per cent and 53.7 per cent of the company respectively. Sudhir Pragjee and I were appointed to the board of Kagiso Media. The shares had struggled for years, but started growing rapidly from 2002. In 2005, we sold our Kagiso Media stake and I used the bulk of the proceeds to fund the development of *Mandela: Long Walk to Freedom*. Many considered the decision foolish but I was committed. Movies were in my blood, my first love. I could never stay away for too long.

In this business – as in most, I suppose – people matter. That was certainly the case with Fani Titi. Our association grew into a strong and binding friendship. 'We would always work hard,' Fani remembers, 'but had great fun all the time. Commercial victories were always followed by sumptuous celebratory evenings. We made money together, but lost some in a few deals as well. Anant has always had a very direct approach, characterised by cast-iron integrity and openness. So at no stage is there any room for confusion as to what the objectives are, and what individual and collective obligations are. Anant's word has always been his bond, and worth more than any legal agreement that can be written, which I don't think he even reads.'

Having ventured into radio, it was a natural progression to seek other opportunities in the media sector. In late 1997 the Independent Broadcasting Authority issued a call for bids for South Africa's first free-to-air television licence. Again we joined Kagiso Media in a consortium that also included Sasani Communications headed by Welcome Msomi, Dali Tambo's African Dream Television, Primedia and banking group Nedcor. We unfortunately lost out to the Midi Television consortium's e.tv. Ten years later, in 2007, we were presented with another opportunity in the television space. This time it was in the pay-TV sector with partners Telkom, Given Mkhari's MSG Afrika Group and WDB Investment Holdings. Sadly, while this bid was successful, the service did not get off the ground as the major shareholder and funder, Telkom, decided not to proceed.

The many relationships I had developed with international distributors and representatives of big movie distribution companies such as UIP – who were unknown and junior in the 1980s – paid off in later years. The same individuals from whom I acquired films in the early years when they were sales executives had since gone on to become heads of studios in Hollywood and elsewhere. I have had long and happy relationships with many of these senior executives, often of 40 years' standing, associations based on friendship and mutual respect. Very often, these relationships and the trust built up made all the difference. One such relationship, which started out one way and grew into both a partnership and long-standing friendship, was with Dennis Cuzen, former CEO of Gallo, the South African record label, which over many decades morphed into a close partnership. Another was with Denzel Washington.

After Nelson Mandela became president, in 1995 some members of Artists for a Free South Africa travelled to South Africa to pay him a visit and I tagged along. The occasion was hosted by Ahmed Kathrada at Tuynhuys, the Cape Town office of the president. One member of the party was Denzel Washington, whom many remembered for his portrayal of Steve Biko in the 1987 film *Cry Freedom*. Due to the political turmoil in South Africa at the time, Denzel hadn't visited the country, the movie having been shot on location in Zimbabwe and Kenya. This time Denzel brought his wife Pauletta and their four kids along. Earlier that day the couple had renewed their wedding vows at St George's Cathedral. It was an intensely private ceremony, presided over by Archbishop Desmond Tutu, and a wonderful example of a full-circle moment. A union of two hearts blessed beyond compare reminding themselves and each other of their commitment. It was on this trip that Denzel, in his private capacity, made a significant donation of $1 million (about $18 million in today's terms) to the Nelson Mandela Children's Fund, and I joined Madiba for a visit to their home in the States when we went there together. Thereafter we flew together to freezing sub-zero Minneapolis for a fundraiser. In 2018 I returned with my daughter Gyana to honour Madiba's 100th birthday with the Minnesota Orchestra to present our film and speak about Madiba. This time in beautiful summer.

21

The King of Pop

In August 1993 journalist Peter Feldman announced in *The Star* newspaper that superstar Michael Jackson was to visit South Africa. Brought over by me, he would give two performances. In his book, *Just the Ticket: My 50 Years in Show Business*, Percy Tucker, founder of Computicket, tells of the wave of national excitement that immediately followed the announcement: 'In subsequent days stories appeared describing how 150 tonnes of equipment would be transported on two 747 cargo aircraft, that additional equipment would arrive by freighter, and that a crew of a few hundred people would be needed to set the whole thing up. At Computicket, we were inundated with calls from as far away as Reunion, Nigeria, Zimbabwe and Zaire.'

The dates had been set – Michael was coming and would be performing on 30 September and 2 October as part of his Dangerous World Tour. All the contracts were signed. Michael's people had given me the green light and tickets were selling fast. The country went mad – in a good way, for a change.

Says Percy, 'Jackson mania hit South Africa and fans queued from the night before booking opened to buy tickets priced at R60, R90 and R150. Pandemonium reigned at some of the Computicket terminals where the crush of patrons was so large that customers were unable to get to the other shops in the malls. Within two hours we had sold almost 70 000 of the 120 000 tickets, and by the end of the first day's booking, takings amounted to some R12 million …'

It was insane. The Computicket system was overloaded. We were in Percy's office and the shows were selling out as fast as they could print the tickets.

And then, almost overnight, a massive personal scandal broke: Michael Jackson was accused of child molestation. Although rumours had been widespread, there had never been any conclusive evidence that this had ever been more than speculation, or vicious gossip initiated by individuals with a particular agenda to discredit the star. Many, certainly his fans, had never given the notion any real consideration, and most believed that it was all blatantly untrue. But these new allegations were to be taken seriously, and there was trouble afoot. The success of Michael's tour was beginning to unravel. What followed was a series of rumours suggesting the cancellation and rescheduling of concerts in Singapore and Bangkok. Would we be next?

The news went viral in a pre-viral world. Two days later his managers cancelled the tour. At the time, the country was gripped by violence. In the three years leading up to 1993 more than 10 000 people had been killed in escalating political unrest in South Africa. Just before the King of Pop was set to come to Johannesburg, 36 people were killed in extreme acts of political violence in townships around the city. Officially, this was the reason Michael pulled out of the agreement, but that was just an excuse. The real reason, of course, was the fallout from the allegations. One of the greatest extravaganzas South Africa would ever see had simply fizzled and spluttered to nothing. There was little I could do, so I refunded all the tickets, every single one. The entire exercise cost me hugely in terms of advance expenses, operational costs and advertising. The lesson was hard learned. Quite possibly it was one of the most trying and draining in my entire professional career. Subsequently, a few years later, Michael spent a few months at the Palace at Sun City as a guest of my friend Jerry Inzerillo and I visited him on several occasions during his stay.

Fast-forward to 1997.

The Michael Jackson HIStory World Tour concert was on! Four years in the making and I couldn't quite believe it was finally happening. Michael and I spent a lot of time together. The King of Pop shared my love for The Tramp, the old British film star in the black bowler hat who made people laugh. It was about the simplicity, I think. Both men were exceptional talents with complex lives.

One afternoon in Cape Town – where the show was being staged at the Green Point Stadium – I was with Michael and his long-trusted security man, Wayne Nagin, at the Table Bay Hotel, where we were staying. Suddenly Michael decided he wanted to go out to buy some books. I took a moment and then I looked at Wayne. This wasn't on the schedule. 'Sure,' Wayne said. 'Let's go.' I was a little taken aback, but I trusted

Wayne – he was the best in the world – and so the three of us made our way to the mall at the V&A Waterfront. Behind us Michael's protection detail, comprising two more guards, followed, but they were quite a way off, so it felt like it was just the three of us casually strolling around a mall, with Table Mountain looming majestically in the background. Michael was in his usual wardrobe but had pulled on a cap. Just Michael Jackson browsing through books at CNA, as one does. After maybe 15 or 20 minutes he'd made his selection, but suddenly there was a buzz in the air. Someone had recognised him.

There were no cellphone cameras, of course, as there would certainly have been today, but a crowd was gathering. Black, white, 'coloured', Indian. South Africans loved Michael Jackson and, after decades of being cut off from the world, spotting your hero in the flesh is a next-level experience. Further confirmation of a sort that, indeed, the wall had come down. Because look … there was the King of Pop. In person. In a Cape Town mall, head down, reading, seemingly oblivious behind his sunglasses. But Wayne and I could sense the excitement and euphoria building – as could the store manager, who decided to shut the doors.

'We'll leave in a few minutes,' said Wayne.

Michael had selected some books, but none of us had cash on us. And we needed to go because now we were in something of a rush – well, Wayne and I were. Not Michael, though; he was enjoying it all.

I asked the manager if he would keep the books aside for us, and I would arrange to pick them up later. By the time we reached the door there must have been 150 to 200 fans gathered outside. I was more than a little stressed. After all, as the tour promoter, Michael Jackson was my responsibility.

Somehow, the two guards had become four. Wayne had seen this kind of thing before. He'd been in the eye of the storm, right beside Michael, for years. So when Wayne said, 'Follow me,' we did. The four security guys created a tunnel effect and we were steered through the crowd, which was growing by the second. People were shouting, the atmosphere electric, the excitement palpable. Finally, we were through and heading back to the hotel less than 100 metres away. Fast. Michael was a giant.

Michael Jackson had touched down in his private jet on 2 October 1997, accompanied by his 160-member entourage, including engineers, lawyers, dancers, chefs and production assistants, while the world's largest aircraft brought in tonnes of equipment. About 1 000 security guards were employed by tour co-promoter Attie van Wyk and Big Concerts, which handled all the local logistics. By the time Michael arrived in South Africa, more than 4.2 million people around the world had already attended the record-breaking tour: 70 cities in 38 countries.

The production was destined to become one of the most spectacular ever witnessed on the African continent, an extravaganza of sound, lights and pure theatre. Michael was set to perform on the largest stage ever erected in South Africa, measuring about 68 metres by 26 metres. The empty stage weighed 200 tonnes and took three days to build. Once set up with gear, the set weighed 550 tonnes, excluding lights and sound, and required 16 crew members to manage.

Tickets ranged from R80 to R350, with an additional 50 special souvenir tickets embedded with holograms at R2 000 each, for the best seats in the house, right in front of the mixing tower. One highlight of the show was a 30-metre statue of Michael.

Until then the biggest concerts the Cape had ever seen were those of Bon Jovi, Tina Turner and Roxette. Michael Jackson dwarfed them all.

I'm in the dressing room before the event in Green Point. Celebrity artists have a rider in their contracts that stipulates the perks and fancies that are necessary for them. Michael's was the most demanding. He requested Sony PlayStation video games, lots of mineral water, plenty of fresh fruit, and flowers with as little pollen as possible. Naturally, we complied. It's all there.

In addition, there is a crowd of 36 000 ecstatic fans.

At 7.30 pm, an announcement in several foreign languages tells screaming fans that history will be made in 30 minutes. The stadium erupts, not unlike a supersonic boom and then, shortly before Michael is to set foot on stage, we get a call.

'He's here.'

The arrival is something of a surprise for Michael.

A global superstar. Someone who outshines the King of Pop himself.

It is Nelson Mandela.

Madiba has brought his granddaughters to the concert and it is here that Nelson meets Michael, each a giant fan of the other. And then, after a 10-minute chat and some photographs, Mandela leaves. He's old, you see. And he's the president. But his granddaughters stay to see the show.

And what a show it was.

Jackson, in a sequinned jacket and black pants, appears on stage in his replica rocket ship to chants of 'Michael! Michael!' With a dramatic flourish, he kicks open the door of the rocket and makes his grand entrance onto the gigantic stage. For onlookers, Michael seems dwarfed by the massive set. Somehow, he looks … alone.

Michael starts the set with a three-song jam of 'Scream', 'They Don't Care About Us' and 'In the Closet', sending the mood through the stratosphere. He ends with 'Heal the World' and then, finally, 'History'. Interspersed between the music is a range of videos and photo montages that show, among others, Michael with Princess Diana and the Jackson Five.

The evening was a triumph and it was repeated with similar success the next day. It took a convoy of 43 trucks to transport the 280 tonnes of stage equipment from Cape Town to Johannesburg and then onwards to Durban for another two magical evenings. A few nights later, before a sell-out crowd in Durban, Michael repeated the set list, the last images being Michael Jackson performing 'Heal the World' with about 20 kids.

On stage in Durban on 15 October 1997, a giant blue earth revolving in the background, Michael, dressed in a black leather jacket and white shirt, looked out on the crazed fans below. 'I love you!' he shouted. 'I love you!'

That was the last world tour concert Michael Jackson performed. On 25 June 2009, the King of Pop died at the age of 50 in Los Angeles. His intended 'This Is It' tour, for which he was rehearsing, was not going to happen. We lost one of the most talented, versatile and complex entertainers of all time. I was proud to have known him and share stories of mutual interest. Most of all I appreciated his musical genius.

22

Love on a jet plane
(A story told by two players)

In the early years I revelled in what I was doing, and knew that marriage and a family would be too much of a distraction. I had been blessed with good relationships that were paying off dividends. But still, like Orson Welles' *Citizen Kane*, I had a nagging feeling that there was something lacking in my life, something deeper and much more personal.

For many years, given my work schedule and the amount of travelling I was doing, personal relationships had been complicated and tricky. I had also made a decision long before to stay away from dating people in entertainment. Relationships in this industry rarely last; the environment doesn't suit sound, long-term prospects. You eat, drink and breathe this business, and a life partner would have found my lifestyle unbearable. She'd have thought it crazy to travel all the way to London, do business and, 12 hours later, fly to New York and then straight back home. The lifestyle was simply not conducive to romance, let alone marriage.

I was a confirmed bachelor. Even my mother was giving up on me, her 40-year-old son who still lived with her whenever he was in the country. This didn't mean that I ever stopped looking for love; it just wasn't a priority. Until one day I found it – in a newspaper.

I had been to visit Madiba in Johannesburg to wish him for his birthday on 18 July 1995, and was on my way home. Paging through the *Daily News*, their front page photo caught my eye and drew my attention. It was a photo of a beautiful woman standing with a cake, wishing Madiba a happy birthday. She had just been crowned Miss KwaZulu-Natal and, according to the newspaper, shared a birthday with Madiba. Her name was Vanashree Moodley.

A fortnight later, at the beginning of August I boarded a plane for Johannesburg, not imagining for a moment that my life was about to change forever. I was standing in the aisle when I noticed her, the same striking woman in the photograph. Later, Vanashree called it serendipity ...

I was on a plane going to Johannesburg for the Miss South Africa beauty pageant at Sun City. As we got up to disembark, this guy starts chatting to me and all I could hear was this American accent coming through. It was like he knew me and I'm thinking, Who are you?

He was wearing a baseball cap, jeans, takkies, very casual. He walked me into the terminal, all the way to the luggage carousel. In those few minutes I told him that we were going to Sun City. He said, 'Oh, my friend runs Sun City ... If you see him, you should say hi to him.' I forgot the name; I mean, I couldn't remember anything he said at all. I forgot about it. Then he called me at the hotel, and left a message on the voicemail.

It said, 'Hi, Vanashree, this is Anant calling from my Durban office.'

Anant? Who is Anant? My roommate and I couldn't figure out if it was Anant, Hanant, Hinant, or whatever. And what does he mean in his Durban office? He didn't leave a number – although to this day he insists he did.

The night of the competition, I got back to my room and my roommate had written me a message: 'Vanashree, you have to call this guy. He wants you to be in his movie.' And I thought, really? What nonsense is this? (She'd written it in yellow highlighter, so I could barely read it.)

The next morning I returned the call and I got an American machine voicemail. I just said, 'It's Vanashree returning your call,' and put the phone down. Within a very short period of time, he called back. 'Oh, hi, congratulations,' he said (I had been crowned First Princess). And then I made the connection. I realised, Oh! That's the guy! The guy I met on the plane, the guy who left the message. And for some reason something just clicked and made sense. You just click sometimes, talking to someone.

We chatted and I mentioned that I wanted to come home to Durban earlier than was scheduled and he said, 'Oh, do you want me to change your flight?'

I laughed and said, 'No, don't do that.'

And then he said: 'If I want to get hold of you in Durban, what's your number?'

It felt right. Plus, I was almost 25 at that stage – I wasn't a child anymore. There was something about Anant that was very unassuming, but down to earth, personable ... You know you can trust him. He has an authenticity about him.

So that week the phone rings at home, it was a Tuesday, I was still in bed. It's Anant on the phone. 'You still in bed?' he says. 'Come on. Get up!' It was like he knew me. And I said, 'Look, I'm having an easy day.'

'Okay,' he said, 'but I'm taking you to dinner tonight.'

At the appointed time he sent a driver to pick me up and it turned out we were having dinner at the house of the American consul, Pamela Bridgewater. She seated us at separate tables. So, firstly, his driver comes to fetch me, and then we get seated at different tables – we barely spoke on our first dinner together. But after the dinner, we went to the Royal Hotel for a drink.

I think it was there that I had my first recollection of who Anant actually was. He was the guy who was supposed to bring Michael Jackson to South Africa in 1993.

He took me home and kissed me goodnight – on the forehead.

And that was it.

The next few days … nothing.

Wednesday, Thursday, Friday.

I remember saying to a friend, 'I met this very interesting guy. And he hasn't called me back. And now it's the weekend and he said he was going overseas.'

So she said, 'Just call him.'

I called his office to speak to him and they wouldn't put me through.

Okay, fine, I said to myself. I gave my name and then I left it. But he did call me back.

'I just called to wish you well because you said you were going overseas,' I said.

And he said, 'I'm actually only leaving on Sunday. What are you doing tomorrow evening?'

This time he sent a friend to pick me up and we went to his beach house where Anant cooked dinner. I was impressed. I think that sealed it. Then it was official.

I have my own version, of course. None of this was planned. It was just how it played out (and is an indication of who I am), although, in retrospect, it is the perfect date strategy.

Vanashree and I spent two years travelling. I introduced her to my friends across the globe. We attended the Oscars in 1997 together, and also the handover of Hong Kong by the British to the Chinese on 1 July 1997. I shared with her my favourite people, places, restaurants, seats on planes and other idiosyncrasies. On one two-week trip she even travelled with no more than hand luggage. That was impressive, but short-lived.

It was in Hong Kong, on my return trip to the US, that I sprang a surprise on Vanashree. Having established that she would meet me and we'd spend a few days there before heading back home, I arranged for her to bring some documents I told her I needed from the office. Unbeknown to her, hidden in among my paperwork was an engagement ring. And so it was that, on the flight back from Hong Kong to Johannesburg, I proposed. Her answer was a resounding yes. Meet on a plane, get engaged on a plane, but not marry on one.

Determined that our wedding – set for 12 December 1997 – would be a private, low-profile event, away from the spotlight (by Indian standards), Vanashree and I spent six weeks orchestrating a traditional Hindu affair at the Durban International Convention Centre. No fancy wedding planner, no overbearing experts determined to have their say, no publicity or media involvement whatsoever – just the two of us, with some close friends, family, associates and the team at Videovision, getting on with things on our own in the six weeks we had at our disposal. Among our guests would be what seemed a large contingent of cabinet ministers, a number of captains of industry – friends I'd made in business over the years – as well as friends and family. At the end of October, Madiba was in Durban, so Vanashree and I went to visit him, mock-up of the wedding invitation in hand, to tell him that we were getting married and to extend an invitation. Of course, we were very apologetic that it was at such short notice. I explained that as much as we would love him to be there, we realised that he was the president; we understood entirely that the enormous demands on his time may mean that he would not be available.

He immediately turned to Vanashree and, in his irrepressible way, said: 'I've been waiting a long time for you to propose to this man. Of course I will be there.'

Ironically, despite our initial determination to keep the whole thing out of the spotlight, it was Madiba who managed to persuade us to relent in some small way. In the lead-up to the wedding, we received a call from his office, urging at least some concession to the media. Madiba's office had been receiving numerous queries regarding the wedding and the president's attendance. In the end Vanashree and I agreed to arrange a holding room for selected journalists and have the media in for when Madiba arrived. We would allow 10 minutes for photographs but no television, and then they'd be ushered right out again before the private ceremony and reception took place. Thanks to the absence of social media and cellphone cameras, to this day there are no images in the public domain of our private moment with our friends and family.

We were married on 12 December 1997 after two years of dating. It was a dream wedding; everything slotted perfectly into place, from the venue to our guests.

Madiba was there as a very special wedding guest. We had become close and I had come to know him well over the years Anant and I had been dating. Whenever Anant and I met him at functions at the Foundation or the Children's Fund, or even at his house in Qunu during Christmas time, he'd say to me, 'You know, nowadays things are differ-ent. The woman can take the first step. Women propose to the men now … The young girls these days, they can make the proposals. They don't have to wait for the men.' He was so funny like that. He was so sweet. It was almost like he was hinting all the time, nudging Anant: What's going on, what's going on, what's going on?

Our wedding day was the first time I saw Anant nervous. I actually had to tell him, 'Smile. Calm down.'

For the first time I think he realised once we were on stage that he had no control over what was going on, and he just had to be there, and you could see it in his face and his body language that he was a bit tense. I kept having to say, 'Just calm down, just smile, take it easy, you know? It's okay.'

Nelson Mandela and Ahmed Kathrada were witnesses and signatories to our marriage certificate. They were like brothers, and both were father figures to us. As a veteran of the struggle and always an avid supporter of my work and my goals, Kathy and I had become close over the years. He was one of the people I most revered and cherished. He and his wife Barbara Hogan were two of my staunchest allies but, more importantly, trusted friends. And so it was natural that I should ask Kathy to officiate as master of ceremonies at our wedding.

When Vanashree walked in with her parents, she stopped at Madiba's table, where he briefly spoke to her, giving advice on the institution of marriage, as he was in the habit of doing. As a wedding gift, he had bought us a huge candelabra, for which he had personally scoured the streets of Durban. He was very proud of it and we were honoured to accept it, but we only heard the full story months later when one of Madiba's security men called to ask whether he could come and see me. Of course I agreed and so he came by. 'I have to tell you this story personally,' he said.

Madiba had apparently been on the presidential plane en route to the wedding when he said to the security detail that he had to make an unscheduled stop at Stuttafords – in the middle of West Street in the centre of town and at peak shopping time – to buy a gift. The request sent his security men into a flurry. This had not been part of the plan and venturing into West Street at that time of the day would inevitably mean all sorts of complications, for which they were not prepared. But what could they say? He was the president. So they drove him into the city, ushered him into the store and, after some deliberation, he selected the candelabra. They waited while he had the present gift-wrapped and finally they carried it to the waiting car. But it didn't end there. No sooner was the president safely ensconced in the car again when he made yet another request. Could they please stop at CNA so that he could buy a wedding card? By this point, I'm sure they must have been apoplectic but, again, they were compelled to honour his request. So Madiba was ferried off to CNA, where he selected a card, paid for it and, back in the car, wrote in it a beautiful message for Vanashree and me.

Vanashree's dress was made by Durban couturier Sid Lakhani. Combining elements of Vanashree's south Indian heritage, my own northern Indian roots and Western influences, it was a champagne gold silk creation with a headdress of seven white orchids. The dress was decorated with over 10 000 pearls and diamanté. Sid also made my outfit, a simple dark blue Nehru suit. After exchanging our vows and garlands, our Hindu wedding rites were conducted by Pundit Roshan Singh. After the ceremony we took our places on the stage, where we were joined by Kathy and Madiba.

At times I got quite emotional, overcome with joy, spellbound by Vanashree's radiance and, at the same time, anxious and stressed – it was a big thing for me to have all my friends and family there, and to be in the process of holy matrimony. Never mind simply ensuring that everything ran smoothly and as planned, I remember feeling like I was walking on air, that I was the luckiest man alive.

The after-party on the night of our wedding was at the Hilton and our reception was held at The Royal the following evening. We then went overseas on honeymoon – although we did nearly miss our flight. One constant cause of stress has always been Anant's travelling habits. He always cuts it so fine, leaving driving to the airport to the very last possible moment. Oh my God, the stress.

The first few times, I'm, like, what the hell is this? I can never do it!

But you know what's the worst thing? After the first two or three times, I was doing the same thing. I was, Why go early? No, get there by the skin of your teeth, get on the plane last and get off first.

Those days there weren't requirements to be there 45 minutes before take-off and stuff like that. It was more like, the plane's leaving at eight, and Anant's walking in at five to eight. It was ridiculous.

Leaving for the honeymoon, the airline staff were actually waiting for us where the car drives in – they were waiting for us right there. It was so funny.

And he has the strangest habits when he watches a movie. I was shocked the first time he took me to the movies; I was, like, what, he didn't even stop at the popcorn and Coke stand? No, he walked straight

*in. And I'm looking at him and he's, like, 'Are you coming?' and I'm,
'What about ...?' And he's, 'Come, come, come – let's go.'*

No popcorn? No chocolate? No Coke?

Nope. Nothing! Maybe a water. Maybe.

*I learned very quickly. After the first few dates to the movies, I'm all,
Aah, this is ridiculous. So I just do it on my own now, get my own snacks.
Weird, weird, weird.*

The moment we got married, Anant said, 'Let's have kids.'

*I'm, like, 'Listen, you waited 43 years to get married. I'm 27 – give me
at least two years or so!'*

Our daughter Gyana was born two years later, and then our son Kiyan
two and a half years after. We'd have dinner together every night and
chat about life, about the world out there. My world became our world.
Suddenly, I had new responsibilities, new insights, and was compelled to
look beyond the immediate. I had to set new goals, lay down rules – for
myself, as a husband and father, and for the children. It was never far
from my mind that the children needed not only encouragement and
nurturing, but also grounding. They would grow up in a far more privileged environment than I had ever known. They needed balance. And it
was our responsibility to provide that.

When it comes to separating public and private, my family and I have
long made peace with the fact that being in the entertainment business
means one opens one's life to scrutiny. As a consequence, you have to
balance the two worlds very carefully, and draw a fine line between private and public. For Vanashree and me, it's always been crucial that we
maintain balance for Gyana and Kiyan, taking into consideration our
own humble roots and the industry that allows us a privileged lifestyle.

It is important to us that, as much as they enjoy a life of privilege, private schools, travelling, getting to know the world and meeting movie stars, politicians and other high-profile individuals, they learn from those experiences rather than take them for granted, that they understand the value of money, and principles and values that come with that. With their mother and me both coming from modest backgrounds, we have tried to instil in them a sense of appreciation and responsibility. We treated them no differently to the way most parents do in virtually every household across the country. From an early age, they were punished for what may have seemed frivolous transgressions at the time, but set the foundation for very clear rules that brought home to them the importance of under-standing the privileged lives they led: there was to be no wasting and they were required to finish their meals; in order to be rewarded they needed to work hard; they understood that nothing comes for free. And, as much as they were never punished with the sjambok as I had been, they nevertheless faced the consequences of any transgressions. If they threw a tantrum or performed inappropriately, they were banished to a corner of a dark room, even sometimes together. They were simply not allowed to get away with that kind of stuff, with anything that indicated that they were ungrateful for the lives they were able to lead.

It was with these lessons in mind, then, that in 2016 we whisked them off on a tour of their history, to experience first-hand what it had been like to grow up in circumstances far removed from their everyday under-standing of their youth. And so we stopped off at various spots so famil-iar to me – the schools I attended, and my childhood homes: the simple tin-roofed, wood-and-iron structure in Quarry Road and then the house in Reservoir Hills, which is truly tiny in comparison to the place they now call home. The local market, the family homes of childhood friends, the tree that had stood in the garden for as long as I could remember.

In this way, they were able to fully understand and appreciate the good fortune that was theirs. They are both now at university and we believe they are well-rounded young people.

23

Who Wants to be a Millionaire?

W*ho Wants to be a Millionaire?* debuted on British television on 4 September 1998, with contestants tackling a series of multiple-choice questions to win big cash prizes, the maximum in most versions of the global show being one million in the local currency.

But before the show became a global hit, its producers wanted to make a movie. I was contacted by my friend and business partner, the British producer on *Sarafina!*, David Thompson of BBC Films.

'Anant,' said David, 'there's this film project, *Eastern Promises*. I think you should take a look at it.'

So I did, and I liked it.

'Yes, let's meet up,' I suggested.

Due to various timing schedules, we finally met up at Heathrow (I was en route to New York) – David Thompson, Paul Smith and me – to discuss their film project. At some point in the conversation Paul mentioned their game show.

The show had been created by David Briggs, Mike Whitehill and Steven Knight, while the concept for the show was developed by UK production house Celador Productions, run by global producer Paul Smith. The show was initially broadcast on the ITV network.

'We're doing a TV show that's just been aired in the UK,' Paul said.

'What's it called?' I asked.

'*Who Wants to be a Millionaire?*'

I shook my head. I hadn't heard of it.

'Hey,' said David, 'it's a big hit here.'

This was just weeks after the show had opened in 1998. They didn't offer any further details, but I was intrigued.

'So, have you done a deal with format rights for South Africa?' I asked.

No, they hadn't.

'Okay,' I said, 'I'll take it. And, while we're at it, let's just include the rights for India and the Middle East too.'

'Great, sure thing.'

Nobody – not even them – had any inkling then that *Who Wants to be a Millionaire?* was going to be the multibillion-dollar global franchise it would become.

I locked it up right there and then.

In the United Kingdom, with Chris Tarrant as host, the show quickly became a massive hit, with one episode watched by more than 19 million viewers. It went on to have a 15-year run before it ended in 2014.

And so it was that in October 1999 we revealed that we would be bringing the spectacularly successful show to South Africans. The local version, hosted by journalist and television presenter Jeremy Maggs, was identical to the British one, with contestants in line to win R1 million if they answered the multiple-choice questions correctly. Although he was initially reluctant to take on this role, Jeremy was the perfect host for our market. We had licensed the show to pay-TV station M-Net, with Videovision Entertainment as producers. We launched on Sunday, 7 November 1999, at 6 pm during their open-time slot. Later it also aired on state broadcaster SABC3. In total, six seasons were made locally, the run ending in 2005. Millions of South Africans were glued to their television screens every Sunday to watch as contestants tried to answer the questions put to them and walk away with R1 million.

We only ever had one contestant win the million: on 19 March 2000 David Paterson, a 60-year-old former teacher from Port Elizabeth, became the sole million-rand winner of the South African show. He was the first winner outside the United States and only the third overall. To top it all, David won outright without needing to resort to his remaining lifeline, the Ask the Audience prompt. He knew the answer before the choices even came up. His R500 000 question was: 'Around the interior of the Voortrekker Monument is an impressive marble frieze. Who designed it?"

Willem H Coetzer was the answer.

And the million-rand question?

'Which musical star was known as Baby Frances Gumm early in her career?'

The answer? Judy Garland.

That clinched it for Paterson.

In the meantime, I'd decided to give away my rights for India and the Middle East. As much as I had an understanding with the creators and producers, I went to Amitabh Bachchan.

'Hey,' I said, 'you know I own this show for India?'

'Yes?'

'Look, Amitabh, I think this is something you should do in India.'

This was not only because of our friendship, but also because we knew by then that this wasn't something we were interested in taking any further ourselves. And much the same was true with the Middle Eastern rights. Someone simply came along, and I said, 'You know, go ahead. Take it and do it.' I put them in touch with the originators and they concluded their own deal. The result was that in 2000 the Indian version of the show, known as *Kaun Banega Crorepati*, debuted, and has been airing ever since, with no fewer than seven winners taking the top prize.

Amitabh was the host for all the seasons except the third when another Bollywood superstar Shah Rukh Khan stepped in. *Millionaire* was Amitabh's first appearance on Indian television and the show was number one in India for years. It also led to the global hit movie *Slumdog Millionaire*, produced by Paul Smith, taking in $380 million at the box office and winning eight Oscars in 2008, including Best Picture.

As the new decade – the new millennium – dawned, we had entered a new phase of growth at Videovision. These were exciting times for us. The previous decade had ended with the wildly successful launch of *Who Wants to be a Millionaire?*, signalling a period of further development, both at home and abroad.

Within 12 months of producing *Millionaire*, we moved straight on to one of the most ambitious, challenging and desirable business ventures we had ever tackled: the creation of our own cinema chain in South Africa. Cinema Starz – one of the first 100 per cent Black-owned undertakings of its kind in the newly democratic country – was the culmination of a passion dating back to the very beginning of my career, when I was pro-hibited from having my films screened in white cinemas and struggled to secure venues as a result.

I had made a brief foray into this space way back in 1983, and it hadn't turned out well. I thought I should take a chance at the cinema exhibition business, but, in my case, it was a mom-and-pop version in a residential area. There was a little building in Reservoir Hills that the owner was try-ing to convert into a cinema and I foolishly thought that I should see if I could make it work. I took a few 16mm projectors and installed them and tried to run a cinema, roping in Sanjeev and Rajan Pather to help me. It was a dismal failure, and after three months I had to give it up. Fortunately I did it on a trial basis, so I did not lose too much. The most important aspect of this venture was the lessons learned in exhibition, even in that short space of time, that boded well for my future in this business.

In the proposal to Sun International for Cinema Starz, I outlined our intention and the vision we had for this ground-breaking venture:

> During the years of apartheid, I successfully operated three cinemas in Durban catering to black audiences. The gross potential at the time was very limited as almost all cinemas were controlled by Ster and Kinekor, which at the time were separate companies. I then opted to go into film production, targeting South African films that could be globally released, as we were excluded from local monopolies. Having achieved this, I believe that the time is right for me to go back to that first love of exhibition, and hence our application to secure these movie complexes at your casinos.
>
> We want to bring the motion picture experience that is the best available anywhere in the world, stadium seating and Dolby digital sound to visitors to your complexes, which will be entirely unique,

combining the aspects of production and distribution ... We are also looking into the state-of-the-art new luxury cinema concept, which includes seats like those on aircraft that would convert to 'love seats' with tip-up arms.

The proposal was met with resounding applause and, endorsed by both President Thabo Mbeki and Nelson Mandela, we launched at the GrandWest Casino complex in Cape Town in December 2000, with the screening of the moving Truth and Reconciliation Commission film, *Long Night's Journey into Day*, the work of Academy Award-nominated filmmakers Frances Reid and Deborah Hoffman and winner of the Grand Jury Prize at the Sundance Film Festival that year. The opening was an extravaganza, a who's who of Cape Town mingling with a scattering of special guests, among them Archbishop Desmond Tutu, CEO of Sun International Peter Bacon and his wife Anneline Kriel-Bacon, Finance Minister Trevor Manuel, Oprah Winfrey, her long-time partner Stedman Graham and her best friend Gayle King. As always, Oprah – the very picture of style and elegance, in black tunic and white trousers, complete with ethnic print scarf and white heels – made it clear that she was very excited to be in Cape Town: 'I'm saying to Anant, so it's Black-owned. Who are the owners? And he says, "I am!" Oh my God!' she exclaimed and gave me a hug.

The new decade was already proving both exciting and rewarding. Just a month later I found myself in Davos receiving the Crystal Award from the World Economic Forum. The Crystal Award recognises personalities who, apart from their individual achievements, have also made outstanding contributions to cross-cultural understanding. Previous recipients of the award include Paulo Coelho, Tao Ho, Lord David Puttnam, Elie Wiesel and Benjamin Zander, as well as South African writers Nadine

Gordimer and Es'kia Mphahlele. In 2001 the award went to four recipients: me, musician Peter Gabriel, West African guitarist Youssou N'Dour and Peruvian writer Mario Vargas Llosa. This was a huge honour, especially in such esteemed company.

The presentation of the 2001 award took place at the closing plenary session of the annual meeting. Quincy Jones, a former recipient, was in attendance. The founder and executive chairman of the World Economic Forum, Prof Klaus Schwab, unveiled the highlight – a surprise video message from Madiba, in which he congratulated me personally. Calling the award 'a unique honour', he said, 'We recall how, in the past, you succeeded against all odds to make films which portrayed the real South Africa. Congratulations on this achievement.'

I'm not generally one who thrives in the limelight and am quite reticent about having attention drawn to me, so as much as the spotlight was now turned on me rather than the stars and celebrities I worked with, I was truly humbled. But the fanfare – and the honours – did not end there. On presenting me with the award, Prof Schwab stated: 'Anant Singh's art is his life's work. He is a filmmaker who has concentrated his work on fighting injustice. First and foremost, Anant Singh has been a sustained and powerful campaigner against apartheid and its legacy.'

I've always been proud of my South African heritage and, in accepting the award, I paid tribute to the many individuals who had worked on my films over the years. It was their work as much as my own that was being honoured with the award. There are thousands of people who have been involved in the work I helped create. They are the unsung heroes of our industries, working passionately and committed to the excellence we all strive for.

In September 2001, I was in New York. I had meetings downtown, in Tribeca, which was close to the World Trade Center. On 9 September, I had an early meeting at 9.30 am at Greenwich Street, and, when I left, I walked down Canal Street as I always did and looked to my right at the two World Trade Center towers, looming large and dwarfing the smaller buildings of Tribeca. I then took the subway uptown to where I had my next meeting and that evening I joined Quincy Jones and the legendary French singer Henri Salvador, hosted by Jean Georges, the world renowned chef, for a stupendous dinner, which went on till past midnight. The next day, 10 September, I left New York for the Toronto Film Festival, where our UK production *Happy Now* was due to screen the next day. On the morning of the 11th when I saw the shocking attack on the World Trade Center on television, it was nerve-wracking. I had been there 48 hours before, at the very same spot! I called Vanashree to let her know that I was safely in Toronto. Then I called my mother and thereafter Quincy. Miraculously, I was able to get through to everybody; within a couple of hours, the entire telecommunications network in North America was shut down. The shock reverberated through all of us that day. And then we got news that the festival was cancelled. My friends decided to stay together to support one another other –Brian Cox, Ruth Vitale, David Thompson and others. In times like these, you want to be with those closest to you. I immediately tried to get out of Toronto to get back home, but obviously all flights were grounded. I decided to just go to the airport, as I had only carry-on baggage and walk from counter to counter asking if they had a flight heading out. If they did, I put myself on a wait list to any destination in Europe or the UK. I was lucky to get the last seat on a Virgin flight going to London later that evening. I took it and happily paid the enormous fare they charged. From London I flew home to South Africa. Many friends of mine remained stranded in Toronto for more than a week. I was delighted and happy to be back home. This was my experience of 9/11.

In January 2002 the World Economic Forum moved its annual meeting to New York to show solidarity with the United States and New Yorkers after the 9/11 attacks. Billed as 'Davos in New York', I was invited by Prof Schwab to produce the opening video presentation to set the tone for the meeting and follow the theme 'Leadership in Fragile Times: A Vision for a Shared Future'. I collaborated with Danny Schechter to produce this and constructed it as a short film entitled *The Darkest Hour is Just before Dawn*.

The aftermath of 9/11 resulted in significant social challenges in the US. Heightened discrimination against Arabs and Muslims in general became prevalent. Juxtaposed to that were the radical Islamists, who took it as an opportunity to intensify their anti-US actions. These issues were the subjects of two films that we subsequently produced. The first of these was the documentary feature *The Journalist and the Jihadi: The Murder of Daniel Pearl*. Radical for its time, it tracked the parallel lives of *Wall Street Journal* reporter Daniel Pearl and jihadi Omar Sheikh. Both highly educated individuals from privileged backgrounds, but vastly different too – one was a humanist who spent most of his career reporting from the Islamic world on a quest to promote cross-cultural understanding; the other was a militant who ultimately chose a deeply violent path. After 9/11, their paths crossed in Pakistan, with tragic consequences, resulting in the murder of Daniel Pearl by Omar Sheikh just four months after 9/11. Co-directed and co-produced by Ramesh Sharma and Ahmed Jamal, the film was nominated for the Emmy Award for Outstanding Investigative Journalism in 2007. Despite Sheikh being convicted for the murder in 2002, a Pakistani court surprisingly overturned his sentence in January 2021.

The second film, made in 2007, was *American East*, which explored the experiences of Arab-Americans living in post-9/11 Los Angeles. The film examined long-held misunderstandings and stereotyping of Arabic/ Islamic culture Americans live by, particularly stereotyping based on ethnicity and religion.

A business must continue to grow and thrive and, if opportunity presents itself, you need to grab it with both hands. Of course, things don't always pan out, but an opportunity not taken is always an opportunity missed forever. We were still firmly in the business of film, but on the odd occasion we ventured into other areas, which were often quite crazy undertakings. This was particularly true in 2002 when Amitabh Bachchan's manager, Kirit Trivedi, Sudhir and I produced another live entertainment extravaganza, the Bollywood spectacular Now or Never, again with Amitabh Bachchan.

Videovision Entertainment, in association with Sahara Television and Sun International's Sugar Mill Casino, once again teamed up with Amitabh and Kirit Trivedi to stage a massive live stadium gig, putting together 10 of Bollywood's greatest stars playing before 60 000 fans at Durban's ABSA Stadium – Shah Rukh Khan, Hrithik Roshan, Sanjay Dutt, Karisma Kapoor, Kareena Kapoor, Sushmita Sen, Rani Mukherjee, Shilpa Shetty and Preity Zinta – led by Bachchan, for one night only, and never done before or since. This was the first and only time that so many top-ranking stars performed together in one show. Its magnitude could only be compared to three individual shows combined into a single mega-show. Ten years after our first show with Amitabh, a number of associates, Kirit among them, returned to South Africa for what was dubbed a 'family reunion'.

The principal performers were supported by a 90-strong troupe of artists, which included leading playback singers, the popular Viju Shah

Orchestra comprising 18 musicians, as well as 25 dancers and six chorus singers. The troupe was joined by local performers. One of these, award-winning Jay Pather's Siwela Sonke Dance Theatre, performed the opening item, a rousing multicultural dance piece to the music from the film *Power of One*. It was exciting to be able to showcase local talent alongside Bollywood's best.

In an address to the media, Amitabh said that South Africa had always had a special place in his heart, ever since his first visit, when he had been overwhelmed by the people and the many fans that Indian cinema had in the country. 'It was a natural choice to hold the biggest live show featuring India's film talent in South Africa,' he said.

It cost us R10 million to stage the show and we made a marginal profit. But, as we have come to know, live entertainment is not just about profit – it is about doing things that are fun too. In many instances, our ventures have not been hugely profitable, but the joy of seeing 60 000 people sharing the same experience in a single venue, faces lit in excitement, is priceless. As rewarding as it is, however, it is also challenging and demanding and the extravaganzas are probably not something we'd do in a hurry again. For me, it was somewhat of a bucket-list entry and clearly, for us, having staged Michael Jackson and Now or Never, there was not much left to do in the arena of live music entertainment. Our job had been done.

That said, in 2018 Gyana dragged me to the Taylor Swift Reputation Concert in New York. I was there reluctantly. It was pouring with rain and I had never listened to any of her songs, other than hearing them when Gyana played her music. But Taylor Swift is an amazing live performer. She reminded me of the power of Michael (Jackson) in the way that she so easily commanded her audience. So never say never … you never know!

24

The Rainbow Nation

In the many decades before apartheid finally collapsed, the film industry in South Africa was largely designed to promote Afrikaner culture
and Afrikaans-language movies – by far the majority made locally up
until then. Before 1994 I had no interest in working in Afrikaans, so I
never did. For me – for us – it was the language of the oppressor, sym-
bolising all the apartheid government stood for and all we were against.
At school, Afrikaans as a subject was compulsory and, attending an all-
Indian school, I rebelled against it. As young as I was, this was my own
little foray into the world of resistance. There was nothing about the
language that intrigued me, inspired me, drew me in – quite the contrary.
It simply made me angry, made me dig my heels in and rebel. The result

was that I failed Afrikaans in my final year at high school, and I had to write a supplementary exam in March the following year in order to get into university.

But then, after the dawn of democracy, I started looking at things a little differently. In 1994, Nelson Mandela embraced FW de Klerk and members of his government, an act almost unconscionable for hard-line resistance fighters, but for me a startling eye-opener. Perhaps it was time to start building bridges, look beyond our blinkers, set our sights on new goals. Perhaps it was time to consider indigenous languages.

So it was that, in 1996, our head of production Helena Spring suggested I take a look at the script of *Paljas*. She had read the book and knew filmmaker Katinka Heyns personally. Of course, my Afrikaans was too sketchy to fully appreciate the mastery of the words, so I had the book translated. And, yes, I agreed. It was exceptional. At the time, films once considered 'too foreign', such as Italy's *Life is Beautiful*, were making great inroads in international cinema. Times were changing and I needed to follow suit. Besides, I wanted to work with the supremely talented Afrikaans-speaking Katinka Heyns. The script, by Katinka's husband, the Afrikaans playwright and writer Chris Barnard, was outstanding and the cinematographer would be another local legend in the industry: Koos Roets. All were Afrikaans.

Ten years earlier I would not have dreamed of touching an Afrikaans film, but we were in a free, united South Africa now and *Paljas* was an Afrikaans film with real integrity telling a universal story. By the end of it, it would be submitted for the 70th Annual Academy Awards for Best Foreign Language Film, the first South African submission for the Oscars since the end of apartheid. It would also be headlined at California's 12th Wine Country Film Festival in 1998, where I was presented with the festival's inaugural Distinguished Film Producer Award – in fact, the same year in which I had been awarded an honorary doctorate from the University of Port Elizabeth. All in all, an auspicious year for me personally and for the South African film industry.

We shot *Paljas* on a farm, Toorwater, just outside the rural Karoo town of Klaarstroom and stayed in a bed-and-breakfast that appeared as though it had been caught in a time warp, stuck in the apartheid past. There were portraits on the walls of Afrikaner leaders, such as DF Malan and HF Verwoerd, some who had caused great harm to the country and its people over the preceding centuries. They must have been rolling in their graves, I told Katinka, at the thought of a Black man sleeping in their house.

Videovision had become skilled at marketing and selling our films overseas and, even more importantly, making money doing so. We were now reaching a much larger global audience on a more regular basis than any of our South African competitors.

South African comedian Leon Schuster – king of the box office, lord of the candid-camera skit and master of disguise – had been making films for decades and his movies invariably turned out to be giant successes at the local box office. But, until 2001, Leon rarely had much success abroad. His films were made largely for local consumption and none of them travelled well internationally. He and I had had some dealings in the early years, most significantly in 1994 when we acquired one of his hit films for international distribution. We went on to sell that film to almost every country in the world. When Leon saw what we could do he suggested that perhaps we could do business together.

Over the years, we established a good relationship. Leon can be hard work at times – as most creative individuals tend to be – but in this business talent trumps pretty much everything else so you make it work. The thing about Leon is that he knows his audience and that's what I admire most about him. Even in arguments about the edit, he's extremely astute and when he agitates for something in a discussion, it's based not on simple likes or dislikes, or personal opinion, but backed up by real thought and careful consideration. It's never 'I don't like that', but rather 'That doesn't work because the timing is off' – a technique mastered by both Peter Sellers and Charlie Chaplin. Leon knows what he's talking about.

Our biggest hits together started with my approaching Leon on a separate matter, not at all related to any of the projects we would work on together later. I had spotted the *Candid Camera*-type skits he had done for TV with Clover, the dairy company, and thought they were really funny.

'Okay,' I said to Leon, 'let's take this and make a movie out of it.'

And so we did.

It was then that he told me about the concept for *Mr Bones* and I liked it. Of course I did. 'But,' I said, 'we need to figure out a way to make it more international.' And so the idea of the African-American golfer coming to South Africa to find his roots was developed, very much along the lines of other hugely successful titles in a similar vein, such as *Crocodile Dundee* and *Coming to America*. It was slapstick comedy at its best, with American actor David Ramsey – who made a name for himself in the *Arrow* TV series as John Diggle/Spartan – playing the lead and Leon in the title role as a white 'witchdoctor'. The film was set at the Million Dollar golf tournament at Sun City.

Mr Bones was released on 30 November 2001 and remained on the theatre circuit for 12 weeks. At the time, it became the second highest-grossing film of all time in South Africa behind *Titanic*, which grossed

R40 million in its entire run over one year. *Mr Bones* was also the biggest budget Schuster film to date. We went all out, doing things never done before in this country. It featured a number of indigenous animals, crazy stunts and special effects using CGI technology generated entirely in South Africa. The big budget and high production values were key ingredients, aimed at ensuring that *Mr Bones* would translate well internationally. And it paid off.

Mr Bones became one of the most successful local films ever made, eventually making R33 million at the local box office and outgrossing blockbusters such as *Harry Potter* and *Lord of the Rings*.

Our next major collaboration with Leon Schuster was *Mama Jack*. This was a slight departure from the usual Schuster fare of entirely candid-camera antics. It had a compelling and funny storyline with a host of visual gags and a cast of interesting characters played by well-known personalities.

Then, in 2007, we decided to forge ahead with a sequel to *Mr Bones*. The public wanted it – they had shown that clearly through box-office attendances of the original – and so did we. *Mr Bones 2* was released in South Africa on 13 November 2008. It was a hit. It went on to outperform the first *Mr Bones*, making *Mr Bones* the most successful film franchise ever created in South Africa. The second film earned just under R35 million at the box office and became the highest-grossing South African film of all time in less than two months, beating the record set by the original *Mr Bones*. It has to be said, though, that contributing to the box-office success of *Mr Bones 2* was the diligent anti-piracy effort of the South African Federation Against Copyright Theft, which meant that the film did not fall victim to piracy. In fact, this was the first time that a local film managed to evade the actions of pirates.

What *Mama Jack* and so many of Leon's other features taught us too, however, was that if you know your audience well, have targeted your market accurately and have a clear vision of the direction in which you want to go, you also know that you're going to tick people off. There are always going to be those beyond your target market, a sector of society that will either write you off as unoriginal and tacky, or even take offence, be personally affronted by what you have to say and what you project onto that giant screen. As a professional, you're aware of the criticism – and the critics can be vicious, believe me – and able to separate the constructive from the destructive. Sometimes, though, you simply fall foul of a bad temper and for the most part you can't do much about that. Leon learned that the hard way.

Over the years, Leon Schuster has taken his share of verbal and physical abuse, negative reactions to what has been considered stereotyping, even suffering beatings from unsuspecting members of the public provoked into losing their temper at a gag his character might be playing. There was the inevitable criticism. There always is. With Leon, there's been an increasing outcry against him disguising himself as Black people, including *Mama Jack*, in his movies. But Leon, as he continues to insist, is an artist, simply pushing buttons.

'I'm a satirist, not a racist,' he says. 'My candid-camera gags are designed to be good, clean fun that is not objectionable to any race or age group. My fans are of all races.'

And he's right in many ways. Indeed, at a movie theatre showing a Schuster film, you'll see every ethnicity. Every age. All laughing their heads off. In the end, we all have our own choices to make.

Like Leon, I am no stranger to criticism, having been on the receiving end of it more than once over the years. Why did I use Whoopi Goldberg and not a local actress in *Sarafina!*? Why did I use a white director – Darrell Roodt – for this or that film? My response is always: Hey, are *you* making the movie? If you want a say, go make your own movie and use whomever you want. Actors play many roles over the course of their careers. Leon doesn't only do Black people – he plays every character, every ethnicity. He does Jewish guys, Afrikaners, Indians. Everyone. At the end of it all, what Leon does best is comedy. And it's art. He's an actor.

I'm reminded of Ben Kingsley doing *Gandhi*.

That was a huge global uproar when Kingsley was cast as the iconic statesman. How dare a white man – albeit one of part-Indian descent – be selected to play Gandhi, perhaps one of the most revered sons of India in living history? The controversy raged on and on until people actually saw the movie and then it was a simple matter of, 'Oh, this guy is good. Maybe even the best. Maybe no one else would have played the man as well.'

I understand why some people can get worked up over all of this. Of course I do. I know that sensitivities abound, issues that have been bubbling under the surface for decades, centuries even. Often they are as a result of years and years of oppression, of discrimination, of marginalisation, and every so often they raise their ugly head and everything boils over. I also understand, however, that at the end of the day it's storytelling. Entertainment.

For me, it has always been a simple matter; my approach is to find the best person for the role. Whether that is a South African or a foreigner. We audition probably a hundred South African actors for almost every leading role we offer. It remains an interesting debate, however – as it should be, of course, because we can never take anything for granted – and one that runs parallel with debates around gender equality and equal pay. Moreover, I have to juggle the economic responsibility to the investors who help get the films made, and sometimes we need star names.

The #MeToo movement and others like it are as relevant as they have always been, and warrant not only awareness but action. Considering all sides of the argument, however, perhaps we all need to simply step back, take a moment and ask whether we are taking issues too far or not far enough. We are in the entertainment business, and *Mr Bones*, for example, has been hailed as one of the funniest films made in South Africa by people across the race spectrum – my own history in the film industry and my body of work demonstrate my personal sensitivity to racial injustice, a principle on which I will never compromise. Context remains all important. Films and television shows such as *Coming to America* and *Mind Your Language* were hugely popular in their time, and yet can be readily criticised for racial stereotyping.

Nelson Mandela was imprisoned on Robben Island on 13 June 1964, the 466th prisoner to arrive at the island prison that year. And so his prisoner number became 466/64. In 2003 this number became a clarion call for global action against the new international crisis that was HIV/AIDS.

AIDS was wreaking havoc in South Africa and the outlook was dire, the state contributing to the catastrophe with its ongoing denial.

Again, it was Nelson Mandela, now an elder statesman, who decided to take up the responsibility and make a difference, going against the Mbeki government's denialist stance. In October 2003 Mandela joined forces with musicians and artists from around the world and called on citizens to join a global campaign in the fight against AIDS in Africa. With this, he launched the iconic 46664 campaign – 'Give one minute of your life to stop AIDS' – in London. It became a worldwide, music-led campaign not only to raise funds but also to increase awareness of the impact of AIDS in Africa. Mandela stated that AIDS was no longer a disease, but a human rights issue.

'A tragedy of unprecedented proportions is unfolding in Africa,' he said when he launched his international awareness programme. 'AIDS today in Africa is claiming more lives than the sum total of all wars, famines and floods and ravages of such deadly diseases as malaria. We must act now for the sake of the world.'

The campaign was driven by Sir Richard Branson and a host of international superstars, among them Sir Bob Geldof and Bono from the Irish rock band U2. I, too, got involved and, at the invitation of Madiba, was appointed to the board set up to manage the campaign and its first event in Cape Town. For our first board meeting at the beginning of 2003, Branson flew us all on his Virgin Atlantic airline to his home in London. Gathered around Richard's dining room table were Brian May and Roger Taylor of Queen, with their manager Jim Beach, as well as Dave Stewart, JF Cecillon, Lizzie Anders, John Samuel (CEO of the Nelson Mandela Foundation) and Iqbal Meer, Madiba's lawyer in London. Together we mapped out a plan for the mega-concert that would launch the campaign and set the ball rolling.

The first 46664 concert was staged in Cape Town on 29 November 2003 and broadcast to over two billion people.

The campaign slogan was simple but telling: 'Awareness and education through entertainment'. Madiba had invited Oprah Winfrey, Beyoncé, Bono, Bob Geldof, Queen, Dave Stewart and Annie Lennox of the Eurythmics, and several African artists, among them Angélique Kidjo, Youssou N'Dour and Yvonne Chaka Chaka. It was a truly earth-shattering event. Geldof, who had championed the famine-starved children of Ethiopia in late 1984 with his song 'Do They Know It's Christmas?' and then organised the Live Aid mega-concert in July 1985, was the first artist on the 46664 stage. He introduced the Cape Town show before launching into Bob Marley's 'Redemption Song' on acoustic guitar.

'The reason that we're here,' said Geldof, 'is 'cause a frail old gentle-man who is one of the few giants of our planet has summoned us here, and you cannot refuse him anything. This is a man whose entire life is characterised by the pursuit of social justice through political action.'

Next up was the indomitable Beyoncé, who performed 'Crazy in Love', followed by her new 4-6-6-6-4 melody. Adding Beyoncé to the line-up had been a major coup, having launched her explosive solo career just five months earlier. As part of the Cape Town experience, we took all the stars to Robben Island. At one point on the ferry Beyoncé was seated just in front of me, where I with sitting with Ahmed Kathrada. Neither had any idea who the other was so I introduced them. I leaned over to Beyoncé: 'I think you should meet this man,' I said. 'His name is Ahmed Kathrada and he was in prison for 26 years with Madiba.' They sat there quietly chatting together for a while. We even had a photo taken. After we had returned to the mainland, Kathy was still a little perplexed: 'Who was that lovely young person I was sitting with?' he asked. He later told me that his grand-nieces and -nephews were shocked that he did not know her or get an autograph.

In the sell-out crowd at the old Green Point Stadium (now the iconic Cape Town Stadium, rebuilt for the soccer World Cup in 2010) sat Madiba, laughing alongside Oprah and Graça Machel, human rights activist, former First Lady of Mozambique and Madiba's wife. As a backdrop to the stage there was a massive, bronzed image of Madiba's face and, later, Mandela himself made his appearance up on stage, dressed in a black shirt with his prison number emblazoned across his chest. At the fundraising dinner the night before the concert, I donated a photograph of Madiba and Muhammad Ali sparring, which was signed by Madiba and all the participating artists. The Irish family band The Corrs bought the picture for $200 000.

'For the 18 years that I was in prison on Robben Island I was supposed to be reduced to that number,' Madiba said. 'Millions infected with HIV/AIDS are in danger of being reduced to mere numbers if we don't act now. They are serving a prison sentence for life.'

In later years we held more concerts, including one on 19 March 2005, hosted at the Fancourt Country Club and Golf Estate in George, that featured Katie Melua, Prime Circle, Annie Lennox, Johnny Clegg, Queen and Paul Rodgers. Will Smith was the host.

The first 46664 events to be staged in Europe took place from 29 April through to 1 May 2005 in Madrid, Spain, and, on 11 June 2005, the 46664 Arctic Concert was held in Tromsø, Norway. I am very proud of the photograph I took of Madiba watching South African iconic group Mafikizolo perform at midnight in Tromsø. A large-format print of this picture adorns the wall of Madiba's post-presidential office at the Nelson Mandela Centre of Memory in Johannesburg. There were more concerts as the awareness drive continued.

Many of my personal interactions with Madiba were less public than such grand staged events. On Madiba's 80th birthday, Kathy, Christo Brand (their B Section prison warder) and I decided to play a trick on him. During his prison years Madiba had been desperate to get his hands on a hair treatment by Pantene – to the extent that Brand had had to get it smuggled in for him. So it was that we decided that, for his birthday, it would be a good idea to source stock of it and present it to him as a birthday gift and as something of a prank. The problem, however, was that the product was no longer available in South Africa, and we had to contact the suppliers in the United States to order it. Then, on the morning of his birthday, the three of us headed over to the house, a giant box and Happy Birthday banner in tow, to meet Madiba and Graça. It brought him great delight, and the five of us roared with laughter at the memory of the old man's vanity back in prison.

Madiba's formal birthday celebrations were held that evening, and it was clear throughout that a romance had blossomed between Madiba and Graça. At some point, Madiba told Kathy that there was to be a special announcement; obviously, Kathy was not at liberty to share the information with me or anyone else that the evening's revelry was to be a double celebration. But we had an idea what it was to be. Graça is an exceptional lady and we saw how she brightened up his life, and the joy Madiba brought to her. We were so happy for them.

Following the announcement that the couple had married, it became something of a long-standing joke of Archbishop Emeritus Desmond Tutu that he had had to chastise Madiba and Graça that, as an unmarried couple, they were setting a bad example to the nation. It is widely reported that Madiba's retort was that this was 'a man in a dress' complaining about his less-than-decorous behaviour.

25

Red Dust

The movie business is a funny business. No matter how much experience you have, you never know for sure how well a project is going to do. Most of the time, you have to make a decision based on very little. Often it's purely the script or the budget and the director and the main actors. That's it.

But you need to make a decision. Are you in or out? Sometimes you just get lucky. In 1991 I brought American actress Kathy Bates to South Africa to star in *Road to Mecca*, a film based on South African playwright Athol Fugard's incredible true story about an elderly woman living in the middle of nowhere, in a small Karoo town in rural South Africa. Fed up with small-minded apartheid ideology, she – along with her black assistant Malgas – escapes into her own world of sculpting in her back yard. In the process, the two create a world of wonder in what is essentially desert. Kathy won the Oscar that year, 1991, for her performance in the 1990 horror, Stephen King's classic, *Misery*. Again, we had a lucky break since Kathy's Hollywood breakthrough came just as she was working on our film.

Another example is the 2004 film version of *Phantom of the Opera*, with Joel Schumacher directing and Gerard Butler as the Phantom. Gerard Butler in a singing role? Our major competitors for the rights to distribute in South Africa were – as always – Ster-Kinekor and Nu Metro, but this time round they didn't even enter a bid. Probably because … Gerard Butler. Singing. We, by contrast, felt that the music was bigger than the cast and so we bought the rights.

Then we struck gold. Not only did Gerard and Joel do a really good job, but, as it happened, theatre legend Pieter Toerien was staging *Phantom of the Opera* in South Africa shortly before the movie was due to come out. Toerien's show was a mega-success locally and the country went *Phantom of the Opera* mad. The timing was entirely coincidental, but it became the boost our movie needed. I suppose that in the game of life you win some and you lose some. With *Phantom*, although it was not the success initially imagined, grossing a modest R4.5 million at the box office, it was nevertheless a tick in the win column.

As much as it's often a matter of hit and miss, movie-making is also incredibly hard work. Always. It's not unusual to spend two, three, sometimes 10 years trying to get a film made. All the public sees is the glitz and glamour at the end of it, the pageantry that is Hollywood, movie stars, cameras and red carpets. It's wonderful, right? Glamorous. Yes, it is all that – but mainly it is a lot of hard work.

In the early 2000s I became intrigued by the story of South Africa's

Truth and Reconciliation Commission, a process that had played out post-apartheid between 1996 and 1999 as a means to provide closure and dispense justice for the victims of apartheid. Hard as it was to have all those festering wounds scratched open and exposed, as a platform it must surely be one of the main reasons for South Africa's relatively peaceful transition from oppression to democracy. It was TRC chairperson Archbishop Emeritus Desmond Tutu who, during a very difficult time in our country, became the country's conscience, the shoulder for a broken nation to rest on. In the process he coined the term 'the Rainbow Nation', but there is no doubt that the load he carried at the time was both heavy and difficult. Much of this was echoed in the award-winning documentary on some of the cases of the TRC, *Long Night's Journey into Day*, which we distributed.

In 2002, the head of BBC Films, David Thompson, brought me a book and, some years after the proceedings were concluded and its findings published, we made a film about the TRC called *Red Dust*. Its story had unnerving echoes of the Boipatong massacre in 1992, when 46 township dwellers were slain by hostel-dwellers at a time when government talks were under way in the run-up to the 1994 general election. *Red Dust* starred Oscar-winning actress Hilary Swank and Chiwetel Ejiofor in the lead roles. We didn't know it at the time, of course, but this was the break that set Tom Hooper up as one of the world's top directors. He went on to win an Oscar for *The King's Speech* and direct the acclaimed film adaptation of the stage musical *Les Misérables*. It also proved a turning point in the fortunes of Chiwetel Ejiofor, who soon garnered worldwide acclaim for his role in *12 Years a Slave*.

In fact, several of our productions with David and the BBC led to meeting young talent who went on to global success. Much the same is true of Paul Greengrass, with whom we had made *The Theory of Flight* with Kenneth Branagh and Helena Bonham Carter in 1997. This, our first collaboration, had come about when the script from a first-time screenwriter landed on my desk. It had been sent to the BBC, and David, having just finished *Cry, the Beloved Country* with me, thought it would be of interest to me. And it was. A powerful script, with a solid story. The female lead, in particular, was a great role, and I was determined to see it through. Top of my list of contenders was Helena and, as she was dating Kenneth Branagh at the time, we managed to score something of a coup by signing both. My next priority was securing a director. And, as it turned out, Paul Greengrass was the man for the job. Paul subsequently went on to direct *The Bourne Supremacy* and others in the Bourne series, as well as *United 93* and the Somali pirate film *Captain Phillips* with Tom Hanks.

Red Dust was an intense suspense drama set during the TRC hearings and explored the decisive struggle to heal the wounds of apartheid atrocities. The film was based on a book by Gillian Slovo, a South African writer who had gone into exile during apartheid. She was the daughter of Joe Slovo, one of the most senior members of the ANC and leader of the South African Communist Party until his death in 1995. We filmed in the Karoo, in the town of Graaff-Reinet. Hilary Swank fell in love – both with the vast expanses of the Karoo, but also with a local stray dog she stumbled across on location. She named the puppy – flea-ridden, starving, ticks in the ears – after the semi-desert in which were shooting, and the two became inseparable. At the end of the shoot, Hilary adopted Karoo and took her home to America, where the actress remains an advocate of dog rescues.

We were just as proud – of Hilary and our movie, which went on to be very well received globally. In June 2004 *Red Dust* closed the inaugural Dubai International Film Festival to a rousing standing ovation.

In attendance at the screening was former chairperson of the TRC, Archbishop Tutu, and various stars and dignitaries.

26

Oscar

'I have this idea …'

It was around June 2003 when I got a call from an excited Darrell Roodt. This energy I'd felt before. When Darrell says, 'I have this idea,' I know better than to disregard it as sometimes he does have a good one. So I nodded, raised an eyebrow, and he proceeded to run his idea by me.

A movie. In isiZulu. About AIDS.

At the time, HIV/AIDS was very topical and very serious in South Africa. Madiba would soon launch his 46664 AIDS-awareness campaign, but the country's president, Thabo Mbeki, was largely in denial about the issue. It was a mess. Even though the message about the seriousness of the disease was well known, people were dying, especially in KwaZulu-Natal. Darrell and I thrashed out the concept, and came up with some ideas. We could tackle it as we'd done *Place of Weeping*, immerse ourselves in a place to such an extent that no matter where you were in the world you would find the same story playing out. We had fought apartheid with our films, so why not step onto the battlefield again, this time against HIV/AIDS.

So Darrell went away, wrote it, and came back to me.

And there it was. *Yesterday*.

The story focuses on a rural woman who contracts AIDS and then follows the community's response to her condition. It is at once chilling, heart-breaking and unforgettable. I was moved beyond words.

'Okay, let me see how we can put this together …'

Easier said than done, however. Many people apparently in the know, including my colleagues and partners at Videovision, shook their heads: Nah, don't do it. Don't make this movie. It's about AIDS and it's in isi-Zulu – nobody will want to see it. It's depressing. Why?

Committing to and deciding whether you want to invest in a project is difficult at the best of times. When making a film, it's almost always the hardest decision to make. Are we in or are we out? Motion pictures can be high risk, and yet they can also be high profit. *Spanglish*, with Adam Sandler, cost Sony over $80 million in 2004 and they lost most of it. *The Blair Witch Project* cost a few hundred thousand dollars to make in 1999 and grossed almost $250 million globally. You really never know. But it helps if you start with a great idea and a strong script. However, even those won't guarantee a great movie. This is why the movie business is so complex and why a company such as Videovision is not listed on any stock exchange – it would simply be too difficult to explain to a board what it would take to make a successful and, hopefully, good film.

Yesterday would not have been made if we had had to explain it to a board. Convince a board of the merits of such a film and do a business plan? Impossible. If you are a listed company, you have a responsibility to shareholders who require fiscally sound business plans – this is not always possible for film projects.

At the end of the day, as a producer, one has creative control. There isn't a right and a wrong. Often it's no more than a question of instinct. With *Yesterday* I just felt it; it had such a powerful message, with such an astonishingly moving storyline. I fell in love with its simplicity, its honesty and its profound strength, especially when it came to the spirit of the women of South Africa. Finally, I said, let's bite the bullet and make it – let's see what happens.

Yesterday was written in English. Darrell then changed it to isiZulu, giving the film an essential truth and authenticity that is hard to capture. Writing the screenplay, Darrell spent two years doing his research in the villages of Zululand. He completely immersed himself in the stories and the people, the villagers for whom this narrative was an everyday reality. In so doing he was able to script a truly authentic screenplay.

After I had read the script, both Darrell and I immediately agreed that our comrade in arms, Leleti Khumalo, should play the lead. After *Sarafina!*, Leleti had gone on to do many wonderful films, among them a role in *Cry, the Beloved Country*. *Yesterday* would be the third big project together for Darrell, Leleti and me. We shot the film with an entirely South African cast over a period of four weeks on location in the beautiful Bergville region of the Drakensberg in KwaZulu-Natal.

When it came to the musical score, Darrell and I had a discussion and it was clear we were both thinking along the very same lines: serendipitous. Having known him from his extraordinary performance in jazz clubs, we immediately agreed on Madala Kunene. Madala, known as the King of the Zulu Guitar, was a local artist. He had no formal qualifications, no training in music theory, but his music was sublime, instantly sweeping the listener away on a tidal wave of heart-rending emotion. Once Madala indicated that he would be happy to take a stab at this opportunity, we ushered him into a studio and showed him the film. There he simply played, nothing pre-rehearsed or researched, simply following the emotions that came to him from the characters and images on screen. And that was it. We had the score for *Yesterday* – beautiful, haunting and emotional.

We premiered at the World AIDS Conference in Bangkok on 14 July 2004 to a resoundingly positive response from academics and others, setting ourselves on the most incredible journey promoting the film and spreading awareness about HIV/AIDS. *Yesterday* was subsequently selected for the prestigious Toronto International Film Festival, which is held annually in September. The most important after Cannes, the festival is also the gateway to the North American film market and hosts over 700 of the world's sales and acquisitions executives.

In 2004, the festival also chose to include *Red Dust* on the programme, so that year we had both films presented at special screenings, marking the first time that South African movies were afforded such high-profile slots within the festival programme.

Writing for the *Chicago Sun-Times*, revered film critic Roger Ebert had the following to say about South Africa's contribution to the festival that year:

> [The] emerging South African film industry ... 10 years after the fall of apartheid and the election of Nelson Mandela as president, is being showcased at this year's Toronto International Film Festival. It's a measure of the maturing South African film scene that there were enough new titles of festival stature to justify the recognition.

A few years ago, there would have been only one or two, such as *Sarafina!* (1992) and *Cry, the Beloved Country* (1995), both made by the pioneers [Anant] Singh and [Darrell] Roodt, both starring Leleti Khumalo.

I have seen four of the films with South Africa connections, and they are among the best films at Toronto this year. Like Australia in the early 1970s, South Africa is finding its voice on the screen ... These films express a new freedom for South African cinema, where every single film no longer has to carry the burden of representing the entire nation to the world.

Following the Toronto festival and the recognition we received there, the magic of show business kicked in. I was in my office in Essenwood Road with our staff all assembled in the screening room on 25 January 2005 when the Academy announced the nominations for the category Best Foreign Language Film: 'Here are the nominees for the Best Foreign Language Film: *Yesterday*, from South Africa ...' The cherry on the top was that ours was the first South African movie to make the shortlist for an Oscar. Madiba sent a message of congratulations, acknowledging what he considered one of our greatest achievements. 'In our fight against HIV/AIDS,' he said, 'we need these kinds of stories which tell us not only about challenges, about difficulties and the tragedies but also, at the same time, those that tell us about hope, and *Yesterday* is about hope. This Oscar nomination highlights *Yesterday* as a South African film and the resulting international exposure will help us in our fight against discrimination and stigma that is attached to the AIDS pandemic.'

While we had always been hopeful, of course, perhaps even quietly optimistic, the nomination went beyond our wildest dreams. Here was a South African film, in an indigenous language, showcasing our country's amazing creative talent in a local story that reverberated across the world.

In this, the 77th Academy Awards, we were up against a phenomenal selection of foreign pictures, among them the German masterpiece *Downfall* and *As It is in Heaven* from Sweden. But the Oscar finally went to the Spanish film *The Sea Inside*. Naturally, we were left a little deflated and disappointed, but happy to have been on this journey. Not only was it genuinely an honour to even be in the race, but the nomination also put our local industry on the map, offering us a global platform. Most moviegoers had never seen a film from South Africa before, let alone one up for an Oscar.

Being associated with the Academy Awards has always been an incredible career and box-office boost; just a nomination creates so many more opportunities. And, indeed, following in the trail we had blazed, the very next year at the 78th annual Academy Awards, for the first time a South African film won an Oscar in the same Foreign Language category. That film was *Tsotsi*, directed by South African Gavin Hood and based on yet another story by legendary playwright Athol Fugard. That Oscar win opened many doors for Gavin and he went on to work on some extraordinary projects from his base in Los Angeles.

It will always be difficult for South African movies successfully to compete with Hollywood on big blockbuster films. There are just too many constraints, making the playing field vastly unbalanced. When you look at scripts, finance and distribution, these are all fundamental parts to making movies and they all require support. In our country – as in others outside America – ongoing government support remains critical if the industry is to grow.

While the state does provide some support, it is quite modest in comparison with competitive countries such as Australia and the UK. In fact, in the UK, creative industries account for the nation's most significant exports. I have never made any secret of the fact that I believe there's no reason why the same should not be true of South Africa. In our current context, it is delinquent of us not to further support our creative arts, particularly in rural areas, where we have such a wealth of talent: from choral singers and potters to weavers and any number of budding entrepreneurs, all of whom could thrive in the absence of middlemen and rise to become income generators not only for themselves but for the nation.

We in South African film have two particular advantages: firstly, small, quality films not dependent on big budgets can be done to a world-class standard in South Africa; and secondly, we are mostly English speaking, which makes it easier to compete for projects on the global market where English is still the main language in the entertainment world.

So, while we may have missed out on an Oscar, we were able to build on not only a growing international awareness of South African film and what we were able to produce, but also draw further accolades for a movie into which we had poured our hearts.

Following its Oscar nomination, in 2006 *Yesterday* was acknowledged with not only a Peabody Award but also an Emmy nomination, the television equivalent of the Oscars, in the category Outstanding Made for Television Movie. The ceremony took place at the Shrine Auditorium in Los Angeles in August, and I attended the event along with Sanjeev and Sudhir, fellow producer Helena Spring, Darrell Roodt and lead star Leleti Khumalo.

Yesterday was up against *Flight 93*, *The Flight That Fought Back*, *Mrs. Harris* and *The Girl in the Café*, the last walking away with final honours. The nomination was not only a tremendously proud moment for all of us and a huge boost for the South African film industry in the wake of *Tsotsi*'s Oscar win, but also an opportunity to spread the message that lies at the very heart of the film's narrative. When Darrell wrote it, he did so with a clear motive; when I decided to produce it, I did so knowing full well what an impact this could have on people ravaged by the disease, both at home and abroad.

Yesterday was endorsed by the Nelson Mandela Foundation, while M-Net and the National Film and Video Foundation were partners. We were able to drive awareness of the disease, and the film became an important weapon in the fight against tackling the stigma and scourge of HIV/AIDS; it became a way to speak to those affected and the communities around them, especially those in denial. No matter where we screened it, or in which language, audiences were moved, allowing us to open a door to education.

We put together an entire HIV/AIDS programme. We went to mines – considered by many to be hotspots – and held screenings for the workers. We experienced the impact of these events. It was both exhilarating and soul-destroying. On the one hand you'd see dimmed eyes light up in recognition, at understanding that fault cannot be assigned when it comes to this disease, and that it is not a death warrant. On the other hand, you could see where denial had taken hold, and the stigma of infection was overriding all else. Some simply stood up and walked out. But for those who did accept their responsibility and admit they needed help, we had counsellors on site who could assist immediately.

This was an exercise in humility, a steadfast belief in striving for the greater good. Fifteen years later, we still screen the film on World AIDS Day and the film continues to be in demand for academic and medical groups.

27

Going for gold

'My greatest regret in life,' Madiba once joked, 'is that I never became the heavyweight boxing champion of the world.'

South Africa's greatest statesman was a keen and competent boxer before his life took a different turn. This was to prove to be something of a blessing to us when, in 2002, Will Smith conducted a promotional tour for his biopic *Ali*, the story of the great Muhammad Ali, which earned him an Oscar nomination for Best Actor. *Ali* had cost about $100 million to make and we secured the South African rights. It was an expensive investment but we wanted it a great deal, especially to work with Will and Michael Mann. Will's performance in this movie was heralded by the champ himself. The film was shot in South Africa and Mozambique where Madiba and Graça met Will, Jamie Foxx and the director, Michael Mann, as well as other members of the production. At the time I was also in discussion with Will about playing Madiba in *Mandela: Long Walk to Freedom* and he was intrigued and challenged by the opportunity.

Getting Will to South Africa was going to be tricky. The costs just to meet the standard stipulations in the star's contract were way out of our ballpark. One of these, for example, required that in the event of him doing promo tours for his films he got a private jet to fly him around. And the contract with director Michael Mann – an exceptional director whose work on *Manhunter*, *The Last of the Mohicans*, *Heat* and *The Insider* I particularly admired – said that whatever Will got Mann also got.

Fortunately, we were able to convince Will to come to South Africa by arranging – among other things – for him to see Nelson Mandela again and visit Robben Island. Most importantly, the premiere was a thank you to the many donors to the Nelson Mandela Foundation. Additionally, in a live auction that Will took over and conducted himself, we raised R1.5 million from a few items that had been donated to the Foundation.

We arranged the African premiere of *Ali* at Monte Casino on Sunday, 3 March 2002, which Madiba attended and, together with Will on one stage, they paid tribute to Muhammad Ali, one of the greatest sportsmen the world had ever seen. Madiba stated how Ali had been his personal hero. The previous evening, Madiba and Will joined us at a boxing match at Carnival City, close to Johannesburg. This wasn't any old match, though. It was the diminutive South African legend Jacob 'Baby Jake' Matlala's final fight – against Colombian Juan Herrera, 10 years his junior. I remember watching and dreading that Baby Jake might lose, especially that evening, with such special fans in attendance. Luckily, he didn't.

During his stay, I took Will and his son Trey to Robben Island, where Ahmed Kathrada led them on a personal tour. Subsequently, Will had the local media in a tizz when he stated how much he loved South Africa and that he was, in fact, looking to buy a house in Cape Town. While he was in the country, we also produced the documentary *Will Smith in Africa*.

Despite all the promotional work done by Will and others on *Ali*, it didn't fare all that well on the local circuit. Once again, as we had already learned, a star doesn't always secure success, not even a mega-star like Will Smith.

Muhammad Ali, like Madiba, has had 'the greatest of all time' appended to his name and he continues to be an inspiration. In 1960, as Cassius Clay, he won gold at the Olympic Games, which were held that year in Rome. At the 1996 Games in Atlanta, it was Ali, then suffering from Parkinson's Disease, who bravely lit the cauldron with the Olympic torch. I was a huge admirer of Ali and avidly watched his fights in a movie theatre and was fortunate to get to know him through our mutual friend, photographer Howard Bingham.

I attended my first Olympic Games in Los Angeles in 1984. My relationship with sport has never really been about sport itself. It is more my association with film and telling the stories of remarkable athletes and heroes, and acknowledging sport's ability to draw excellence, whether from an individual athlete or a team, pushing themselves to be the best in the world. And, as Thomas Bach, president of the International Olympic Committee (IOC) once reminded me, it was after all Nelson Mandela who said: 'Sport has the power to change the world.' Sam Ramsamy had introduced me to Thomas when he visited South Africa on sports development projects.

The 1992 Olympic Games in Barcelona saw South Africa competing after decades of isolation. I was not there personally, but avidly watched the events on television. This was an extra special occasion as Madiba attended the games prior to him becoming president two years later, but he was given head-of-state status. It was amazing to see Madiba in the Stand of Honour, while Sam proudly led Team South Africa at the Opening Ceremony.

I attended the 2000 Olympic Games in Sydney and went early to join Madiba at a pre-Games anti-racism human rights conference. Madiba was very upset that Australian Prime Minister John Howard did not accept the conclusion of the 1997 'Bringing Them Home' report that genocide had been practised against the indigenous people of Australia, the Aboriginals.

Having attended Sydney and seeing how the Olympic movement worked and witnessing for myself sporting excellence at its best being celebrated, I came to appreciate this world event in a different way. Until then I'd perceived the Olympics largely as a television sports event. Now I realised that it was actually a quite exceptional initiative by Baron Pierre de Coubertin, who had the vision to reintroduce the modern Games after a 1 500-year hiatus. In ancient times, an Olympic Truce was announced before and during the Olympic festivals in warring regions of Greece and beyond to enable all of the athletes to come together to achieve sporting excellence. In recent years under the leadership of Thomas Bach, the Olympic movement has been able to embrace many areas of social development, gender and ethnic diversity and peace, as we saw with the combined North and South Korean teams in the PyeongChang Winter Games 2018. We've also seen the formation of the refugee team to compete in the Olympics since 2016 in Rio, an amazing initiative supported by the United Nations.

Combining my great love for sport and film, I started with the Zola Budd story and *Go for Gold* in 1984, but then expanded to a series of films on South African Olympians, including double gold-winning swimmer Penny Heyns, 800-metre silver-winning runner Hezekiél Sepeng and marathon gold-winner Josia Thugwane. Today, my involvement in the world of sport is one way to distract myself from my day job. As much as I love making movies, I don't want to do it all the time; I also love meeting interesting people from other walks of life, including great athletes, and use my knowledge to further the celebration and legacy of their excellence. I explored this quest for excellence in *The Long Run*. The film was set against the backdrop of the Comrades Marathon, which is considered to be one of the world's most gruelling ultramarathons. Armin Mueller-Stahl portrays a demanding, seemingly over the hill coach who, in his heyday, had aspirations of winning the Comrades, but remained unsuccessful. He discovers a promising, spirited young runner, played by South African actress Nthati Moshesh, and sets her on a training programme to run the famous marathon.

Apart from the sport-themed international films we distributed, such as *Power of the Game*, among the other stories we told that echoed my own passion for both sport and storytelling was *More than Just a Game*, a docudrama focusing on organised football among prisoners on Robben Island that led to the formation of the Makana Football Club, run under FIFA rules. Another was the documentary *Once in a Lifetime*, which captures the excitement and jubilation of the 2010 FIFA World Cup, the first World Cup to be hosted on African soil.

In 1995, the City of Cape Town decided to bid to host the Olympic Games in 2004, and I offered my support. We worked closely with the Bid Committee and the National Olympic Committee of South Africa (NOCSA) on the bid. I produced the film and audiovisual presentation to be shown to the IOC at its 1997 session in Switzerland, as well as all the material that was shown on South African television in the lead-up to the 2000 Games in Sydney. This included infomercials featuring South African medallists who had done South Africa proud since our re-entry into international sport.

My first visit to the IOC in Lausanne, Switzerland, was when I joined Madiba and then NOCSA president Sam Ramsamy there in 1997 as part of a delegation presenting Cape Town's bid to host the 2004 Olympics. Despite the best efforts of all involved, ultimately our bid failed and the 2004 Olympics was hosted by Athens, Greece. On 15 May 2004, I returned to FIFA House in Zürich, Switzerland, again with Madiba for the announcement of the host nation for the 2010 Soccer World Cup when it was revealed that the tournament would be hosted in South Africa. It was so exciting to be there in person.

In 2015 I was appointed to the Olympic Channel Commission by IOC president Thomas Bach. One year later, in August 2016 I was elected as an individual member to the IOC.

The membership of the IOC is a diverse and global community of not more than 115 members in total. Thomas Bach appointed me in 2018 to chair the Communications Commission of the IOC. I became a member of the Digital and Technology Commission, and in 2019 I was appointed to chair the jury of the Olympic Golden Rings Awards – a television award for the best TV programme of the Olympic Games coverage.

I am also honoured to be a member of the IOC's Coordination Commission for the Olympic Games Los Angeles 2028. The Games is not only the biggest sporting event in the world, but it also showcases the power of sport to contribute to building a better world. It is exciting for me to share and learn in this dynamic organisation and to forge new friendships.

In August 2021 I was once again privileged to be at the 2020 Olympic Games, held in Tokyo a year after schedule as a result of the COVID-19 pandemic. At the opening ceremony at the National Stadium, I was proud to see our Rainbow Nation being represented by an amazing integrated and diverse group of athletes.

It was an honour, especially, to be part of the celebration of our country's Olympic successes, being led by women in the medal count. Tatjana Schoenmaker, who set a new world record in the 200 metres breaststroke, became the first South African woman to win an Olympic gold medal in 25 years; she also won silver for the 100 metres breaststroke. I was pleased to meet her and present her with her silver medal – I told her I was going to be back with a gold medal for her in the 200 metres. It was such a proud and emotional moment for us both. And then there was Bianca Buitendag, who won a silver medal for surfing. How wonderful to celebrate these women who brought honour to our country, as well as all the women of South Africa, just ahead of Women's Day, which is celebrated on 9 August in South Africa. Women are, and have always been, the anchors of our society.

28

Pirates on the Cape Flats

M aking movies is always risky, and distribution even more so. Hit and miss, that's the name of the game. What doesn't change is that it takes dedication, perseverance and extraordinary commitment to the dream, the bigger picture. For me, that commitment meant putting our money where our mouths were. It saw us taking a huge new step: building our own film studio.

Diversification was always part of our palette and I had wanted to build film studios in South Africa for some time. My initial plan was to build in Durban and grow our industry there, so I approached the city and, remarkably, all political parties voted in favour of my proposal. This was to build a film studio complex with entertainment and tourism elements in Durban, much like Universal City in Los Angeles.

With the idea first mooted in 2002, it was in December of the following year that we bought a piece of land on the beachfront in Durban, an old army base known as Natal Command, with the plan to build a huge film studio there. Not only would it be the first in Africa but it would serve as a pivotal hub for all the creative arts in a single location. I wanted to make Durban the motion picture capital of South Africa. We had been in the business for 30 years and were making significant progress, but we felt a studio would mean a quantum leap forward, especially for Durban, my home town, which was still largely being left behind by the film industry. By 2004 the South African film industry was worth R7.7 billion per year and 70 to 80 per cent of that was going to Cape Town and Johannesburg; only a minuscule amount of work was coming to Durban.

Filmmaking has always had a massive multiplier effect on local businesses, be it car rentals, legal services, tourism, you name it. *The Lord of the Rings*, for example, had a significant impact on New Zealand, as did *Game of Thrones* on countries such as Ireland and Croatia, where a lot of the work was filmed. Soon after we'd signed, however, someone came along and tried to extort a piece of that pie for personal gain, bringing an action against the city and provincial government for not following due process. The matter would drag on for 10 years, a decade of legal tussle that went all the way through to the Constitutional Court, which finally ruled in our favour.

Meanwhile, the film tax rebate had been reintroduced by national government so I knew the timing was right. I couldn't stand the delay of the protracted process and my Durban plan was at a frustrating standstill. I began to look elsewhere. The Western Cape government had recently put out a request for proposals for film studios. It came to our attention that a group in Cape Town was also looking at setting up a studio. There was an option for a 200-hectare piece of land that was perfectly suited, close to both the airport and the city, so we took a major interest. Even though I had funded the project for two years, I invited well-known businessman Marcel Golding, head of e.tv, the commercial free-to-air television channel, to become our partner.

The result was a film studio in Cape Town called Dreamworld, known today as Cape Town Film Studios.

The initial proposal incorporated a number of components, which together represented a commitment in excess of R400 million. The development progressed in phases, Phase One being three sound stages, various production and digital facilities and outdoor back-lot areas. In addition, we offered much more than sound stages – we were committed to developing a complete 'one-stop-shop' production facility that would help local producers clinch deals and result in the studio becoming home to South African production. At the time, the Western Cape was attracting up to 25 per cent of all national film activity and 58 per cent of all commercials filmed in the country. It was estimated that the film industry in the Cape was worth R2 billion a year in direct and indirect economic spin-offs, and that the industry in the province had the potential to grow to R7.7 billion per annum, with the entire South African industry reaching a value of over R10 billion per annum.

Things had clearly changed since the 1980s, when Johannesburg had been the hub for all things film and television. Cape Town had not even been on the radar back then. Now it was the centre.

Naturally, we remained committed to Durban too, confident that there was no conflict of interest between Videovision Entertainment's involvement in both the Durban and Cape Town studios. I likened it to the Australia-based Fox Studios in Sydney, Melbourne and the Gold Coast, or Toronto and Vancouver. Having studio facilities in two cities increases the economies of scale, giving the industry a competitive edge previously lacking. It also gives filmmakers access to a variety of locations without the inconvenience of irritations such as long-distance travelling. The studios would provide much-needed film infrastructure and change the face of the industry in Cape Town and South Africa.

In February 2004 we finally won the bid to build the studios when the provincial government of the Western Cape and the City of Cape Town appointed Dreamworld as the developer. With the bidding process concluded, the development of the studios could now commence. We built the studios at a cost of R 500 million, competing against studios in Europe and America previously built for hundreds of millions of dollars. Cape Town Film Studios is world class and in much demand. Today, it is majority owned by two South African companies – Videovision and eMedia – with the Western Cape government owning a further 10 per cent. Having employed some 88 000 individuals in the first eight years of operation, it has since led to a number of expansions and its growth continues.

Cape Town Film Studios began hosting productions in August 2010 when work began on *Dredd*, the 3D action film based on the comic book character Judge Dredd, even before the building was fully completed.

If you happened to be driving along the N2 highway away from Cape Town in 2019 you might have been startled by a strange sight looming up on your left: giant eighteenth-century pirate ships dotted on the horizon, seemingly stranded on dry land, landlocked, and surrounded by fields and mountains in the distance. These ships were the gigantic sets of the popular global television series *Black Sails*, which emerged as the number-one hit on Starz, the US pay-TV channel. The vessels were built on the lot at Cape Town Film Studios. On the same lot were replicas of sandy Caribbean beaches, old towns of the American West, a set built for a Stephen King feature, and Nelson Mandela's prison cell.

The studio has become the most successful in the developing world, attracting big names from Hollywood to South Africa. We're very proud of what has been accomplished and what is still being done there. Some of the major projects shot on the set were Stephen King's *The Dark Tower*, the Ryan Reynolds/Denzel Washington spy thriller *Safe House*, *Tomb Raider 3*, *Mad Max: Fury Road*, Ridley Scott's *Raised by Wolves*, *Doctor Who*, *Inside Man 2*, *Around the World in 80 Days* and *Black Beauty*, among others. Another major project shot at the studios was, of course, *Mandela: Long Walk to Freedom*.

Over the years, we have created thousands of jobs at the studios and almost all the crews are locally hired. Since these different worlds all have to be built from scratch, the studios spawned something of a manufacturing industry of its own. Many people from the neighbouring townships work on the projects the studio takes on. They have been trained as painters, carpenters, artisans, costume-makers, metalworkers and landscapers. The sets on the back lot are recycled and reused. The Robben Island prison for *Mandela: Long Walk to Freedom*, for instance, was converted into a hospital for *Eye in the Sky*, the British drone-themed thriller.

The studio is a catalyst for production, especially international production, in South Africa. Branching out into the studio world has also created an entirely new way for the country to venture further into the global film industry. In essence, it helps us keep our finger on the pulse of the industry worldwide, and with many big international studios coming to Cape Town to use our sound stages, it's become a really good way of keeping in touch and building relationships.

The studio doesn't make a lot of money but it is a very important asset. It brings with it many other benefits, including outside influences that have positively impacted on the studios and the economy. Today the South African government helps drive the industry, most significantly by way of its programme offering 20 per cent tax rebates, which is crucial in attracting film projects from Hollywood and elsewhere. Of course, South Africa's weak currency, which has been drastically devalued in the past few years, offers another advantage for filmmaking for export purposes. In the interim, the impact on industry growth has been significant.

The amount of business that has gone through the studio to date has surpassed all our expectations, serving as a catalyst to growing the international production film industry, especially in the Western Cape. The facility is fully booked for years in advance; it often has to turn work away. In 2019 alone a total of R2.38 billion was spent in the Cape in film and media production, creating the equivalent of 2 265 full-time jobs. This was largely due to the presence of Cape Town Film Studios in the region.

Dreamworld had thus become our dream world, perhaps one of the pinnacles of a lifelong passion that started in a 16mm film rental shop in Durban, and found expression in so many different ways over the years. It is a very personal achievement for me. Over time, the business has expanded to become involved in almost every aspect of the film industry, from studios to production, distribution and exhibition. The development of Cape Town Film Studios is something I look back on with a deep sense of pride. This initiative is led by Sudhir Pragjee on behalf of Videovision and Khalik Sheriff for eMedia.

In 2014, my friend Robert Lantos talked to me about getting involved in a series of films with him as executive producer. It was an opportunity to work with him again and it also made business sense. The films produced included the thriller *Remember*, starring Oscar winners Christopher Plummer and Martin Landau; the sci-fi drama *Clara* with Patrick J. Adams; *Through Black Spruce*, which focused on the story of a woman from the indigenous Canadian Indian tribe the Cree; and the Tim Roth and Clive Owen starrer, *The Song of Names*, adapted from the novel by Norman Lebrecht, which I executive produced.

In 2015, we shot the film *Shepherds and Butchers* in Cape Town, directed by Oliver Schmitz and starring Steve Coogan. This courtroom drama is set in South Africa in the late 1980s and is about a successful lawyer who faces his biggest test when he agrees to defend a prison guard who has killed seven men. The crux of the story is a compelling charge against the death penalty. This is a human rights issue and a controversial topic, but we made a statement against capital punishment with the film. In December of that year, I travelled to Miami with Brian Cox to meet the Bee Gees' Barry Gibb to discuss composing a song for the film. The result was the song 'Angels', composed by Barry Gibb and written by him, Stephen Gibb and Ashley Gibb. The song was performed by internationally renowned musician Vusi Mahlasela who is known as 'The Voice' of South Africa. We premiered *Shepherds and Butchers* at the Berlin Film Festival in February 2016 where the film won the Panorama Audience Award for Fiction Films.

Beyond movies, we retained our interest in media and radio broadcasting. In 2012, we ventured back into radio, acquiring a licence for a new Cape Town radio station, Cape Town Radio (Pty) Ltd, of which I was joint chairperson along with businessman Dr Ernest Messina, following a 30-month application process.

We were very excited about the prospect of setting up a brand-new station in Cape Town, one aimed at meeting the needs of all listeners in the region. The format we were offering was fresh and unique – and we believed it would add to the diversity of radio content in the city. The new radio station was Smile FM and its task was to focus on good news, music and talk, a format established following extensive research. Smile FM, broadcast at 90.4FM, became a massive success. By 2019 it boasted more than 200 000 listeners.

We had come a long way since the Free State.

29

Life, death and fatherhood

Losing your father at a young age sharpens your thinking on the complex issues like life and death. One of the things that struck me, even as a young boy, was that when someone dies there is a natural, almost welcome, period of grieving, of mourning. There's a death and everyone's there – for a couple of days, weeks or even months. But then it's over and everyone gets on with their lives. All people, even mourners, need to refocus on their own world. This is fine. It's natural. It's to be expected. But suddenly you're alone. Very alone. And lonely. And you learn to accept that too, and live with it.

For me, the one in the middle of it at such a young age, that was the most difficult part to comprehend and assimilate, that I, too, would have to simply get on with my life. There were just three of us when my dad died: Mummy, Sanjeev and me. I was just 13, Sanjeev only 10. We were blessed by the love and support we had from some of our extended family and friends – which continues even today – but still I had to make that journey and come to the realisation that life goes on, even for a 13-year-old. Even for a grieving son, mother or brother.

The thing about death is that it also brings clarity about what really matters. About what is really important, what the priorities ought to be. Along the way, as we set off to work day after day after day, labour away at our desks, raise families, maintain homes, make ends meet, we can sometimes forget what life is really all about. And it's none of those things.

This is the theme that shines through in *Citizen Kane*, and the whole notion of Rosebud: *At the end of your life's journey, what is most important in life? What supersedes all else?* Of course, we can never have everything – and nor should we. We can't have our bread buttered on both sides.

When you live in the world of entertainment, as I do, maintaining a fully private life, away from prying eyes and the attention of the public, is not easy. It comes with the territory. I have to be both mindful and respectful of what I have. I have to find a balance, so I make accommodations.

Over time, as with Kane's sought-after sleigh, I have come to place more value on that which is most required of me and which I have least of: time. I try to apportion that most valuable, invisible commodity so that I do not waste it on things that, in the end, do not matter. Time spent with friends and family and building relationships, not for the business or professional value they may promise, but for their intrinsic value and the intangible riches and enrichment they bring. When I think about the sheer joy and peace I feel when I am surrounded by people I love and who love me back, I realise these are the investments that ultimately pay off. Simplicity, honesty, humility, respect – these are values to live by, the exact pillars that were instilled in us as children. And to be able to spend time with those who inspire, teach or share their wisdoms is a gift to cherish. With some of my films and the stories that guided me, I tried to create a legacy of timelessness.

Often, when I'm at my desk in my office at home, I look up and see the piece of art, my pewter construction that I'd made when I was 11 years old. It brings back a rush of memories of when my dad was still around. I remember how proud we both were when I completed it. For almost everyone else it is meaningless and worthless. For me it's an irreplaceable memory, my own Rosebud, and I am grateful to have found it.

Becoming a father in my 40s opened an entirely new chapter of my life, an unexplored parenting adventure and a level of happiness that I had not known existed. From the moment our children were born I started taking photos of them and making videos, desperate to capture each moment. Perhaps subliminally I was making up for the time and memories of my own father that I lost out on and the film and photos that were lost over the years. I never edited the footage of my kids and when they were in their teens I handed them a hard drive of the footage, capturing their lives and our lives together, hundreds of hours. And because I was determined to ensure that they didn't lose what I had lost, I made sure that there were multiple copies and hard drives.

Vanashree and I have always made our children an integral part of our lives; our friends are their friends and our lives and travels are theirs too. We have seen the world together and it has been both deep and satisfying to share experiences with our children and see life through their eyes. We have tried through it all to be role models and to give unreservedly, without expecting anything in return. With the many demands that the movie industry makes on those who operate within it come many challenges and it can be difficult to maintain a balance when raising a family. But, with time, I have found it easier, and more fulfilling than I could imagine. We spend as much time with our children as possible and when I am away the understanding is clear: if they need me, I will be there as soon as humanly possible. In the meantime, technology allows us to speak to or see each other daily.

Being an older father, the kids like to joke about my age, making wisecracks about my grey hair (or my lack of hair!), the spread of fine lines across my forehead, the creases around my eyes. The joys of ageing. But perhaps the kids have also kept me young, and made our lives infinitely more interesting and challenging at the same time.

Our daughter Gyana was born on 6 February 2000, a very exciting time to have her come into the world at the dawn of a new century. She was not only our introduction to parenthood, but also a long-awaited addition to the Singh clan. Her birth was greeted with enormous joy, from the families as well as those in our immediate circle and beyond. Vanashree received a call of congratulations at the hospital from Madiba – he was always so thoughtful. Gyana's first trip overseas was when she was seven months old, to the Sydney Olympics.

Gyana chose to study abroad, first in Switzerland, at Franklin University, and more recently at the University of Southern California, in Los Angeles. She is majoring in Business Administration with an emphasis on Finance at the Marshall Business School, with internships at Investec, Ernest & Young, Woolworths and recently in Wealth Management at Glenmede in New York. Today she is a headstrong and brilliant young woman. I like to push her buttons and she, in turn, likes to describe me as a 'drama king'. She believes it's a good thing that I'm behind the camera rather than in front of it.

We have shared many special friendships, including that with Graça and Madiba – although as a toddler Gyana had a funny way of showing it. Madiba was always the ultimate grandfather figure, everyone's Tata. He loved children and they all loved him, but for the first two years of Gyana's life she would start crying whenever he held her. Madiba wanted her to love him, but she would have none of it. Luckily, he was amused. Then one day, when she was about two years old, we spent the day with him at his home in Qunu in the Eastern Cape and slowly they became friends. The screaming finally stopped.

Our son Kiyan arrived on 4 August 2002, an arrival that kept us on our toes until the very last moment. Twelve hours before, Vanashree and I had attended the Gold Cup horse race in Durban and then had dinner at home, finishing at about two in the morning. Just a few hours later, we found ourselves heading off to the hospital, with our son determined to make his appearance as soon as he could. The excitement of a day at the races had done the trick. He probably felt he was missing out.

Since that auspicious start, Kiyan has smashed me in the face – as young boys do – and nearly broke my nose when he accidentally hit me with an iPad. I fled the room groaning, clutching my nose. When I returned with a bloodied napkin held to my face he was mortified. He frantically scrambled around trying to find the number for our doctor until I relented – and showed him that the blood was ketchup.

Dropping Kiyan off at boarding school in the KwaZulu-Natal Midlands was one of the hardest things Vanashree and I have ever had to do. Leaving our young 13-year-old son in the care of others was a wrench but it turned out to be the best decision – a decision Kiyan himself had made – and he flourished in the environment. He developed into a well-rounded young man. Kiyan and I share a love for sports and we've attended soccer and rugby World Cups as well as the Olympic

Games together, watching, cheering, sharing great moments of victory and defeat. It's moments like those that remain etched in our memory, moments I never got to share with my own father, which make them all the more precious to me.

Kiyan represented KwaZulu-Natal in table tennis and he has also excelled in music. He was appointed deputy lead chorister for the Michaelhouse choir and was an enthusiastic member of the school's marimba band and an avid pianist. He composes his own scores and music and has now enrolled at New York University's Steinhardt School to study music/business.

Gyana and Kiyan used to say occasionally that I travelled too much, which made me feel really bad. It's not a good feeling when you worry that your children might be feeling abandoned, or distanced from you. It was especially difficult when Vanashree and I travelled together; the children were young and didn't fully understand why I was away so often. It got better in later years as they grew older. When I was travelling on my own I took comfort in knowing that Vanashree was always there. We also had support from both their grandmothers whenever she and I travelled together. One year we passed on attending the Oscars because Kiyan made a comment about me leaving *again*. When I look back on it now I realise that it wasn't a difficult decision to make at all.

I've always been a keen swimmer. I once won a trophy for swimming at high school. I'm no gold medallist, but I get by. Swimming runs in the family and dates back to those early decades when we were growing up in our corrugated iron houses on the banks of the Umgeni River in Springfield, where Uncle BB established the Durban Indian Surf Lifesaving Club. My family were all big swimmers back then. Sanjeev and I were also taught to swim in the Umgeni, tossed in by our uncles as youngsters and helped until we could manage to keep our heads above the water. I never imagined that all that time I spent in the water would one day save my life.

The sea was a significant part of our lives. In 2011 we spent the Easter weekend at our beach house in Tongaat, north of Durban. Over the years the family enjoyed many weekends there. I bought the place in 1993 when it was the only area where people of colour could own beach property and it's remained our getaway, one of our very special places as a family. As usual, the weather was sublime and the kids, Vanashree and I spent a fair amount of time on the beach that weekend. At around lunchtime on Easter Monday, we were strolling along the beach in front of Beach Bums, the local beach pub. Kiyan was fishing. Gyana and some friends were with him and Vanashree and I joined them a short while later.

We were walking together along the beach when I noticed that there was somebody in the sea who was either fooling around or experiencing difficulties. The man was waving his hand furiously. As can be expected, the weather being what it was, the beach was busy and stunned onlookers were beginning to point at him.

Unfortunately, as it is a fairly remote beach, there were no lifesavers on duty. I shouted out to ask whether anyone knew if he could swim. No one seemed to know. I had to assume he was in trouble – there was clearly no time to hesitate – so I dashed into the water and swam out to him, grabbing a boogie board abandoned on the sand on the way. It took probably no more than three minutes, four at most. The young man was about 80 metres from the beach, the treacherous ocean churning like a washing machine, waves thumping down in increased frequency as the tide turned. I quickly realised that he was not fooling around – this guy was in real trouble. Over the years, I had come to know Tongaat beach well; the times of the tides and the currents, the habits of the ocean and the games it plays. I had learned these things the hard way – I still have many scars to prove it. I was thus all too aware of the power of the ocean, but with the board at hand I felt fairly confident that I could reach him and bring us both back safely to shore.

By the time I finally reached him, he had begun to sink, his arms flailing as he struggled desperately to stay afloat. Eventually, I managed to haul him up to the surface and keep his head free of the water. Then I tried to drag him onto the board, calling to him to help as the waves crashed around us, and the currents pulled in different directions. By this time, I think, he had already swallowed too much water. He seemed in a coma-like state, unresponsive, despite his eyes being wide open, the whites of his eyes stark against the dark ocean. I held on tight, my wrists and knuckles aching as I tried to manoeuvre him up alongside me, all the time water leaking from his mouth and nostrils.

It was a sad and terrifying sight. In fact, the entire situation was becoming frightening. By now I, too, was struggling to stay above water. I knew that if I didn't do something quickly, we'd both be in serious trouble. But the ocean, angry and stubborn, refused to play along. Struggling in the churning waves, trying simultaneously to manage the drowning man (he was very heavy), the board and myself, no sooner had I succeeded in hoisting him up onto the board than he slipped back off, his apparently lifeless body sinking beneath the waves again.

I was rapidly realising that I wasn't going to make it out on my own. Already floundering and now desperate to keep my own head above water, I knew I was going to have difficulty getting back to the shore. If I was going to get back to safety, I was going to need help, even with the board. I knew that much. So it was with huge relief that, in the chaos and raging turbulence, I noticed a lone figure making his way towards me. Fortunately, a good Samaritan, a friend of a friend, who was at the beach, got wind that we were in the ocean and in trouble. He was an excellent swimmer and immediately headed out to us, finally managing to help us along by guiding us through the currents.

My experience with the ocean, especially in Tongaat, came into play that day; the rule was – as it always is – do not panic. You may be swept out to sea, but you will be pulled back eventually. The key is to stay calm and keep your head above water. It's no use trying to swim against the currents. You stand no chance against that kind of resistance.

In those long moments – I had no idea how long we had been out there – a stirring set of circumstances and emotions came to the fore: bravery, tragedy, sadness, ambivalence and loss. All of them playing out on the beach in front of my children.

We tried to locate the drowned man's family but, tragically, while there were some who claimed to know him, no one was able to tell us who he was. The next day, or perhaps it was the day after, word got out and his mother and family came to Tongaat. Understandably, they were distraught, especially given that he was only 26 years old and, as it turned out, the only breadwinner of the family.

The body was not found immediately; generally, it can take about four or five days for a body to wash up. It was a day or two later that Mr Ngcobo's body washed up at La Mercy, about 10 kilometres down the coast from Tongaat, bringing his family some closure.

I've often thought about that day, whether I could have saved him had I reacted a minute or two earlier, if I had acted faster or made an even greater effort. But I have come to the conclusion that the answer is probably not. In the young man's panic, to all of us standing on the beach that day it looked as though he was just fooling around. He hadn't been. But I had done the best I could. And, had it not been for that one person who cared enough to swim in after us, I may well have suffered the same fate.

The experience, terrifying as it was, highlighted the fragility of life for me and my family. Gyana and Kiyan had witnessed it all playing out in front of them and, although initially troubled by the experience, it taught them a lot too. A hard life lesson to learn, but a lesson none the less.

One golden rule, a universal truth and a basic life lesson we can all learn from, is to never, ever underestimate the power of that which is greater than you. For me personally, this tragic episode brought on some hard introspection and raised some interesting questions, among the many issues of self-doubt: was it irresponsible of me to have just dived in and swum out by myself like that? What about the others around me? What about my children and my family? What about my life? What if I had drowned too? Or was it the responsible thing to do?

Looking back on it now, I think my actions may simply have been instinctive, a lesson taught by my father, a moral imperative: if it seems right, if it's the right thing to do, then do it – irrespective of the consequences, or how others may respond. You have a duty to do what is right. I've thought long and hard about this and, at the end of it all, I have made peace with the fact that, yes, if it had to happen again, I'd do exactly the same. Without hesitation.

I have tried to live my life with relative simplicity, especially given my profession, with value-based decisions. I have tried to help where I'm able to and to give back to communities and organisations. These values have served me well.

30

Long Walk to Freedom

Nelson Mandela began writing his autobiography in 1974. He did not have the luxury of sitting back and taking stock, of reflecting on a life well lived, surrounded by friends and family. He was prisoner number 46664 and he wrote in secret in a cell on Robben Island. By day he broke rocks in the island's notorious limestone quarry and at night he secretly wrote.

'The manuscript Madiba wrote on Robben Island was not as dense as *Long Walk to Freedom*, which was much more developed and researched, but it was used as the basis for his book,' said Ahmed Kathrada, who was one of the seven political prisoners sentenced alongside Mandela in the Rivonia Trial. 'We had been in prison for 10 years. We thought that the time had come for us to make a political statement and that getting Madiba to write his autobiography would be the way. This was kept a secret even from ANC people, except those of us who were directly involved. The process was that he would write whatever he could and give it to me for my comments, which I would write in the margin, and then pass on to Walter Sisulu for his comments. Then, with our comments, Madiba would write the final version and send it to Mac [Maharaj] and Laloo [Chiba] who – in minuscule writing – reduced 600 pages to 50 double-sided pages.'

Because Maharaj was to be released first after serving a 12-year sentence, the job of smuggling the manuscript off the island fell to him. Once he reached his destination, the plan was to send Kathy a postcard confirming that it had been safely delivered and that they could destroy the original, which they had compressed into small plastic containers and buried in the prison garden.

'We thought we were safe and didn't destroy it, but when the prison authorities decided to build a wall through the garden they came across the original document,' said Kathy. The original document was presumably destroyed because it has never been recovered. Fortunately, they make a handwritten duplicate.

In late 1994, I was shooting *Cry, the Beloved Country* and when I visited Madiba to show him some stills, he gave me an exclusive preview of his autobiography. I was now more convinced that it should be an epic motion picture. He requested that I assist in staging the launch of his book and create a video for the event at the Saxon Hotel, which I was proud to do.

The full and official autobiography, *Long Walk to Freedom*, was published shortly after Mandela was inaugurated as the first president of a democratic South Africa. The book became an instant global bestseller.

The film rights, much coveted across the world, were aggressively sought after by studios and film producers. But, Mandela jokingly assured South Africans in a quip quoted in *The Star* newspaper in December 1994, he had no interest in playing himself. 'I'm no actor,' he said with a laugh. It might not be widely known but he'd actually already appeared on the silver screen – in a cameo role in Spike Lee's *Malcolm* X, which was released in 1992. He told me that he had been annoyed to have had only one scene in a classroom with no dialogue; it was a 10-second scene that required six takes.

Thanks to Fatima Meer, I had been communicating with Madiba while he was in prison and, of course, we had had that first eventful meeting in her home shortly after his release. By the time the book came out he had seen *Sarafina!* in 1992 and in 1995 he attended the premiere of *Cry, the Beloved Country*. Previously, our talks had centred around Fatima's book about his life, *Higher than Hope*, but with the publishing of the official autobiography, it made more sense, and would add more gravitas, to base the movie on *Long Walk to Freedom*. 'Anant,' Madiba said to me, 'you are the person I want to make a movie about my life.' And he was true to his word. On acquiring the rights, I was both humbled and honoured when Mandela entrusted his story to me. Giving me his public endorsement, he declared at the time: 'Anant Singh is a producer I respect very much and, when we were considering various offers, I personally opted for him. He is a man of tremendous ability.'

As thrilling as it was for me, it was also a daunting and terrifying task. Madiba had chosen me and with that honour and trust came huge responsibility. I promised him I would make the film to the best of my ability but told him it might take a while. I felt it was essential that we tell his story in the best possible way and at a time I believed would be right. I had a responsibility not only to Madiba but to the nation, to portray his legacy in a motion picture that would be a fitting tribute. There would be no compromise.

It certainly did take a while, and quite a lot longer than I had imagined – 25 years in total. The formal contract granting me the rights to *Long Walk* was signed on 30 March 1996, so by the time production commenced in May 2012, I had been involved in the development of this movie for 16 years and, prior to that, eight years developing Fatima's *Higher than Hope*. You could say this was my own Long Walk. There were many sceptics who were convinced it would never happen, but Madiba himself remained steadfast in his support and never pressured me. He was nothing less than gracious throughout the process, always insisting, 'I trust you to do the best you can – don't bother me.'

As custodian of the film rights, it was my responsibility to convey the morality, power and strength of Madiba's life story and to make the film a reality. This was a feat not without its challenges when it comes to one of the most remarkable leaders the world has ever seen. For one, by helping to document Madiba's legacy, we also had to acknowledge the roles played by his comrades and colleagues who had endured so much fighting for our liberation under atrocious conditions, never wavering from their integrity, values, humanity and sense of morality. In this we were guided and inspired by Madiba's own words: 'Acknowledge our problems and challenges and then proceed to tackle them with determination and in a spirit of optimism.'

The first announcement regarding *Long Walk to Freedom* was made at the 1998 Cannes Film Festival. With a budget of $40 million to $50 million, the plan was to release the movie in 1999 to coincide with Mandela stepping down in October, at the end of his term as president of South Africa. The original director attached to the project was Shekhar Kapur; other early directors I had discussions with were Anthony Minghella,

Darrell Roodt and Tom Hooper. This process was long, with many missteps along the way in the never-ending puzzle of alignment needed for success, just to get it done.

In fact, our journey had only just begun. Several elements needed to come together before cameras could roll. As with all film productions, there had to be a screenplay on which all agreed, as well as a director, suitable actors and financiers willing to put up the money. For every movie, it is no mean feat to line them all up at the same time. The usual order is that the screenplay attracts a director, both attract actors and the entire package, all of these together, attracts financiers. This project was thus subject to all the usual filmmaking delays: stars who showed interest for a while, but never quite committed; directors who came on board, demanded new drafts, and then slipped away. With *Mandela: Long Walk to Freedom*, we saw at least five directors and actors come and go over time. There were multiple challenges, including problems with availability, uncertainty over the screenplay and competing projects.

When I started on *Mandela: Long Walk to Freedom* Morgan Freeman was the preferred choice to portray Mandela. In the years that followed I facilitated maybe five meetings between Madiba and Morgan. Morgan went on to play Madiba in Clint Eastwood's film *Invictus*. He had been well prepared for the role thanks to all the work we had already done, and had had the benefit of what I'd set up – but there were no hard feelings. Other actors in contention for the role were Denzel Washington, Djimon Hounsou, Will Smith, Chiwetel Ejiofor, John Kani and a host of other South Africans.

When we finally had our team, it was many years since we had started the process and, ironically, it marked a reunion of sorts for me.

The screenwriter was William 'Bill' Nicholson, the director was Justin Chadwick and the producer was David Thompson. We had all worked together before – David and I on *Sarafina!*, *Red Dust*, *Bravo Two Zero* and many other films. Bill had penned the *Sarafina!* screenplay (other screen credits of his included *Shadowlands*, *Gladiator* and *Les Misérables*). I had approached David in 1996 to suggest he write the screenplay for *Long Walk*. From the start, we agreed the new project was too important to get wrong. This was a story for the world. David and I had been the producers of Justin's multiple-award-winning *The First Grader*, which had been shot in Kenya and starred Naomie Harris. Justin also directed *The Other Boleyn Girl*.

We were confident that we had assembled a formidable team. Bill had been with me all along, persevering with the script since 1997. 'For a writer,' said Bill, in an on-set interview, 'the movie business is strange in many ways, none more so than the intense relationships that are formed over the stressful months of making a film. I've learned over the years that these friendships do not outlast the project. When the day comes that I'm no longer required, I become invisible. The phone stops ringing … Anant is the great exception. I've worked with him since I was brought in to write *Sarafina!* We lived through the decades-long gestation of *Mandela: Long Walk to Freedom* together. In all those years, when a phone call or an email came through from Anant, my heart lifted. It's hard to explain how unusual this is; I think it's to do with his positive energy …'

In the making of *Long Walk*, we were fortunate to have Ahmed Kathrada on board as an adviser. Kathy visited us during pre-production at the Cape Town Film Studios on the day we started shooting. He reminded me that that day had been one of the darkest in their lives: it was on that day, in 1971, that the prisoners on Robben Island had been pulled out of their cells at midnight, made to strip down and humiliated and threatened. The scene is in the film. Kathy was one of our greatest supporters and stood by me all those 16 years of waiting and planning and preparing. He was always accessible and generous with his advice, and without him we would never have reached the end.

Justin had just finished directing *The First Grader* when I spoke to him about the Mandela project. His remarks right upfront were that he – along with so many of us – was concerned about the challenges of fitting so much life into just two hours. On 9 September 2011, when *The First Grader* premiered in Johannesburg, I invited Kathy and Barbara and several other activists who had been close to Madiba to the premiere in order to introduce them all to Justin. Hugh Masekela was also there, as was Zenani Mandela. The connection was immediate, and it wasn't long before Justin was signed up and ready for the challenge.

Production designer Johnny Breedt – who worked with Justin on *The First Grader* – was already on board. I had pulled him into the project from the very start, some 15 years earlier, and he had lived the process with me. Along the way he had done extensive research, accumulating thousands of images, books and historical references, even generating sketches of proposed sets.

Between them, Bill and Justin agreed that *Long Walk to Freedom* would be a love story at its heart, but also a film about belief, of never giving up, of being both selfless and strong. Those themes would be the very core of the movie.

Our co-operation was not, however, without incident. On our first research trip together, we visited Robben Island, Pollsmoor Prison and then Victor Verster Prison. On the Pollsmoor trip, the car carrying Kathy, Bill and me spun out of control and careened into a rock. Kathy was unscathed and I suffered a few broken ribs and some whiplash, but Bill was hurt, breaking his nose and dislocating his shoulder. To add insult to his injuries, this meant that Bill was unable to meet Mandela as planned – and, in fact, sadly he never did. Bill stuck with me on the project all those years, in the end writing no fewer than 33 drafts of the screenplay before we reached the final version. With each draft we believed we were only months away from starting production, but it didn't turn out that way.

It was such a difficult and complex task to condense Mandela's life story, with all its intricacies – politics, the struggle, his personal life – into a two-hour film. An average screenplay is only about 120 pages long. It was insane to think we could incorporate it all, so it was always a case of what to keep in and what to leave out, where to start and where to end. We could have easily made a 10-hour miniseries and still not covered half the story.

I had to keep motivating Bill, assuring him that, despite the passing years, the movie was going to be made. Letting it go was never an option. I had promised Madiba, and I was going to keep that promise, but not before I had all the elements in place first and I felt it was ready. Every screenplay draft over the years was important. It was vital that the film portrayed Madiba's journey in a way that would be a fitting tribute to his extraordinary life. We were also keenly aware that the onus was on us to make a film that would satisfy South African audiences, who have always felt a degree of proprietorship over the life of Mandela.

Madiba himself never wavered in his support of the project, his only instruction – which he stated repeatedly – being that he did not want to be treated like a saint. We were to showcase him, warts and all, as a flesh and blood human being, with a beating heart, with all the faults: 'I have weaknesses and strengths,' he said. 'I am like every man; I have made mistakes. Show me for what I am.'

With that said, he made it clear right from the start that he had no wish to vet the screenplay, or to have any influence over the resulting film. Still, the problems facing us were immense. Too much material for one film, too complex a political story, too many key characters. Add to that the iconic nature of the man himself and no one was in any doubt that we had our work cut out for us.

Bill's job was to conjure up scenes with Mandela, put words into his mouth, track his political evolution, imagine his love affairs, and at times rewrite his often lengthy speeches. Two speeches in the film are in Mandela's own words, though heavily edited; the others are dramatised versions of statements he made and beliefs he held.

We had decided – along with Justin – that Mandela and Winnie's love story would be at the heart of the film, their tragedy a metaphor for the struggle for freedom. Through their parallel lives, we could represent the two paths to liberation: Mandela isolated on Robben Island, learning to forgive, and Winnie, tortured beyond endurance, learning to hate. It was only once we had established that love story as the basis of our narrative that the project finally shifted into focus.

Throughout the planning process, one pivotal question remained: who to star in the lead roles of Nelson and Winnie Mandela? Eventually, casting director Shaheen Baig suggested Idris Elba for the Mandela role. Justin and I had seen and loved *The Wire*, a television series in which Idris had starred, and I arranged for Justin to meet him in Canada, where he was shooting the film *Pacific Rim*. I joined on the phone and privately spoke to him at the end of the discussions and we both concluded that our intentions were the same. Idris, a brave, instinctive actor, came on board shortly afterwards. What clinched it for me was when Idris told me he had grown up with his father, a unionist at Ford in the UK, talking about Mandela and what he stood for.

It had taken many years to find the right actor to play the complex and daunting role of Nelson Mandela and Idris was our man. He was the best actor for the role – he had the talent, the passion, the African roots and the growing star power. This was validated when the Londoner won the Golden Globe for Best Actor for his role in *Luther* in 2012. Beyond Idris's obvious talent and the skill he brings to his roles, it was also comforting to note that his personality, gravitas and charisma were very similar to that of Madiba at age 40.

In the casting of Idris, there was – not surprisingly – some criticism that we had not gone with a South African actor. This was an issue we had all predicted; it's hard, after all, to justify not championing the cause of Africa, and its struggle for equality, especially considering the legacy of the very man we were portraying. But, as I have always insisted, the role must come first, and everything else second. Actors earn a living portraying other people – it's what they do. And we believed we had found someone who would do the role justice. Actors are selected for certain roles because they are right for the character and have all the attributes required to play the role. I had no doubt that Idris was the only actor available at the time able to deliver the incredibly diverse and complex demands of the role.

Of course, with the casting of the male lead consuming all our time, we also had to find the perfect foil to Mandela. The character of Winnie Mandela was a formidable and complex one, and playing her would be demanding for any actor. There were so many facets to her. We needed a versatile actress who would be able to assimilate the character and *become* Winnie. My instinct told me that Naomie Harris could pull it off effortlessly and she was thus the only person to whom I offered the role. I had produced *The First Grader*, in which she starred, three years before we embarked on *Long Walk to Freedom*, and I approached her when we were seated next to each other at dinner during the world premiere in Toronto in 2010 – before we cast Idris. Initially, as she told me much later, she'd thought it was just talk, the way producers try to win over stars with the promise of career-making opportunities, promises that never materialise. But I knew that Naomie had the magic we needed, and I had no intention of making false promises.

I had known Winnie since the mid-1980s, having been introduced to her by our mutual friend, Fatima Meer. I had great admiration for her and had learned a lot about her personal struggle directly from Fatima. In cinematic terms, Winnie's story is, in fact, far more interesting than Madiba's, specifically during the period he was in prison. Naturally this influenced the journey we travelled. Over the years I had several discussions with Winnie about her portrayal, as we went through multiple drafts of the screenplay. I promised her I would handle it honestly and try to show some of the issues she had to deal with. Although she assured me that she trusted me, I'm sure she must have been quietly apprehensive.

As part of Naomie's research, I arranged that she meet Winnie for dinner.

'What do you want people to take away from this film?' Naomie asked her. 'How do you want people to see you?'

Winnie's response was unreserved. 'I don't want you to think in those terms,' she said. 'I want you to be totally free to interpret my life as you think fit.'

That, said Naomie, was very liberating.

Naomie has more costume changes than any other character in the film – 45 in total – from soft, feminine dresses to Black Panther-style leather jackets. In real life Winnie 'used her clothing almost as a weapon of defiance' was how costume designer Diana Cilliers saw it. 'She dressed in the colours of the ANC when the ANC was banned. She dressed in

African traditional clothing as a statement of solidarity with the prisoners – she very much used clothing as part of her cause.'

When the movie was eventually complete, Winnie and I watched it together, alone, just the two of us. As the credits began to roll, she turned to me, took me in her arms and gave me a kiss. 'Thank you,' she said. 'Don't change anything.' And her admiration for Naomie knew no bounds. 'This girl,' she said, 'this girl has to have some African blood in her.' I was happy that I did not have to do battle with this giant who took on the apartheid regime's most feared torturer, Major Theunis Jacobus Swanepoel.

Casting could not end with the characters of Nelson and Winnie, of course. In the end there were over 110 speaking roles in *Long Walk to Freedom*. Other key roles to be cast were Walter Sisulu, Govan Mbeki, Ahmed Kathrada, Oliver Tambo and Chief Albert Luthuli, just to name a few. All of these roles were played by South African actors, the cream of the country's acting talent. Tony Kgoroge – who also starred in *The First Grader* – stepped into the shoes of Walter Sisulu, Riaad Moosa inhabited the role of Ahmed Kathrada, and Govan Mbeki was played by Fana Mokoena. They all came together, unified, a tight crew. Whenever I met Sisulu, Kathrada and Madiba together in real life, I experienced a spirit and camaraderie; I felt that this same spirit existed among the three actors who played them in the film. That was important, because that is the energy that ultimately reveals itself on screen. In addition to the Robben Island prisoners, we had a remarkable cast playing other characters central to Mandela's life. The younger Mandela (age 16 to 23) was portrayed by Atandwa Kani, son of acclaimed actor John Kani, and Siza Pini played Mandela as a child.

Finally, with the all-important task of casting behind us, we moved into production. As it turned out, *Long Walk* became by far the biggest undertaking by an art department on any film shoot in South Africa. Mandela's story covers more than seven decades, and the film features him from his childhood in a rural village to his life as a young lawyer, his imprisonment and then election as president. While we were compelled to cast two young actors as the child and teenage Mandela, Idris – at the age of 40 – was able to play the bulk of Mandela's life, spanning his years from 23 through to 76.

Having just one actor carrying a film is always a risk, but Idris pulled it off with aplomb. When he came on to do the scene in which he addresses the nation on television – the first time he was playing the old Madiba – the impact was extraordinary; he walked into the room and *ping!* Done on the first take. He had clinched the spirit of it, echoing in perfect pitch Madiba's voice, his mannerisms and movement. I don't know quite how he found these, but something unexplainable seemed to take over. He just sailed into the part and made it his own from day one. This is an incredibly difficult thing to do for any actor, let alone one who is playing a man whose every move, every gesture, every sound clip was followed by millions all over the world. When Idris finished that scene, you could hear a pin drop, before spontaneous applause broke out. He had done his homework. Watching the footage of that first scene we knew we had something truly special. In addition to Madiba's characteristic accent – which could so easily have evolved into pure caricature, comedy even – Idris had the presence, the charm and the dignity, all the qualities we know of Madiba. He had nailed it.

Casting Idris allowed us the advantage of having a single actor playing Madiba virtually throughout, but that also meant that one of the most important aspects was ageing him so that he resembled the Madiba everyone knew. For the job, I interviewed the top four make-up artists in the world, including Rick Baker and Greg Cannon. Mark Coulier was someone I liked; he was based in the UK, but worked across the globe and was also the most affordable. The devil, of course, is in the detail and when you make compromises, they show. In order to get everything just right, we left no stone unturned – the wig for the older Madiba alone cost $12 000. Mark did a phenomenal job and Idris was also very patient, having to get up at 4 am to be in make-up for up to five hours before starting his day on set. Prosthetic pieces for the make-up would be trashed at the end of the day, so each had to be made up and ready for the next day. Mark went on to win the 2012 Oscar for Best Achievement in Makeup for his work with Meryl Streep on *The Iron Lady*, and won again in 2015 for his work on *The Grand Budapest Hotel*. We had some exceptional South Africans in the makeup department: hair and makeup designer Meg Tanner was one, and Clinton Smith as prosthetics supervisor was another.

Every effort was taken to make this movie as authentic as possible, whether it was the way Mandela folded his handkerchief, his wardrobe or 1940s' Johannesburg. We looked at the hats people wore, the cars they drove. Every detail mattered and production designer Johnny Breedt brought his best work to this production. The movie had 283 scenes and 200 sets, each with a minimum of two or three set pieces. There were 12 000 extras, 141 cast members – including seven leads – and a timeline spanning more than five decades. We used 350 action vehicles, from cars dating back to the early 1920s, spanning all the decades leading up to the 1990s. By the time we were ready to film a scene we would have had up to 80 individuals who had been working in preparation since 3.30 am.

The entire shoot took us 81 days to complete. Shooting on Robben Island proved to be a logistical nightmare. Because it is a national museum with thousands of tourists visiting every day, we were only permitted to film in certain areas at specific times. Because of this we decided to shoot only the areas that were of good screen value, such as wide establishing shots and some exteriors. Under Johnny's guidance, we then set about the mammoth task of recreating Robben Island at the Cape Town studios. The construction team consisted of over 25 local freelance film crew, more than 100 local labourers and over 20 contractors recreating the entire B Section where prisoners had been held. Recreating the cells in that way allowed for some cheating in order to make filming easier. Some of the cells were built bigger than the originals, something we would never have been able to achieve on Robben Island but a necessary evil to enable the crew to be able to move from one corridor to the next and shoot 360 degrees on the set. Because the island is now a heritage site and doesn't look the same as it did decades ago, we also needed to recreate the limestone quarry; this we did at a nearby sand quarry.

In the interests of authenticity, Idris – ever the professional and determined to bring truth to his portrayal – insisted on spending a night in Madiba's cell on Robben Island. It was a noble gesture, but one that left him more than a little rattled as he had to be locked in for the night. In the stillness of a dark, essentially abandoned island and alone in the dark, damp cells with such a turbulent and tragic history, the experience terrified him. Over the course of the night, during which he was left alone on the island, he heard noises – footsteps, a distinct presence he could not account for. To top it all, his cellphone refused to connect to the network.

The Cape Town Film Studios, which had opened just 14 months earlier, turned out to be a giant turn of fortune in our favour. South Africa has always boasted superb locations, great technical and creative resources, but studios were the missing link. Having this resource for *Long Walk* made an enormous difference to the end product.

We engaged professional construction companies that used industrial equipment to excavate an area of some 15 000 square metres on the back lot in order to clear a space for the sets. A road construction company laid tar-surfaced streets for Orlando township with 20 period homes for exterior shots. Critically, shooting at the studios also enabled the production to maintain control over riot scenes featuring army tanks and petrol bombs in township streets. These were central to the story, but re-enacting such violence and carting military hardware into public spaces were not viable options. Apart from the physical danger to civilians and related risks, these events remain disturbing for township residents and we couldn't in good conscience subject local communities to that kind of trauma. Johnny managed to track down the only working Casspir left in Johannesburg (the rest of these much-feared armoured vehicles used by the police during the apartheid era were sold to the Congo), and this is the one used in the riot scenes in which young boys hurl rocks – for our purposes, painted stones – at the vehicle.

Authenticity was key. Every single element of every single frame had to be not only believable but true to the original context. Our art department housed more than 300 books and 5 000 photographs that served as aids and reference tools for actors, the director, the costume department and researchers throughout the movie. The behind-the-scenes making of the movie, *Beyond Long Walk*, was itself four hours long.

The surrounds of Mandela's home village of Qunu had changed so drastically since the 1920s that the team had to identify a new location, one as breath-taking as the Transkei decades before. The answer was the magnificent Drakensberg in KwaZulu-Natal.

Kliptown, situated in an older part of Soweto, served as a base to shoot the many scenes set in Soweto, and the team built 30 sets there. The script also called for scenes to be shot in Sophiatown, a multicultural suburb in Johannesburg that no longer existed. Given its proximity to central Johannesburg, the apartheid government had razed the shantytown to the ground decades before, dispossessing this unique community of their homes. This brutal act of destruction was vital to the narrative and an integral element of the film. Justin wanted to approach the demolition scene in a substantial and gritty way so Johnny managed to locate a ruin at an old mine. His team set about adding to what remained of the mine, transforming it into a semi-ruined Sophiatown. But the team was taking no short cuts, so we built it all for real, with bricks and cement. The result was that when the bulldozers slammed into those structures, their collapse was authentic – all dust and crumbling walls and flying debris, a chilling reminder of what had transpired in reality in the demolishing of Sophiatown.

The beautiful musical score for *Long Walk* was composed by Alex Heffes (with whom we had worked on *The First Grader*), with additional music contributions by Caiphus Semenya and recorded at the iconic Abbey Road Studios in England with a 50-piece orchestra. As production was drawing to a close, we set about securing someone to write a song. Our quest ended with one of the greatest rock groups in the world, Irish band U2, and a new song, 'Ordinary Love', written by frontman Bono and performed by the band. Having gotten to know each other through the 46664 concerts, Bono was an activist and had long been a close friend of Madiba's, so when thoughts turned to music, for me he was the perfect choice. 'If there's anyone to do it,' I said, 'then it should be Bono.'

I travelled to New York to screen the film for Bono and The Edge, and the band members who were in town at the time. Bono was blown away, spellbound, and immediately agreed to be involved. He wrote two songs, both of which I loved, but Bono wasn't convinced – he is his own harshest critic – and he dumped them. 'Okay,' I said, eyes wide, 'it's your call.' I really wasn't sure how this would pan out. Before he went off to start again, Bono wanted to know more about the Mandela/Winnie love story. He was on holiday (and his manager had made it very clear that Bono never works during his vacation), but so determined was he to get this right, to capture exactly the mood of that love story, that he was prepared to devote as much time to the project as it needed. He wanted to understand the nature of their relationship.

'Okay, this is how it worked,' I told him. 'They would write letters to each other, but those letters were restricted. I can send you copies, if you'd like?'

'Please do,' Bono said. And I did.

So it was that 'Ordinary Love' was composed, emanating from the poignant and heart-wrenching letters of love between Winnie and Nelson Mandela, both in solitary confinement.

At the end of the day, our film was not a complete historical record and in two hours of film there was no way that it could be. But what it does, I think, is important. It tries to pass on to the next generation the extraordinary achievement of a man who dared to forgive his enemies. It tries to make people who have never heard of apartheid and care nothing for South Africa care about this man – Nelson Mandela – and what he came to stand for. I suppose it is, in its own way, the creation of a legend. But at the core of that legend is truth.

31

A crowning moment, a devastating blow

*L*ong *Walk to Freedom* took just over two years from the start of production to finish. When production ended, I showed portions of it to Winnie, Zindzi and Zenani and they agreed that we should take the opportunity to show Madiba snippets of the film and stills from some of the scenes. In December 2012 I made my way to Mandela's home in Qunu in the Eastern Cape. He was quite frail by then, part of the house serving as a private hospital, but he still had that sparkle in his eye.

'Is that me?' he smiled, looking at a picture from a scene in which Idris Elba is wearing one of his famous Madiba shirts, sporting grey hair and an aged face. 'He looks just like me,' he said. I nodded and explained to him the prosthetics involved in ageing Idris. He laughed. Before I left I held his index finger and showed him how to flip through the iPad and left the device with him so that he could sift through all the footage, including nostalgic memories of his friends and family, many of whom he joyfully recognised instantly.

The world premiere was at the Toronto International Film Festival on 7 September 2013. We received a 10-minute standing ovation from the audience at the end. The film was due for release in South Africa on 28 November and its London premiere was scheduled for 5 December.

Going into the project, I had raised the funds almost entirely in South Africa, to ensure that we would not have to answer to a studio or some other outside force determined to impose stars or structure conditions or angles to the story. This meant that when the day finally came, we could forge ahead and not have to wait any longer for all the pieces to fall into place. The plan worked well, but then I had to get the film distributed in the US. We were in post-production, and I figured that I would show the movie first, and only make a deal once we were done. But then I started to second-guess myself. *What if people don't like it when it's finished?*

So I put together 40 minutes of scenes from the film and, in February 2013, flew to London, New York and Los Angeles to screen the cut for various companies. Harvey Weinstein had called me in October the previous year to ask whether he could see the film and I had put him off. All of my instincts were telling me No, no, no. My first stop was London, and although Harvey lives in New York, he happened to be in London at the time and he knew I was in town. He was keen to see the film, he said, and this time I relented. We set up a screening. Thirty minutes into the screening, he said, 'I want this.' By the time it was over he was ready to sign on the dotted line.

Harvey being Harvey, the negotiations took no more than 24 hours to be finalised, contracts and leveraging done, and by 3 am the next morning we'd closed the deal. He had agreed to virtually all the creative aspects. As uncertain as I was about the arrangement – the terms could actually have been better – I also knew that I had an obligation to investors. The thing was, when Harvey was committed and passionate, he and his company were a formidable force. On the flip side of that, when he got a bee in his bonnet and things didn't work out, he was extremely hard to work with. With *Mandela: Long Walk to Freedom* the experience turned out to be the latter.

As we went through the process with Harvey, we also undertook several 'test screenings' with recruited audiences, the first of which was on 12 February 2013 in Reading in the UK. This was followed by screening in New Rochelle, New York, on 24 April and another in Los Angeles. The screening that stood out most for me was the one in Birmingham, Alabama. It was quite a task getting there so I convinced Harvey to pay for a private plane to make that 90-minute journey, together with the Weinstein Company's distribution executives Erik Lomis and Nicole Quenqua. It was fascinating to be in Birmingham, the home of the US liberation movement, and to experience a middle-class screening where the integrated audience really loved the film. On the way back, we stopped at one of the many barbeque rib places and took the ribs with us on the plane as our dinner, giving us quite a Southern experience.

Despite the exceptionally successful screening in Toronto, Harvey decided he wanted to make changes. He had a nickname in the industry: 'Harvey Scissorhands'. He liked being in charge and liked to have a say in the final cut, despite the convention that what the director says goes. Usually the director, the producer and the investor jointly decide on what's in and what's out. The unanticipated issue we now encountered was that Harvey appeared to have the director in his pocket – he had signed Justin to go direct to his next project, *Tulip Fever*. I was thus outnumbered and outvoted. Harvey felt that the process that he and Justin were embarking upon would make the film better and generate better reviews. He also arranged for the projector to fail about 40 minutes into the press screening in Toronto – which he finally admitted doing to me some time later – which was very unfortunate, as I had no doubt that it would have screened very well.

The result was that the final product wasn't entirely what I had wanted. For instance, one cut Harvey insisted on was a popular scene depicting the 1988 Wembley concert celebrating Madiba's 70th birthday and demanding his release from prison. Harvey wanted it gone. I couldn't fathom his reasoning, but there were three people making the final decisions – me, Harvey and Justin – and Justin backed Harvey. We remained resolute, allowing him only to change the US version, for which he had distribution rights.

When releasing a big film, it is essential that we have test screenings with different audiences to determine how the film will be received in the market. Sometimes, we use the feedback we receive to edit the film to enhance its audience potential. We undertook extensive test screenings with *Long Walk* in diverse communities in London, New York, Los Angeles and, of course, Birmingham, Albama.

The other key markets for *Long Walk* were the UK and Europe. David Thompson, our UK partner, had discussed the film with Cameron McCracken, head of Pathé Films in London. Pathé was very keen to get involved and became associated with the film very early on while we were shooting. This led to a very successful partnership with Pathé as the distributor in the UK and France; they also handled the international sales. Pathé and its founders, Sophie and Jerome Seydoux, hosted the French premiere in partnership with UNESCO on 2 December 2013, which I was delighted to attend.

After all the bruising battles, all the elements had finally fallen into place and we had still made a film we could all be proud of, one we could take to global audiences to enable them to experience South African history through Madiba's eyes. Harvey only held the rights for North America, so we released our original version in every other market.

The first time I had any association with Barack and Michelle Obama was in 2008, shortly before his first-term election when director Danny Schechter and I had made a feature documentary on his campaign trail. With Obama being the first black US presidential candidate, and with South Africa having emerged from the apartheid era, I felt that Obama's story was worth telling, certainly worth recording. It turned out to be very well received, particularly after his ascendancy to the Oval Office. A short while thereafter I was privileged to attend a lunch with him in New York. Following the successful premiere of *Mandela: Long Walk to Freedom* in Johannesburg on 3 November, we were invited to the White House for a special screening with the US president on 7 November.

It was an exceptional honour to have a screening hosted by President Obama at the White House, another first for a South African film, especially since it held a special global significance. Both Madiba and President Obama were statesmen responsible for major paradigm shifts in their respective countries and enjoyed special places in the hearts of their people. Vanashree and I were invited, along with Mandela's daughters, Zindzi and Zenani, lead actors Idris Elba and Naomie Harris and director Justin Chadwick. Also in attendance were Harvey and his fashion-designer wife Georgina Chapman, as well as Ted Sarandos of Netflix and former US ambassador to South Africa Donald Gips.

Speaking at the screening, Obama explained how Madiba had influenced not only him but many people all over the world. He said he was proud to host the screening at the White House and to have Mandela family members as well as the filmmakers present.

Within a month of opening, it was clear that *Long Walk* was going to do well at the box office. It had seen a record opening day on 28 November when it opened at cinemas in South Africa and had emerged from the weekend as the highest-grossing film in the country, raking in R4.4 million. In the process, it had outperformed Leon Schuster's latest offering, *Schuks! Your Country Needs You*, which earned R3.6 million that weekend. (*Long Walk to Freedom* also outgrossed the opening-weekend box office of some of the biggest studio films of the year, including *The Hunger Games: Catching Fire*, *World War Z* and *The Hangover Part III*.)

I had visited a few cinemas over the opening weekend and, having experienced the emotional response to the film first-hand, I was really pleased with the reaction, from critics and audiences. For me, as a filmmaker, all boded well for the movie and for us. When it opened in the United States on 29 November, the day after the South African opening, it earned an average of $25 076 per screen, the highest over that weekend.

A week later, on 5 December 2013, the film premiered in London. It was a Royal Charity event and the Duke and Duchess of Cambridge were in attendance. Vanashree and I were there, as were Zenani and Zindzi Mandela.

Tragically, as the audience was watching Madiba's life play out on the big screen in London that evening, in Johannesburg the final curtain on his life was coming down. So surreal, so bittersweet.

About halfway through the movie I was alerted to Madiba's passing. I left my seat immediately and made my way to the foyer of the cinema. I had an important decision to make. My instinct was to end the screening right there, but Zenani and Zindzi both asked me to allow it to continue – 'as Madiba would have wanted,' they said – and to wait until the film had finished before making any announcement. And so, with a heavy heart, I took the decision to wait.

A row behind the Duke and Duchess of Cambridge sat some of those who had helped me make the movie. Gyana and Kiyan were there too, neither of them aware of the passing of Madiba, despite the quiet commotion. Prince William was handed a phone by one of his aides to read a message. Then Kate was seen to be quietly crying. Some thought her tears were because of the emotional scene unfolding on the screen.

When the film ended, I made my way to the stage, but the audience was on its feet, applauding, giving the film a resounding ovation. I stood there, alongside a distraught Idris Elba, who whispered to me that it felt like he had lost his father, waiting for the applause to die down. No doubt they thought we had taken to the spotlight to receive our accolades and I had to quieten them, struggling to get my emotions under control. As a hush fell over the Odeon, I broke the sad news.

That moment was the most challenging of my life, not only because this was Nelson Mandela, who had meant so much to his country and the world, but because it was also a deeply personal loss. My friend, mentor and bright light, for me and millions of others, was no more. I would never see or talk to Madiba again.

For a moment there was a stunned silence. Some in the audience started to weep, others were visibly saddened, haunted by the emotions of what they had just witnessed on screen come to this, the passing of Nelson Mandela. For the first time, a member of the royal family departed from royal protocol when Prince William, before he left the theatre with the distraught Duchess of Cambridge by his side, took a moment to acknowledge Madiba and his legacy. 'I just want to say it's obviously extreme and tragic news. We were just reminded of what an extraordinary and inspiring man Nelson Mandela was and my thoughts and prayers are with him and his family right now,' he said.

On hearing the news, Vanashree had returned to the hotel to support and be with Zindzi and Zenani, to comfort them and be there for the two sisters who had just lost their father. After arranging for Gyana and Kiyan to be taken care of by friends, I joined them there and began to make arrangements to have us all flown back to South Africa. The after-party was cancelled and mourners gathered where they could, paying their own respects to the man whose life they had been celebrating just hours before.

That night back at the Mandarin Oriental Hotel, we stayed up until the small hours making emergency plans to get back home, Vanashree and I shuttled between our room, to be there for our children who were then 13 and 11, and those of Zindzi and Zenani. We took some comfort that we were all together and able to support each other. The next morning, before we left to return to South Africa, I headed to South Africa House, the scene of much protest action in some of the darkest years of apartheid. Now it was a place of mourning, with thousands of individuals gravitating there to pay their respects to the late statesman, laying flowers and cards and kneeling in prayer, saluting a giant.

The world became a much smaller, poorer and sadder place the day Nelson Rolihlahla Mandela died. The guiding light, freedom fighter, and first president of the new South Africa had brought peace and freedom to a country that had been ravaged and pillaged for centuries, and had shown the world what true forgiveness and love meant. His broad smile, incisive intelligence, humility and vast vision welcomed all South Africans and their friends around the world to help build a land that belonged to all who live in it. His work and very existence gave us faith in the potential of human beings, and our capacity to forge a more just future together.

We all returned home together and went directly to Madiba's house in Johannesburg to pay our respects to Graça and to Winnie.

I had played but a bit part in his life – one I was indeed most privileged to play. He had played a major part in mine. Nelson Mandela was a great man and South Africans will forever be indebted to him for the role he played in unifying the country. It was, however, inevitable that his day would come. It is now up to the rest of us, not only South Africans, but the global village, to strive to continue the unfinished work to which he dedicated his life – the creation of a society forged in reconciliation and partnership, and rooted in justice. A world of equality and peace and unity and justice.

This is what I continue to dedicate my life to.

Although it was clear that he had been ailing for some time, the death of Mandela still came as a terrible blow. We had decided on the movie's release date some seven months before, so the London premiere coinciding with such a significant and tragic event left us rattled. It came as a huge shock to us – as it did for the public at large.

The entire period immediately after Mandela's death was surreal. His spirit was everywhere. Once again, for a few fleeting moments, Madiba magic engulfed the world with an outpouring of global support and admiration for the man. We all followed the show of love, the expressions of profound sadness, that seemed to come from every corner of the globe, from kings and queens, presidents and clergymen and clergy-women, and from ordinary everyday people who identified with his story.

Suddenly the viewings of *Long Walk to Freedom* took on another dimension – as a mark of respect, we had pulled the film from theatres in South Africa on 6 December, returning it the following day – and watching it now was an even more emotional experience. A deep one. I sat in on a few public viewings and was overwhelmed by the public's reaction. Everyone who ventured into those cinemas to see this film left with a profound sense of loss and a far deeper understanding – we like to think – of the man and his story. That made all the hard work worth it.

Our initial plan for *Mandela: Long Walk to Freedom* in America was a limited release on Thanksgiving weekend, followed by the big release – 1 000 theatres – on Christmas Day, the conventional date on which movies come up for critical acclaim. By then, however, a global sense of 'Mandela fatigue' had set in. After his death the whole world had joined in to celebrate the man and his legacy. The press and broadcast media were flooded with material on the late statesman. Various documentaries and reams of old film footage were shown on repeat. Perhaps people were also somewhat reluctant to spend their holiday weekend watching a movie that may have left them remorseful or sad. This was how we saw it after our own analysis over the weeks that followed, and that's the only explanation that makes any sense when I look now at the performance of the movie. Before Madiba's passing the exit polls had been great and viewers were very impressed; afterwards not so much. Attendance figures dipped considerably. The film had cost $35 million to make and in the end its total box-office takings amounted to no more than two-thirds of the cost. It did, however, go on to do well on television once it was licensed to Netflix, and continues to play on television screens globally.

Naturally, the passing of a global icon left the world a little shell-shocked. The outpouring of grief and adulation lasted for months, and lingered still by the time awards season came around. We had hoped to see our film feature in certain categories and so it was disappointing when the only Academy Award nomination we got was Best Original Song for U2's 'Ordinary Love'. The song was performed live by the group at that year's 86th Academy Awards, but it didn't win, the Oscar going instead to 'Let it Go' from the animation hit *Frozen*. The view – and this view was echoed by Harvey Weinstein – was that the Academy would accommodate only one provocative production focused on issues of race, and so the Oscar for Best Picture that year went to *12 Years a Slave*. Alfonso Cuarón won for Best Directing for *Gravity*.

Long Walk was, however, nominated for three Golden Globes: Idris for Best Actor (Motion Picture Drama), Alex Heffes for Best Original Score and U2 for Best Original Song. We felt honoured – this was the first time a South African film had come up for three Golden Globes. And it was U2 who walked away with the award, the first for a South African movie.

In accepting their award for Best Original Song, U2 guitarist David Evans, The Edge, said, 'We have been working for President Mandela since the 70s, when we were teenagers, when we did our very first concert against the apartheid movement, so it's taken us 35 years to write this song.' In his acceptance speech, Bono stated: 'This really is personal for us – very, very personal. This man turned our life upside down, right side up, a man who refused to hate, not because he didn't have rage or anger or all these things, but because he thought love would do a better job. And we wrote a love story – or a love song, rather – because that's kind of what's extraordinary about the film. It is this kind of dysfunctional love story. And that's why you should see it ... You know about the global statesman, you don't know about the man. That's why you should see this film.'

I was ecstatic for Bono and U2, but sad for the rest of our team who had worked so hard on this production. Each and every crew and cast member had knuckled down to contribute his or her expertise to make the best possible movie. The story resonated – and continues to resonate – with every South African and everyone felt a sense of pride and owner-ship. We were one big family and, regardless of the position held by any single individual, we all felt privileged to have had this once-in-a-lifetime opportunity to work on this remarkable story. As filmmakers we could only hope to leave a legacy for South Africa's future generations that told of the man who helped fight for their democracy. We remain confi-dent that we were able to tell that story in a way that was both true and accurate, so that those in a world 50 or 100 years from now can see this film and say, 'You know, that was an amazing journey. You can't believe that actually happened.' Madiba's story stands apart and above, and *Mandela: Long Walk to Freedom* is a cinematic acknowledgement that will hopefully inspire generations to come. That's the beauty of film. Like Madiba, it offers a lasting message that transcends time and place.

Saying my final goodbye to Madiba on 15 December 2013 at his home village, Qunu, in the Transkei, was another roller-coaster. Idris, Vanashree and I were privileged to be included in the Mandela family retinue and we flew with them from Johannesburg. We relived the sorrow and loss we first felt in London on 5 December, but here in Qunu it was far more difficult, knowing that this marked the physical end of Madiba. This immeasurable loss aptly captured in Ahmed Kathrada's emotional speech, which he delivered while trying very hard to hold back his tears, mirrored what we were feeling, especially these words: 'While we may be drowned in sorrow and grief, we must be proud and grateful that after the long walk paved with obstacles and suffering, we salute you as a fighter for freedom to the end.' This is the way I felt about both Madiba and Kathy.

Most importantly, it was the special privilege and joy that I, and later my family, were able to be a small part of and to share, understand and appreciate Madiba as a great man and friend. There are so many little things that I remember: being in his room when he made his own bed, the perfectly stacked newspapers after being read early in the morning, the humility of the father figure to all his staff, his love for all his children not to miss the big ones, flying together, taking off his shoes on a flight, the many telephone calls, him visiting our home for a meal and so many other memories in South Africa and around the world. Like any human relationships, we had disagreements too.

Death, as I had so painfully learned with my father all those years ago, eventually catches up with everyone. Just four years after the passing of Madiba, on 28 March 2017, we lost Ahmed Kathrada.

Ours had been a long and happy association, one that grew from my own unreserved admiration for him as a struggle stalwart to a deep and rewarding friendship as I got to know the man, the husband and friend. Over the years, Kathy became a father figure to me, one I'd turn to for help and advice, one in whom I could confide whenever I felt overwhelmed or uncertain. He was the most honest, sincere, caring, loving human being I had ever met.

As a family, we had taken many trips with Kathy and Barbara, both at home and abroad: New York, Los Angeles, London and a particularly memorable one to Budapest. This destination had been top of his bucket list ever since the nine months he had spent there working at the head-quarters of the World Federation of Democratic Youth in the early 1950s. He had been desperate to return and often spoke of it. Finally, in May 2016, I was able to make that happen with the help of my friend Robert Lantos, who introduced me to many people in his native Hungary. It remains one of my greatest thrills to have experienced with Kathy the Budapest that he knew and to visit the places etched in his memory, with him as my guide. We didn't know it then, of course, but this was to be his last international trip. It was always such a treat to spend time with both Kathy and Barbara on all of the overseas trips and holidays we took together.

On 28 March 2017 I was in Cape Town to accept an honorary doctorate from the Cape Peninsula University of Technology. Kathy was in attendance each time I received such accolade. On this occasion he had been unable to accompany me as he was in hospital, but I felt that he was there in spirit. This time it was just Kiyan and I with Eddie Daniels, a former Robben Island prisoner and close friend of Madiba and Kathy's. We were alone that morning at the Table Bay Hotel when I received news of Kathy's passing. I had lost another father. On one of my visits to Kathy during his illness, Barbara had mentioned that he was unsteady on his feet, and I suggested that he use a walking stick. In his witty way, he responded by saying that he didn't need one because Barbara was his support!

It was a glorious Cape Town day. Just beyond the window the bay sparkled in the sunshine and off in the distance was Robben Island, where Kathy had spent so many wasted years. How bittersweet that day was for me. In many ways it was surreal, our joy tempered by the grief that threatened to overwhelm us. As soon as I was done at the university, my doctorate in hand, Kiyan and I, with Eddie Daniels, boarded a plane and flew to Johannesburg to join Barbara and other family members for the funeral and memorial service. Vanashree and Gyana joined us there to say goodbye to a very special human being who brought brightness into so many lives as he emerged from the gloom of prison.

32

Speaking up and speaking out

During apartheid, I chose film as my voice. Films such as *Place of Weeping* and *The Stick*, and the messages they carried, spread across the South African and global landscape, providing insight into the dynamics of being South African during that turbulent era.

I have always been proud to be a Black South African. For me, the years 1990 to 1994 were filled with possibility. But then reality slowly set in. Following the initial euphoria, challenges rose to meet us at almost every turn. If it wasn't the task of establishing an equitable dispensation, then it was the issue of white privilege and the legacy of apartheid, of tackling the HIV/AIDS pandemic glibly glossed over by some in government, then the steady but rapid decline of state entities, the years of state capture, rampant corruption and ineptitude in almost every sphere of government. But still ... still. Despite the many challenges we face here in South Africa, I am no Afro-pessimist. I travel an enormous amount and still there is no place I would rather live. I sometimes think South Africans fail to appreciate what a special and beautiful country we live in – and that goes not only for the affluent, but South Africans from all walks of life, on every step of the socio-political and economic ladders. It is special because of its people. The problem is partly that, after the initial high following Mandela's release and the emergence of the new era of democracy, we all – I suppose, inevitably – settled to a lower level of intensity and satisfaction. After 1994 we became complacent in this new democracy of ours.

Following Nelson Mandela's single term in office, the country was led by Thabo Mbeki, who was then replaced by Jacob Zuma. Under Zuma's presidency the political and economic landscape of the country declined considerably. In what has been termed the Nine Wasted Years, with state capture and corruption taking centre stage, the once proud ANC saw many of its senior leaders implicated almost daily in media reports of corruption. This led to stalwarts, including Ahmed Kathrada and his wife Barbara Hogan, taking a very public stance against the Zuma presidency. Barbara, in her own right, held strong views politically and was always guided by her conscience to do the right thing, which ultimately led to her being fired as a cabinet minister by Zuma in 2010. Many honest and committed politicians and activists of the struggle, like Barbara, were brushed aside, ignored, criticised and even ostracised.

In late 2015, I felt driven to take a stand, to add my voice to those who had already stood up against the dire circumstances in which the country found itself. In a public statement issued on 14 December, I outlined my personal views on the events that were unfolding around the firing of Finance Minister Nhlanhla Nene and the subsequent collapse of the rand and our financial markets. My statement was published widely in the press, mainstream media and social media.

> During the apartheid era, I chose to remain in the country and contribute to the struggle against apartheid, using whatever resources were available to me. I turned to the medium of film to speak out against the regime ... I have always been proud to be a Black South African, and the watershed years of 1990 and 1994 were the most memorable. These years were filled with an immense hope and pride. What we thought impossible, became possible. Our dreams were becoming realities, recognising the damage caused by apartheid and the high levels of poverty and inequality for the majority in our country. Today this hope and pride in our rainbow nation has been eroded to a point of despair.
>
> How did we get here? Why do we find ourselves in this predicament? And where do we go to now?
>
> I do not have the answers to these questions. But each of us, as South Africans, has to use our rights as enshrined in our Constitution to take more control of our destiny. We have to do this as a united nation, and we have to do it now. We owe it to the young people of our country and future generations.
>
> In the past few days, the South African nation experienced one of the lowest points in our history. It is a low point that we never believed possible in our country ... The time has come for all of us to take our collective responsibility seriously and exercise the rights afforded to us by our democratic order.

On 19 February 2018, the country was still in a very dark place when

I took up my pen again and wrote an imploring open letter about what was happening in my country. Zuma had finally resigned and been replaced by Cyril Ramaphosa. I started off quoting the Reverend Theophilus Msimangu from Alan Paton's, *Cry, the Beloved Country*: 'I see only hope for our country, and that is when white men and black men, desiring neither power nor money, but desiring only the good for their country, come together to work for it.' Reflecting on these words, I wrote about the love I have for my beloved South Africa.

For almost the entire past decade we have lived our lives amidst a national tragedy. How is it possible that our beloved rainbow nation could have disappeared into an abyss of sadness, greed, corruption and inhumanity?

I do not have the answers to the questions ...

It was fascinating to observe the transformation now taking place in South Africa [after Jacob Zuma's resignation] and our nation enters a new phase of recovery and, once again, of hope. I commend President Cyril Ramaphosa and all those involved, including opposition parties, in peacefully navigating this process, and again we hope, we all hope, that this time events will ultimately result in an outcome beneficial to all the people of our country ...

All South Africans should follow Nelson Mandela's example and embark upon a selfless journey to improve the lives of the less fortunate, by making a meaningful contribution, no matter how small, by committing ourselves and partnering with government and its programmes to make our land beautiful and beloved again.

In 1994, in his inauguration speech, Madiba said: 'Never, never and never again shall it be that this beautiful land will again experience the oppression of one by another and suffer the indignity of being the skunk of the world.'

I will hasten to add that we should never allow corruption, greed, inhumanity and disrespect by any individual against the well-being of our people.

And then, right in the middle of an unparalleled global crisis following the outbreak of the COVID-19 pandemic spreading across the globe at such an alarming rate that it sent the world into a tailspin the likes of which we had never seen before, there emerged once again the ugly head of racism that seems never to be too far from the surface. With much of the world in an unprecedented lockdown, frustrations began to brew, tempers flared, fists flew, violence in every form rising to claim further victims. While the horror of George Floyd's murder in the US played out in the international arena, the growing tide of discontent that followed spread across the globe.

On Youth Day, 16 June 2020, I wrote in the *Daily Maverick*, on the aching resonance here in South Africa of the Floyd tragedy.

In the past weeks, we have seen people around the world stand up against the brutality that led to the killing of George Floyd, Rayshard Brooks and so many others whose names are not known to us. The tipping point for our freedom may have been in 1976, but it would be another two decades before those ideals were realised. I hope that the actions and introspections required today provide quicker outcomes. We simply cannot continue to lose any more lives.

The last 20 days since the slaying of George Floyd in the USA has been a revelation, with an outpouring of humanity all around the world, a solidarity that is long overdue.

As a South African, I reflect on my life as part of the oppressed majority that endured the harshness of legislated racism: apartheid. Brutality, oppression and violent authority were the tools of perpetrators, those who had the protection of the law and who used it very effectively, that cost thousands of, mostly, black people their lives.

My body of work in film has been largely dedicated to telling stories, stories that celebrate the people and events of our liberation. One such narrative is that of the black youth who rebelled against the authorities when they were forced to learn Afrikaans, the language of the oppressors.

On 16 June 1976, a cold winter's day, students in Soweto marched to deliver a petition to the Education authorities. It was then that everything fell apart. They were met with police brutality, 69 individuals killed for their convictions. We salute these young heroes, the 44th anniversary of one of the most harrowing incidents in South Africa's history. *Sarafina!* was the film I made saluting those young heroes. These teenagers put their lives on the line and were at the forefront of the liberation – they are the heroes of our struggle.

What is of significance today is that now there are protests around the world, and we are able to see the unanimity of support from all race groups, particularly among the youth, in the almost global stand against discrimination, gender-based and all forms of violence. It is these individuals who are taking the future into their hands, and that this is finally finding a foothold in other sectors, such as the environment, and in support for green resources, bodes very well for the future.

Good values, ethics, morals and kindness have been subjugated by arrogance, greed, hypocrisy and dishonesty. And it is this that has led to the growth of the right-wing nationalism in so many countries around the world.

Ubuntu is a South African saying, a notion that suggests that *I am* simply *because you are*. That we are all connected, that we need each other to exist. That our every action has an effect on the humanity of the world. Today, ubuntu is more relevant than it has ever been.

The world seemed to be reeling, not only under the injustices and racial violence that continued to play out in the international arena, but under the sudden and startling changes people were experiencing in their every-day lives. COVID-19 was taking its terrible toll on the bodies, minds and spirit of people across the world, from every walk of life. In efforts to stem the growing tide of infections and prevent as far as possible the spread of the virus, many countries went into strict lockdown, limiting social interaction and restricting movement to only the essential. South Africans, with armoured vehicles roaming the streets, the police ever-present in scenes terrifyingly familiar to the country's state of emergency in the 1980s, were urged to #StayHome, the lockdown effectively threat-ening not only lives but livelihoods. It was a terrible time, especially for those already vulnerable – the elderly and infirm, those living hand to mouth, already barely able to survive on the pittance brought in by cas-ual labour and piece work – but also for those whose livelihoods suffered as a result of the shutdown of factories and services, retail and manufac-turing, production and distribution.

For many, it felt like the end of times, and it was hard even for me – ever the optimist – to stay rational and sensible, to maintain a balance between facing up to the realities of what all of this presented and keep-ing a positive look.

For me, one of the lowest points came right in the thick of it, on Monday, 13 July 2020, with the sudden and devastating passing of Zindzi Mandela at the age of just 59. It was a severe blow for me personally, but for those who knew her, who loved her and had followed the arc of her life, hers was a loss that was indescribable – particularly in such trying times when it seemed that the whole world was already out of kilter.

Zindzi Mandela was a friend, a sister, an activist and an inspiring lady. She was also her mother's daughter, a firebrand who was not afraid to take on the apartheid regime when both Madiba and Winnie were either incarcerated or unable to speak for themselves. Having known her for so many years, and having worked closely with her and the family in the long run-up to the release of the movie of her father's life, Zindzi's passing left me with a deep and profound sense of grief. In a message I sent out to friends, family and colleagues in the industry on the day she passed, I tried to convey at least some of what she had come to mean to all of us.

Another fearless, shining light of the Mandela family has left us. We will miss her love, her dignity, her humanity and her care for all those around her.

Zindzi was, and always will be, a special friend and inspiration, especially having had her alongside from early on when the plans for the film began to formulate, while Madiba was in prison, to being awarded the film rights to *Mandela: Long Walk to Freedom*. She was always accessible and generous with advice …

Not only was she a daughter, sister, mother, grandmother and wife, she was also a deep thinker, a diplomat and poet. She had shared poems with me. In 1978, at the age of 18, she published the anthology *Black As I Am*, which was profound. One of the poems in this collection, 'A Tree Was Chopped Down', is especially appropriate today.

Zindzi's passing was tragic and her loss heartfelt, but it also helped put so much of what we were experiencing at this tumultuous time – me personally, South Africans generally and indeed the entire world – into some perspective. There is not a day to be lost, for there is never a guarantee of tomorrow.

In July 2021, I was once again on my way to attend the Olympics, this time in Tokyo. As exciting and energising as it was to be at the Opening Ceremony in lockdown, without spectators and in all its splendour and feel the pride of being South African, at the same time my mind was sombre. Back home unprecedented scenes of social unrest and widespread looting of stores in areas in Gauteng and my home province KwaZulu-Natal, were making the headlines no country wants to see. Sparked initially by protests in some quarters by supporters of Jacob Zuma who, in defiance of a court order, had begun a 15-month prison sentence for contempt of court, the chaos that erupted was deeply concerning to me on many levels. How the rest of the world was perceiving us at that moment was starkly shown in the many articles I read in the international media. Closer to home was how in KwaZulu-Natal the unrest had escalated, with distressing racial overtones.

I felt moved to put my own thoughts in writing and share them on social media.

> As depressing and somewhat despairing as these reports may be, it is a reality that we have to face and deal with as a nation. It is our collective responsibility to find solutions to mitigate falling deeper into this abyss.
>
> Over the past several weeks I've been thinking about and trying to

assess how I can meaningfully contribute to the process towards reconciliation and healing given the significant pain, insecurity, anguish
and loss of life that has occurred in our beautiful land. In the past,
I've used the vehicle of film and narrative storytelling to do this, but
I feel that given the urgency and the timing, for now, I would like to
share my feelings. Whilst there have been many commentators and
journalists who have criticised the events around the unrest, and laid
blame on many different possible causes, we have to acknowledge
that these events have occurred, and we now need to look to the
future and try to find ways of making sure this doesn't happen again.
Social cohesion and the ability for different ethnic groups to peacefully coexist should be natural, but social inequality and disparity
in people's lives are huge factors that threaten our nation, especially
given the economic conditions, the high unemployment rate and the
human instinct to survive in a peaceful manner.

We cannot allow for lawlessness and criminality from people in
power, politicians, law enforcement personnel and those in other
organs of state, nor can the public at large try to take the law into
their own hands. Unfortunately, this dire situation was not managed
well or handled efficiently by the authorities, so understandably private citizenry needed to, and did, come together to protect themselves and their property.

Our president has received enormous criticism for his, and his government's handling of the situation, and I hope that a more positive
roadmap will emerge as we, as a country, deal with the desperate
state of affairs brought about by the ravages of COVID-19, and the
resulting economic and social challenges, and endemic corruption
that has been perpetuated.

As a result of the unrest, people were traumatised, many were displaced and left homeless and for the first time in my memory, there was a threat to food security, with no access to basic foodstuffs due to supply lines being disrupted and shops closed. In this unprecedented time, ordinary people stepped up to the plate and helped with the desperate situations that emerged and helped find solutions. We need to celebrate these loving and caring South Africans. They are the heroes of the day.

I am firmly of the view that lawlessness cannot be condoned and perpetrators of crimes, including the much-publicised killings, must be brought to book and face the full might of the law. What is of concern to me is what is being described as the 'Phoenix Massacre'. This seems like a deliberate attempt to put a wedge between Africans and Indians as part of a political agenda. While freedom of speech is a basic right of our democracy, the media must be alive to any agenda that is counter-productive to nation-building and the rule of law.

All of this was exacerbated by the flurry of posts on social media platforms, some of which were designed to create dissent, while some were exaggerated to incite violence and instil fear. In some instances, it was difficult to determine which posts were fake and which were real! We have seen how dangerous this tool is, and the influence it had on politics in the United States under Donald Trump. Social media platforms have built algorithms into their systems to detect content that could be offensive, including hate speech, racism and the incitement of violence. We have to implement the same while protecting freedom of speech.

Our country needs to go through a process of rejuvenation of morality. We need to especially tackle the damage that has been done through the propagation of 'greed is good' which has become ingrained in the psychological mindset of some people. Most people in our nation are honest, hardworking South Africans, of all race groups, all of whom yearn for 'a better life'. Unfortunately, this has not been achieved in any meaningful way to impact on the majority of our fellow citizens. I believe that every South African, from all walks of life, be it those that are privileged, to the middle class and the general man in the street, need to come together and contribute to the upliftment of our society in any way they can. Their contributions need not necessarily be financial only, but could also be the psychological support needed for our people to change their thought processes and make a paradigm shift.

South Africa's success on an international platform like the Olympic Games shows our potential to be the best. South Africa is a beautiful land with beautiful people. Our nation needs to come together to find solutions for economic equality and a prosperous future. We all have to work harder to achieve this.

Together, we will be strong! Together, we shall overcome!

Can these letters make a difference? I do not know. But they can do no harm and I hope they give the reader food for thought.

33

An appetite for risk

Creating content and producing movies is extremely satisfying, but it is also hard work, and requires courage and perseverance. To achieve success in the movie business, it's important that you're able to conceptualise a film from a story, a book, a script or someone's life. But you also need strong partnerships, loyal and honest ones, on which you can rely time and time again. Success is hard to achieve alone.

The business of film is a collaborative endeavour that sees hundreds, sometimes thousands, of players coming together, all completely committed to the product. It is like a family for the duration of the production. Sometimes they are friends, at other times simply acquaintances or colleagues who share the same vision, the same goals. I have built sound and lasting business relationships over decades because of friendships, and a large part of our success has been achieved with the support of others who are equally committed. But even then, in many instances, there are those – particularly investors – who are unable to see past the challenges, to think outside the box, and see potential.

'No one will go see it' was something I heard many times over the years, followed by energetic efforts to dissuade me. This was the case with *Place of Weeping* and with *Yesterday*. It applied to some of our other ventures too. These are the times when you need to have the will and the courage of your convictions to forge ahead regardless. It's always something of a gamble. Sometimes your gambles don't work; sometimes they pay off handsomely. So one has to follow one's instinct and passion.

Another lesson hard learned during my time in the movie business is that, in the quest for success, you cannot shy away from taking risks. The anti-apartheid films I made were difficult projects. Even though their messages were well received, enormous effort was demanded to ensure that they saw the light of day. Some Hollywood studios even warned against them; there's no audience for them, they said. Nevertheless, I persevered. I had a goal, a vision and a determination to see those stories told on film. It was this combination that established me as a filmmaker with credibility, and some gravitas.

Competitors and critics would say I think differently about films, but what they actually mean is I am prepared to produce what they would consider to be unimportant. And they're right. Filmmaking is a business, an entertainment business, and so, yes, sometimes I make commercial films. The fact is that if it weren't for films that made money, it would be impossible to make the more important ones that don't make money but carry a stronger, important message. Films such as *Deadly Passion* and *The Mangler* funded films like *The Stick*, *Cry, the Beloved Country* and *Sarafina!*. That's the way it works. We are in the storytelling and entertainment business.

Making motion pictures is like having children. You try your best, work hard and your commitment to each is the same. Some films turn out better than others, but locked in your memory are the ones that brought joy and satisfaction, despite the long road, the hard work and sleepless nights. For me, my career highlights include *Place of Weeping* and *The Stick*, then *Sarafina!* and *Cry, the Beloved Country*, and of course *Mandela: Long Walk to Freedom*. Even as I say that it feels like I'm unfairly favouring one over another when, deep down, I know that of the over 100 films I have produced thus far each has its own qualities, its own truths.

Videovision remained active in television. In 2018 I tackled yet another challenge, something that had appealed to me for a long time – the idea of a daily television show. I had worked with Leleti Khumalo for many years and I greatly admire her talents, so when she called one day to tell me she had an idea she wanted to pitch, I was happy to hear her out. She and Duma Ndlovu of Word of Mouth Pictures, with whom I had also worked, were collaborating on a project, a television series titled *Imbewu: The Seed*. It was a story about two families from different cultural backgrounds – one African and the other Indian – an original authentic story about people in Durban and its rich and colourful diversity.

Naturally, I was excited at the opportunity and presented it to Khalik Sheriff and the e.tv team (our partners at Cape Town Film Studios), who were equally enthusiastic, and, on 16 April 2018, we launched the series on e.tv to great acclaim. The series, shot entirely in Durban with Leleti, Duma and myself as executive producers, is set in KwaZulu-Natal and reflects the multicultural environment that makes Durban and the broader province of KwaZulu-Natal unique, crossing the cultural divide between Zulu and Indian, promoting social cohesion in South Africa and showcasing a hybrid of cultures in South Africa today. The show became immensely popular. By December 2018 – eight months since its launch – each episode was being watched daily by almost 4 million South Africans.

In late 2018, Angus Gibson, who received an Oscar nomination for the documentary *Mandela* in 1996, presented his film *Back of the Moon* to us. The film is an ode to the multicultural melting pot of Sophiatown, which was destroyed by the apartheid government, and I immediately felt that we should be involved. Angus did an amazing job crafting an authentic period film, bringing Sophiatown to life and celebrating its rich legacy. It had its world premiere at the Durban International Film Festival in 2019, where it won the Best South African Feature Film award, followed by the Best International Narrative Feature award from the prestigious Black Film Festival of Montreal in 2020.

Ramesh Sharma, with whom I produced *The Journalist and the Jihadi: The Murder of Daniel Pearl*, had been developing a documentary feature that explored the global impact of the teachings of Mahatma Gandhi and approached me with the project sometime in 2018. The 150th anniversary of Gandhi's birth was to be commemorated globally in October 2019 and I got involved as producer on the film. The film, *Ahimsa – Gandhi: The Power of the Powerless*, is a fascinating account of the impact of the Gandhian message of non-violence worldwide: how it inspired Martin Luther King Jr, Václav Havel, Barack Obama, Nelson Mandela and other leaders. We were fortunate to have the beautiful song 'Ahimsa' written by Bono and A.R. Rahman, which was performed by U2 and AR Rahman for the end titles of the film. In June 2021, the film won Best Documentary Feature Award at the 21st New York Indian Film Festival.

Shortly before the COVID-19 lockdown in March 2020, we decided to resurrect an experimental film that Darrell Roodt and I had worked on some years before. Made in the mode of a silent film, it was called *Don't Give Up*. With themes of poverty and homelessness, it is the story of a woman – played by Leleti Khumalo – who begs at a busy street intersection to eke out a living for herself and her two sons. We were fortunate to secure Oscar-nominated composer Philip Glass to score the film and have Peter Gabriel's hit song, 'Don't Give Up', as the title song.

In 2020 we teamed up with Bomb Productions, headed by Teboho Mahlatsi, Angus Gibson and Desireé Markgraaff, with whom we worked on *Back of the Moon*, to develop an exciting show set against the backdrop of the fashion industry. *House of Zwide* premiered on e.tv on 19 July 2021 and on its first day attracted a whopping 4 million-plus viewers – a remarkable achievement for a brand-new television show!

As the landscape of film began to change, with DVD and conventional television viewing declining, streaming services luring viewers and film choices being made by algorithms, Videovision branched out into other endeavours, occasionally some that were quite far removed from film. One of these was real estate – a five-hectare property on the beach at Umhlanga, the site of the Southern Sun group's Umhlanga Rocks Hotel. This was arguably the finest piece of real estate in the country, initially developed in the 1960s by Sol Kerzner after he built one of his first hotels here. Our idea was to develop the site into a R3.5 billion, seven-star property called The Pearls of Umhlanga. We formed a consortium with other partners and bought the site from Southern Sun for R150 million. Today The Pearls is an iconic residential resort, an ambitious and highly successful development that has transformed the shoreline of the city I call home. And it started with my approach to head of Southern Sun Hotels, Helder Pereira (Jimmy's son), asking to buy the land next to the Beverly Hills Hotel to build a home.

More than 20 years since I came up with the idea of building a movie studio complex in Durban, the eThekwini Film Studios is finally becoming a reality. First there was the 10-year delay brought about by the legal dispute that went all the way to the Constitutional Court (which found in our favour), and then the Cape Town Film Studios, which took our focus away from Durban for a while. But my dream of being able to bring the creative and economic benefits of the film industry to Durban never went away.

Our vision is a R7.5 billion mixed-use development that will include modern film studios, a hotel, residential units and a movie-themed retail area. The architects and concept designers, Creative Kingdom, are on board and set to see Film City come to fruition. The team was headed by world-renowned architectural creative talents (the now late) Eduardo Robles and Thanu Boonyawatana, who were responsible for such landmarks as the Palace of the Lost City, the Palm Islands in Dubai, the first Ferrari Hotel in Spain and The Pearls. Despite the long wait, the project is another dream come true, one in which patience, despite the challenges, is paying off.

When completed, the Durban studio will not only be an enormous economic injection for the city, but will also be the actualisation of my long-held vision for a creative industries hub for the province. Over the decades, we've seen some extraordinary talent come out of KwaZulu-Natal – Ladysmith Black Mambazo, Gcina Mhlophe, Leleti Khumalo, Lebo M, Sibongile Khumalo – and I am determined that Film City will continue to nurture that talent locally. It's going to be a space for creative geniuses to enjoy, a space where artists, sculptors, potters, musicians and traditional crafters can hone their talents and sell their works. It's taken a long time, but it's beginning to emerge.

When it comes to local filmmaking, there is no reason why South Africa cannot be a significant global competitor. We have the stories and the backdrop; as a largely English-speaking nation, with great creative and technical talents, we can comfortably accommodate international relationships beneficial to us as well as a far broader market. We could, for example, readily have made *Black Panther* here in South Africa. What we don't always have are sufficient financial resources. Yes, we do have government support, but is that enough? The answer is, quite simply, no. And so we don't want to be scaring off those who have money to invest and spend; we need to attract them to our shores and demonstrate our multiple skills and versatility.

We have a more than plentiful supply of our own stories and we need to keep telling them. But we need also to be mindful of that eternal balance between being pragmatic and commercial versus the creative voice that is common to all filmmakers. Sometimes it is enough to make a film that is a creative triumph but bombs at the box office, but we have to be clever and creative with our choices too. We have to try to understand what the audience wants and will react to.

I think we may have exhausted the cinema of liberation. *Sarafina!* spoke to that. *Place of Weeping* spoke to that. So did *Cry, the Beloved Country* and many others, not just my films. But they were also timeless and very human stories. *Mandela: Long Walk to Freedom* remains a story of the triumph of the human spirit. I am very proud of these and that they will be around for decades to come.

In South Africa, the movie-making market appears to continue to be limited to genres of comedy, action or romance. It's not impossible to see success beyond those areas, but it is harder. One of the challenges faced by local films and thus the struggle to diversify is because there are so few channels to get movies to the public. Access to audience is a key factor, one that has the ability to propel the local industry to greater heights if it is well managed. And now, with streaming services such as Netflix and Amazon producing here, I trust that the growth will continue, especially with the new and young creative talents emerging.

I've been fortunate in my career in film – luckier than most. I've had films nominated for Emmys and Oscars, BAFTAs and Golden Globes, but still the bright lights of Hollywood can't tear me away from the place I love. I love most things about South Africa. There is nowhere else I would rather be. As I said, it's a place where you can dream, where you can succeed, where you can make your own destiny. As I sit today, on the southern tip of Africa in 2021, through the medium of technology the world has become an integrated space. People no longer see boundaries. I hope my story helps in some small way to illustrate the significance of that. It is also my hope that many more young women and men embrace the opportunities of their passions.

Lady Luck has smiled on me, and without her, none of this would have been possible.

Over the years I have learned – often the hard way – that success requires hard work, faith and a lot of patience. It can take years to shift from idea to fruition. It's frustrating at times but, ultimately, as Madiba said, 'It always seems impossible until it's done.'

Afterword and acknowledgements

This book began during the March 2020 lockdown, as I was going through old files, photographs and archived videos, reliving and revisiting my life and its memories. I have had to piece together my journey as accurately as possible because memory is not my strong point, particularly because I tend not to dwell on things. It has been fascinating to revisit, reflect and realise how fortunate I have been.

Life and destiny have very different and very distinctive pathways for each one of us; our trajectories vary, a turning point triggered by a single incident, a decision taken at a particular point that sets each of us on an entirely different path. For better or worse, no one knows, nor does it really matter.

Of course, I owe my being and where I am today first to my family – my father and especially my mother, my wife, my children – and to my country. Thanks to each of them for filling my life with joy.

Even though we struggled under the legalised racism of the apartheid regime, many of the challenges that presented themselves to me as a person of colour, growing up and working my way into an industry designed by, and supportive of 'whites only', made me want to achieve and succeed even more. Failure was not an option – courage and tenacity were everything.

I am also very fortunate to have had many special people through my life who have moulded me, shouted at me, guided me and taken care of me when I needed their support: my father, who guided us in our formative early years, giving us a solid grounding and steady foundation and introducing us to the moving image; my mother, who to this day continues to be blindly supportive, and for lovingly raising us. Her commitment to my brother Sanjeev and me, and our families, has always gone way beyond her paternal obligations. She sacrificed most of her adult life to ensure our well-being and growth. No one can ask for anything more, and words cannot express the gratitude I have for her support and guidance. In her twilight years, I dedicate the song 'Thank You, Mama' to her – from *Sarafina!*, sung by Miriam Makeba and Leleti Khumalo – saluting her love and wishing her continued good health.

Many friends and family members were there for me through the difficult early years and, as time progressed, many more stepped up to the plate. Eddie Falconer, AK Rajab, Jimmy Pereira, Tim Ord, Larry Kulpath and Jonsy Singh became generous mentors. The guiding hands of Fatima and Ismail Meer, Winnie Madikizela-Mandela, Graça Machel, Ahmed Kathrada, His Holiness the Dalai Lama, Leah and Archbishop Desmond Tutu and Reverend Leon Sullivan inspired and helped ignite my politicisation and saw me expand my knowledge – and, most importantly, led to my meeting Nelson Mandela, which changed and enriched my life forever. There are many people who made some contribution to inspire, enrich or just be there for me, some are mentioned and there are so many who are not mentioned. I am deeply appreciative of all of them.

My wife Vanashree has so blessed my life that I can scarcely find the words. It is through the life that we have enjoyed together, the love and memories that we share, that I have been able to find the greatest fulfilment. I thank her for her love, support, guidance and tolerance over the past 25 years. In the process of raising our two children, Gyana and Kiyan, I learned to appreciate the hard work that goes into parenting and understand, now more than ever, the challenges my mother had to endure. The future now belongs to Gyana and Kiyan, and their generation. Seeing life through their eyes gives one a fascinatingly fresh view of life in the new millennium. Their approach and outlook continues to impress me each day.

The legacy of my grandparents, Parvati and Bunsee Singh and Rajpali and Morty Moonilal, provided sound foundations for my family.

I also acknowledge my other family, the Videovision team, especially the early partners, Sanjeev Singh, who left his job at Unilever to join me in 1981. Bravely, he too followed his passion for film, considering the uncertain future of the film industry at the time. It has been a great journey for us both to be together as part of Videovision.

Equally so for Sudhir Pragjee, who joined in 1988, and brought with him a solid foundation in accounting and business and guided our diversification. In 1990 he brought in Robert Naidoo to build on the foundations to support the accounting and business affairs team. Thank you both and your teams.

Thank you to Nilesh Singh, who also joined us formally in 1990, for overseeing our radio interests, media and communications; and for guiding and leading the process of every aspect of this book from the research through to getting it published.

To my exceptional executive assistant, Taryn Collier, thank you for your patience, support and for always being there for me and my family.

Of course, the rest of the small Videovision family, the current team, Avisha Gounden, Ronnie Govender, Thoko Khanyile, Sumeet Maharaj, Lwazi Mgwaba, Precious Mpulo, Rajan Pather, Marleen Pillay, Sharon

Ramiah, Teddy Ravjee and all past team members are an integral part of my journey.

I have also had the good fortune of meeting and interacting with many individuals around the world who made time for me and continue to inspire me: Junaid Ahmed, Rowley Arenstein, Amitabh Bachchan, Claudia and Thomas Bach, Bono, Brian Cox, Dennis Cuzen, Eddie Daniels, Peter Dignan, Dan Fellman, Richard Forlee, Teddy Forstmann, Tom Freston, Pravin Gordhan, Whoopi Goldberg, Laurence Graff, Celia Gritten, Alan Grodin, Sello Hatang, Hal Hess, Tiffany and Charles Heung, Ann Hung, Mo Ibrahim, Prudence and Jerry Inzerillo, Barry Irwin, Paul Janssen, Richard Jeffery, Michael Katz, Sol Kerzner, Leleti Khumalo, Steve Koseff, Robert Lantos, Mac Maharaj, Ritchie Mohamed, Aaron Ndwandwe, Rosalind Neville, William Nicholson, Mickey Nivelli, Rosanna Oliva, Harry and Bridget Oppenheimer, Sugan Palanee, Helga and Sam Ramsamy, Darrell Roodt, Dezi Rorich, Hilde and Klaus Schwab, Danny Schechter, Tokyo Sexwale, Khalik Sherriff, Bill Shields, Kanoo Soni, Helena Spring and her Videovision team, David Stern, Gerry Stone, Jim Taiclet, Moses Tembe, Jimmy Thomopoulos, David Thompson, Fani Titi, Prof Phillip Tobias, Harry Alan Towers, Chris Tucker, Patrick Wachsberger, Pauletta and Denzel Washington and so many others.

Then, the many unsung heroes who were there in the beginning and friends who in small ways helped me grow and flourish, those who did little things that meant a lot, like giving me a ride home after 7 pm, so I did not have to take a bus, just being there as a friend or to give me support in some way: Charlene Africa, Lionel Calvert, Mohamed Cassimjee, Pickey Dass, Sabitha Dass, Dr Solly Ismail, Vicky Jacobs, Gora Kadodia, Subby and VS Maharaj, Vinod 'Wally' Mistri, Shan Moodley, Chris Naidoo, Dave Naidoo, Raj Naidoo, Satchi Naidoo, Shorty Naran, Mike Narsey,

Dino Pather, Snowy and Tabu Pillay, Ishrath Rajab, Rajesh Rajkumar, Ian van Rooyen, Reshma Sathiparsad, Chandra, Nikita and Tasha Singh, Dhina Singh, Inder Singh, Niru Singh, Prem Singh and Yasmin Singh.

My appreciation to James-Brent Styan who helped me begin writing this book, and to Sean Fraser for his contribution, as well as Laura Lanktree, Lois O'Brien, Maya Mavjee and Peter Dennison for their advice and support.

My gratitude goes to Barbara Hogan and Quincy Jones for accepting and so lovingly writing the foreword and the prelude to the book. Barbara, your thoughtful and heartfelt words mean so much to me. Thank you both and I await your memoirs. And thank you to Gcina Mhlophe and Deepak Chopra for their generosity and support of this book.

A special thank you to the Pan Macmillan team: Terry Morris for agreeing to publish this book and for her support during the publishing process. To Andrea Nattrass for her astute guidance and hand-holding from the editing all the way through to publishing, and to their exceptional team for delivering this book.

I could not have wished for a finer editor than Alison Lowry, whose editorial genius ensured that my vision for this book was achieved with precise and prudent insight to make your experience as a reader better. Without her and Pan Macmillan there wouldn't have been a book. For this I am truly grateful.

I was not certain that this memoir would ever be published. I started working on it initially simply as an exercise to go down memory lane, and was unsure whether my journey would be worthy of a book. I do not take lightly that people have to spend their valuable time reading what I have to say. But slowly, as I progressed and with the support of others, I felt a little more comfortable to let go and to share. In writing it, I share my life's journey with you and deliver a glimpse, a slice of life of a South African through the challenging years of our history. It is my hope that this may inspire and guide young people in some way. If this is achieved, I will be happy.

My life is film, and a creative family of thousands who have so loyally and lovingly shared my passion and helped create the magic that is a large part of this book, my life and my films. Thank you.

It's been a hell of a Walk, but it does not seem that Long.

Anant Singh
Durban
October 2021

Chapter photographs

Prologue: Prince William, Duke of Cambridge, and Anant at the Royal Film Performance in London of *Mandela: Long Walk To Freedom*; in the background are Zindzi Mandela and Kiyan (son) (5 December 2013).

1 Even the circus was in on it: Sanjeev (brother) and Anant (1964/65).

2 Sundays, bladdy Sundays: Sanil Singh (cousin), Sanjeev, Raj Naidoo (friend), Vinodh Singh (cousin) and Anant (1966/67).

3 Early days: Anant in his Sastri College uniform (1969).

4 Sink or swim: Hareenbrun (father), holding Sanjeev with Anant in the background (1959/60).

5 The path less travelled: Trip to Rhodesia with Hareebrun, Bhagoobhai Bhikha (a family friend), Anant, Niru (aunt), Bhindoo (mother) and Sanjeev (1966).

6 James Bond, Basie Smit and the Durban Vice Squad: Movie poster for *Live and Let Die* (1973).

7 The arts of persuasion and distribution: Anant, Brian Cox and Paul Janssen at the Cannes Office (1988).

8 The vision that was video: Anant on the set of *Deadly Passion* (1984).

9 Lights, camera, action: Anant on the set of *The Stick* with Paul Witte and Darrell Roodt (1987).

10 *Place of Weeping*: Anant and Darrell Roodt at the Carnegie Theatre in New York, which was showing *Place of Weeping* (1986).

11 Censored: Censorship certificate for the James Bond film, *Live and Let Die* (1973).

12 *The Stick*: Ambush marketing for *The Stick* in Cannes (May 1987).

13 Who bans the Chippendales?: Chippendales logo (1990).

14 Meeting Mandela: Anant with Nelson Mandela (1994).

15 Exit, followed by an elephant: Amitabh Bachchan on the rooftop of Chatsworth Centre in Durban (3 January 1991).

16 Whoopi, Leroy and Harvey Weinstein: A typical crowd at the Cannes Film Festival.

17 *Sarafina!*: Mbongeni Ngema, Miriam Makeba, Leleti Khumalo, Whoopi Goldberg, Darrell Roodt and Anant on the steps of the Palais de Festival in Cannes (11 May 1992).

18 Towards the new millennium: Anant at the Rose Bowl in Los Angeles attending the FIFA World Cup Final (16 July 1994).

19 *Cry, the Beloved Country*: *Cry, the Beloved Country* premiere in New York with Richard Harris, Nelson Mandela, James Earl Jones and Anant (23 October 1995).

20 More than just business: New Radio Consortium members: Johnny Clegg, Fani Titi, Reuben Shapiro, Anant, Jack Shapiro and Sudhir Pragjee (1996).

21 The King of Pop: Michael Jackson and Anant at the CNA at the V&A Waterfront, Cape Town (October 1997).

22 Love on a jet plane: Vanashree Moodley and Anant (1996).

23 *Who Wants to be a Millionaire?*: Anant on the set of *Who Wants to be a Millionaire?* with host, Jeremy Maggs (1999).

24 The Rainbow Nation: Anant with Archbishop Emeritus Desmond Tutu, who described South Africa as the Rainbow Nation (2000).

CHAPTER PHOTOGRAPHS

25 *Red Dust*: The stars of *Red Dust*, Hilary Swank and Chiwetel Ejiofor (2003).

26 Oscar: Anant and Vanashree (wife) at the Academy Awards (2003).

27 Going for gold: IOC President Thomas Bach inducts Anant as a member of the IOC in Rio de Janeiro on 4 August 2016 (photo courtesy of IOC/Ian Jones).

28 Pirates on the Cape Flats: An aerial view of Cape Town Film Studios.

29 Life, death and fatherhood: Anant on the beach in Tongaat (2020).

30 *Long Walk to Freedom*: Ahmed Kathrada, Nelson Mandela and Anant (November 2000).

31 A crowning moment, a devastating blow: Zenani Mandela, Anant and Zindzi Mandela at the Royal Film Performance of *Mandela: Long Walk To Freedom* in London (5 December 2013).

32 Speaking up and speaking out: Anant delivering a TEDx address at the London Business School (9 July 2015).

33 An appetite for risk: Anant in Durban (13 October 2021).